Balance Sheets and the Lendi

Balance Sheets and the Lending Banker

An Assessment of Accounting Statements and their Interpretation in Relation to Bank Advances

J. H. Clemens
Fellow of the Institute of Bankers
Associate of the Chartered Institute of Secretaries

and

L. S. Dyer
Fellow of the Institute of Bankers

LONDON
EUROPA PUBLICATIONS LIMITED

Europa Publications Limited
18 Bedford Square, London, WC1B 3JN

Sixth Edition

First Published 1949
Sixth Edition 1986

British Library Cataloguing in Publication Data

Clemens, J. H.

Balance sheets and the lending banker: an assessment of accounting statements and their interpretation in relation to bank advances.—6th edition

1. Financial statements
I. Title II. Dyer, L. S.
657'.33'024332 HF5681.B2

ISBN: 0-946653-29-1

Made and printed in England by
Staples Printers Rochester Limited,
Love Lane, Rochester, Kent.

Contents

List of Illustrative Examples

List of Balance Sheets Discussed

(These balance sheets are in the Appendices at the back of the book.)

From the Preface to the First Edition

This book was originally planned as a study of accounting statements from the special point of view of the banker. Its emphasis is upon accounts rather than on bank lending. Indeed, lending depends on so many factors other than accounts and figures produced to the banker that the wider subject of bank lending requires more exhaustive treatment than is possible within the limited purpose of this book.

Financial ratios and certain detailed calculations are explained in Chapters 10, 11 and 18. It is not suggested that the lending banker would have the need, or indeed the time, to extract these ratios or make such calculations *as a matter of regular routine*. But in cases calling for exceptional closeness of control, the extra information thus obtainable can be invaluable.

The three goals of study are knowledge, understanding and wisdom. Knowledge is the reward of the industrious; understanding the prize of the thoughtful: but the crown of wisdom comes only, as a free gift, to an elect few. Wisdom cannot be taught. The author, however, earnestly hopes that the argument of this book will, in some measure, add to the reader's knowledge, understanding.

J. H. CLEMENS
Southgate, N.14, 1949

Preface to the Sixth Edition

Since the fifth edition was published in 1977 there have been numerous developments in accountancy and several Companies Acts. Now that the consolidating Companies Act 1985 is in operation it seems an appropriate time to update the text through a new edition.

The book starts with an introduction to financial statements describing the planning process leading to the preparation of estimated figures, cash projections and monthly figures. Bankers are now laying more stress on this aspect of control of lending. This leads naturally to the appraisal of balance sheets and other financial statements.

There has been a slight rearrangement of the chapters in this edition to form a more flowing sequence and the whole text has been revised in the light of the Companies Act 1985 and accounting developments.

Two new chapters have been added:

> Chapter 21. The Requirements for Company Accounts. This deals with the requirements called for under the Companies Act 1985, the Statements of Standard Accounting Practice and the Stock Exchange.
>
> Chapter 22. Statements of Standard Accounting Practice (SSAPs). This explains and gives a banker's view on the effect of every current SSAP.

This edition has, therefore, been devised to be an up-to-date work of reference for the practising banker as well as covering the requirements of the student banker.

STUART DYER

CHAPTER 1

Introduction to Financial Statements

Management accounting – Planning process – Estimated profit and loss accounts – Cash projections – Profit and loss and cash statements – Cash management – Estimated balance sheets – Sources and application of funds

This book, as the title suggests, is mostly about balance sheets, but it cannot be restricted to balance sheets alone, as there are many other financial statements which necessarily have to be produced for businesses to run efficiently.

An examination will be made of the items which appear in balance sheets and profit and loss accounts, and their interrelation. Of course, to produce profit and loss accounts it is often necessary to have manufacturing accounts, trading accounts and also appropriation accounts, and these will also be examined. Unfortunately these various accounts and balance sheets are produced at the end of trading periods and the final production of these accounts is very often well after the end of such periods, and much of the information contained in them is by then out of date.

It might well be asked why, when such figures refer to a period in the past, bankers are so interested in them. The speed of change increases each year, and it would be as well to question whether a banker is using out-of-date methods in assessing lending propositions when he looks at balance sheets and profit and loss accounts. Surely it would be better for a banker to know what is actually going on at the time a proposition is put to him rather than what happened in a period well past which may have no relationship to the present one.

Management accounting

Fortunately forward-looking accountants have been tackling the accountancy aspects of this problem for many years, and management accounting now plays an important part in the mangement of large businesses.

To make correct decisions, proprietors of businesses need to know how their businesses are faring, for which they need to be supplied regularly with figures. Management accounting methods enable this to be done and it would be as well, therefore, to spend some time examining these methods to see what help they can be to the lending banker before proceeding with the detailed examination of balance sheets and profit and loss account items. It will be seen that there is a close relationship between historical accounts and management accounts, and one relies on the other for a complete understanding of the finances of businesses.

Let us first of all consider the situation of a man who wishes to start a business on his own. Naturally he would have to weigh very thoroughly whether he could withstand the drop in income from his giving up employment, and whether he could replace this from the profits of his own business. He would have to weigh carefully what turnover he could support on the available resources of money, labour and ability, and he would have to estimate carefully his expenses and the profit he would make. In fact, what he would have to do would be to look at the current position from the start of the business, and continue it through until the end of a trading period. He would also have to estimate what his profit and loss account and balance sheet would look like at the end of the trading period.

This would mean that he would have to look particularly at his cash position, and see whether there would be sufficient cash (either his own money, an arranged overdraft, or credit to be received) to meet his monthly liabilities, and leave an amount in hand for contingencies.

We see that a man in this position would have to do a considerable amount of estimating. He would have to work out the budget to which he hoped to keep, and this budget would have to be related to a cash projection showing his position month by month. This, of course, is not easy to do, and in the light of experience it would no doubt be found that some of the estimates would be incorrect. However, after the first year of trading, and using the experience gained, the estimates for the second year should be much more accurate. This, of course, is planning and budgeting in its simplest form, but it is so very necessary when resources are limited.

Over recent years the world has been plagued by rapid inflationary trends, and estimates and costs now quickly get out of hand. Proper budgeting and planning is therefore more necessary than ever in all organizations. Unfortunately, it is not done on as wide a scale as it should be, and although we find that many men starting their own businesses plan minutely for the first year or two, they then stop planning and merely clear the work that comes before them. The good habits of the first few years are not continued, and often this leads to a lack of control, particularly over finance, which then causes hardship.

The planning process

In large organizations detailed planning and budgetary control is done, but there are many possible methods and no one method is suitable for every company. Each company must work out a system which is suitable for its particular needs. This necessarily means that there will be many different methods but, even so, there will be a similarity between them all.

To understand the planning process perhaps we should consider how it might be done in a manufacturing company. Raw materials have to be bought and converted into finished goods. Sales have to be made. It is therefore necessary to estimate what sales can be achieved, and if the manufacturing capacity is sufficient to make the required number of goods, and to make them at a price sufficient to enable a good profit to be made.

The planning process cannot be made in isolation. The sales department will have to be brought in and the manufacturing and financial departments. Costs of raw materials will have to be assessed. Added to this will be wages, factory expenses, repairs, depreciation and overheads and all the other expenses necessary in a manufacturing organization. Account will also have to be taken of all the expenses on administration, finance and sales; a chart will have to be drawn up of how much material will have to be bought each month, what sales will have to be achieved each month, and what finance will be required to support these levels of manufacture and sales. The planning process will therefore be one of estimates from departments amalgamated by the financial department, and probably then returned to the original department for further comments.

It may well be that what the salesman wishes to achieve cannot be produced at a satisfactory cost by the manufacturing department, or perhaps the finance available is insufficient for the proposed level of activity. Aspects outside merely financial considerations such as labour relations and the quality and quantity of the work force will also have to be considered. Additionally many companies draw up contingency plans in case the prepared plan cannot be achieved.

At this stage a budget can be produced with a cash projection and, subsequently, actual figures can be produced on a monthly basis which can be compared with the budget. Enquiries should immediately be made into any variances to see how they occurred, whether it affects the overall plan, and if alterations should be made.

We therefore see that the original plan is not one that must be adhered to at all costs, but one which must be looked at, and considered in the light of all surrounding circumstances, to try and achieve a successful business enterprise.

This is the only way in which to run a successful business and it would seem that a banker should therefore be more interested in budgeted figures, cash projections and estimated profits than in out-of-date balance sheets and profit and loss accounts. However, it is ironic that the businesses that really need to plan do little of it and so cannot supply their bankers with this vital management accounting information, whereas the successful businesses can produce their historical balance sheets and profit and loss accounts which show such strength and ability that a banker has no need to ask for mangement accounts. Nevertheless, times are changing, and we shall undoubtedly see more businesses planning in detail in the future as sophisticated systems come into more general use. Bankers are now asking regularly for cash projections to support lending propositions for both overdrafts and longer term loans, and a knowledge of management accounting methods is becoming essential to a banker.

Now let us follow the planning process through by examining some figures. In the following examples where a figure appears in brackets, i.e. (£5,000), this means that it is a negative amount, i.e. if £42,000 is taken from £37,000 the figure will be shown as (£5,000). Similarly brackets will be used for figures for a bank overdraft to distinguish them from a credit amount at the bank. There is no standardized form of financial statements as companies will decide for themselves which specific points need emphasizing and the presentation will emphasize such points. Also detailed figures will be available to the financial section of the company, and abbreviated figures may well be sufficient for the senior management in the knowledge that such additional information required can always be supplied.

Estimated profit and loss accounts

As previously mentioned, after all the estimates have been received from all departments and an agreed plan has been prepared, an estimated profit and loss account is drawn up (Example 1). It will be seen that the estimated profit and loss account has been prepared for a six-month period only, and this may be a wise procedure. Some companies have such well-established and regular business that they are able to forecast for twelve months ahead, but conditions change rapidly, and in times of change it is not easy to look so far ahead.

It will be seen that it has been decided that sales of £240,000 are possible, and that after expenses of manufacturing and trading there will be a gross profit of £104,000 which, after costs of administration and other expenses, will produce a net profit after tax, of £12,000. This estimated profit and loss account forms the basis of further financial statements, and the next stage will be for the company accountant to transcribe the figures on to an estimated monthly profit and loss basis, shown in Example 2.

The figures, as shown in Example 1, appear in the last column under the total figure, and then these figures are assigned to the specific months.

A banker should examine the individual items carefully. It will be seen that the company's stocks of raw materials and finished goods increase gradually over the six-month period, and that purchases and factory expenses are spread evenly throughout the period, as also are depreciation and finance charges. The administration and other expenses are also spread in a fairly even way. The monthly profit increases throughout the six-month period, and this can be related to a large extent to the increase in sales over the period.

In the first three months the profit figures are small, with sales around £36,000 to £37,000 per month. In the last three months the sales rise to betweeen £42,000 and £45,000, increasing profit. It seems, therefore, as if the company's profits are very sensitive to sales over and above the amount of £37,000 per month. This, however, should be queried with the company as the change is dramatic, and thus will give a banker a better understanding of the work of the company.

EXAMPLE 1

Estimated profit and loss account for six months' period

1st January to 30th June

	£	£	£
Sales			240,000
Stock of raw materials at 1st January		20,000	
Stock of finished goods at 1st January		12,000	
Work in progress at 1st January		5,000	
		37,000	
Less			
Stock of raw materials at 30th June	22,000		
Stock of finished goods at 30th June	14,000		
Work in progress at 30th June	6,000		
		42,000	
		(5,000)	
Add			
Purchases of raw materials	80,000		
Carriage inwards	2,000		
Factory wages and salaries	25,000		
Factory overheads	22,000		
Depreciation of machinery	12,000		
		141,000	
Cost of sales		136,000	136,000
Gross profit			104,000
Less			
Wages and salaries – administration staff	20,000		
Wages and salaries – sales staff	24,000		
Administration expenses	14,000		
Distribution expenses	11,000		
Finance charges	3,000		
Sales commission	2,000		
Depreciation of office equipment	2,000		
Other expenses	6,000		82,000
Net profit on ordinary activities before tax			22,000
Tax			10,000
Net profit on ordinary activities after tax			£12,000

EXAMPLE 2

Estimated monthly profit and loss account for six months' period 1st January to 30th June

	January	February	March	April	May	June	Totals
	£	£	£	£	£	£	
Opening stock of raw materials	20,000	20,000	21,000	22,000	22,000	22,000	
Work in progress	5,000	5,000	5,000	5,000	6,000	6,000	
Stock of finished goods	12,000	12,000	12,000	12,000	12,000	13,000	
Opening stocks (1)	£37,000	£37,000	£38,000	£39,000	£40,000	£41,000	
Closing stock of raw materials	20,000	21,000	22,000	22,000	22,000	22,000	
Work in progress	5,000	5,000	5,000	6,000	6,000	6,000	
Stock of finished goods	12,000	12,000	12,000	12,000	13,000	14,000	
Closing stocks (2)	£37,000	£38,000	£39,000	£40,000	£41,000	£42,000	
Alteration in level of stocks (1 minus 2)	—	(1,000)	(1,000)	(1,000)	(1,000)	(1,000)	(5,000)
Add Purchases	13,000	13,000	13,000	14,000	13,000	14,000	80,000
Carriage inwards	300	300	400	300	300	400	2,000
Factory wages and salaries	4,000	4,000	4,000	4,000	4,500	4,500	25,000
Factory overheads	3,000	3,700	3,800	4,000	4,000	3,500	22,000
Depreciation of machinery	2,000	2,000	2,000	2,000	2,000	2,000	12,000
Cost of sales	£22,300	£22,000	£22,200	£23,300	£22,800	£23,400	£136,000
Sales	37,000	36,000	37,000	42,000	42,500	45,500	240,000
Less Cost of sales	22,300	22,000	22,200	23,300	22,800	23,400	136,000
Gross profit	£14,700	£14,000	£14,800	£18,700	£19,700	£22,100	£104,000
Less Wages and salaries – administration staff	3,300	3,300	3,300	3,300	3,400	3,400	20,000
Wages and salaries – sales staff	4,000	4,000	4,000	4,000	4,000	4,000	24,000
Administration expenses	2,300	2,300	2,300	2,400	2,300	2,400	14,000
Distribution expenses	1,500	1,700	1,800	2,000	2,000	2,000	11,000
Finance charges	500	500	500	500	500	500	3,000
Sales commission	300	300	320	330	350	400	2,000
Depreciation of office equipment	300	300	300	300	400	400	2,000
Other expenses	1,000	1,000	1,000	1,000	1,000	1,000	6,000
Total expenditure	£13,200	£13,400	£13,520	£13,830	£13,950	£14,100	£82,000
Net profit on ordinary activities before tax	1,500	600	1,280	4,870	5,750	8,000	22,000
Tax	690	285	590	2,205	2,610	3,620	10,000
Net profit on ordinary activities after tax	£810	£315	£690	£2,665	£3,140	£4,380	£12,000

I mentioned that depreciation and finance charges were spread evenly over the period. It would be wrong to put such expenses all in one month as this would upset completely the profit figures for that month, and would give incorrect figures for the remaining months also. The figures are, therefore, produced on the normal accrual principle used in accounting, but related to monthly periods.

Cash projections

The next stage for the company accountant is to produce a cash projection to show if there is enough cash available to carry out the proposed plan. To do this the accountant will have to take into account the actual payments and receipts expected in each month. For example, depreciation will not appear at all in a cash projection, as this is a book entry and does not affect cash. Finance charges will appear in the month in which they are paid, and any bonus schemes or sales commission will also appear in the month in which payments are made. It must also be kept in mind that sales are not the same as debtors. Sales are made in one month and the money collected from debtors appears in subsequent months. Similarly purchases are obtained on credit and the creditors paid later.

Example 3 shows a cash projection following from the monthly profit and loss account.

There is an overdraft at the beginning of January of £10,000, but at the end of June a credit of £1,800 appears. This improvement in the company's cash position of £11,800 might at first be thought to reflect the £12,000 net profit shown on the estimated profit and loss account. However, it is merely a coincidence, because the payments in and the payments out each month are the actual sums relating to that month and refer only to cash items.

As mentioned, depreciation is not included in the cash projection, and as we look at the figures there is also an amount of £8,000 for tax paid in January. This tax refers to a previous period, and the tax due in the current period will not be paid until later.

A banker, when looking at a cash projection, must not merely look at the bank balance. For example, in the present instance the customer could well have asked the banker for an overdraft of £24,000 which he would utilize by the end of March, and then provide repayment by the end of June. A banker would be very naïve if he was prepared to accept these figures without comparing them with the estimated profit and loss account; detailed consideration of the individual figures is always worthwhile.

In the present instance we see that receipts form cash sales and debtors start at £35,000 in January with a gradual increase to £42,500 in June, and this follows fairly well the amount of sales shown in the estimated profit and loss account. If we now look at cash purchases and creditors, they start at £14,000, which is in excess of the purchase of £13,000 shown in the profit and loss account, but it must be kept in mind that the payments

EXAMPLE 3

Cash projection for six months' period 1st January to 30th June

	January	February	March	April	May	June
	£	£	£	£	£	£
Bank balance at start of month	(10,000)	(11,700)	(22,500)	(23,220)	(12,720)	(320)
Add RECEIPTS						
Cash sales	500	500	500	500	500	500
Debtors	35,000	36,000	37,000	38,000	40,000	42,000
Sub-total	25,500	24,800	15,000	15,280	27,780	42,180
Less PAYMENTS						
Cash purchases	1,000	1,000	1,000	1,000	1,000	1,000
Creditors	13,000	10,000	10,000	10,000	10,000	8,000
Factory wages and salaries	3,500	3,500	5,000	4,000	4,000	5,000
Factory overheads	2,000	2,500	6,000	2,500	2,500	6,500
Wages and salaries – administration staff	3,000	3,000	3,900	3,000	3,000	4,100
Wages and salaries – sales staff	3,500	3,500	5,000	3,500	3,500	5,000
Administration expenses	1,500	2,000	3,000	2,000	2,000	3,000
Distribution expenses	1,200	1,300	1,400	1,500	1,600	1,700
Finance charges	—	—	—	—	—	3,000
Sales commission	—	—	920	—	—	1,080
Tax	8,000	—	—	—	—	—
Capital expenditure	—	20,000	—	—	—	—
Other expenses	500	500	2,000	500	500	2,000
Total payments	£37,200	£47,300	£38,220	£28,000	£28,100	£40,380
Bank balance at end of month	(£11,700)	(£22,500)	(£23,220)	(£12,720)	(£320)	£1,800

may refer to purchases over the last month or so. Subsequently the cash projection shows the amount paid to creditors as only £10,000 and, in fact, reducing to £8,000 in June, whereas this is much different from that indicated in the monthly profit and loss account. It looks as if payments are being held back from creditors, and it would be as well for a banker to ask if this is possible without creditors complaining, and to obtain a proper explanation.

It will be seen from the cash projection that wages, salaries and other expenses are not even throughout the six months, but have been accounted for in the months in which the wages and expenses have to be paid. A rough check should be made of these figures to see if they accord with the estimated profit and loss account. If they are wildly different then an explanation should be called for.

In February there is a capital expenditure of £20,000 and this, of course, does not appear in the estimated profit and loss account because it is a balance sheet item.

By this detailed examination of the figures, and by comparison with the estimated profit and loss account, a banker will see that although it is estimated that a net profit of £22,000 before tax is to be generated in the six-month period a payment of £20,000 on capital equipment is contemplated, £8,000 is to be paid in tax, and at the same time the banking overdraft is to be repaid completely. This does not make sense, and it looks very much as if payments to creditors are to be delayed so that capital expenditure can be made. A full explanation from the company seems called for at this stage.

Monthly profit and loss statements

During the financial period under review the company's accountant will prepare profit and loss statements for each month showing estimated figures compared with actual figures. We will consider a statement (Example 4) on these lines for the month of February, and work on the basis that the figures for January were more or less as projected (only £100 better than expected over all items).

Figures for the month of February are compared, and also the cumulative figures for the year to date. If we look at the February figures we see that the opening and closing stocks are as predicted, but the expenses for the purchases and factory overheads were £900 more than forecast. As sales were £1,000 less than predicted, gross profit was down by £1,900 (£1,000 short in income, plus £900 additional expenses). The other expenditure for the month shows that £300 more than forecast had to be incurred so that overall the actual results were £2,200 worse than forecast and a loss for the month of £1,600 was incurred instead of the budgeted profit of £600.

If we now look at the cumulative figures for the year to date it will be seen that the total of the differences is almost the same as the differences

EXAMPLE 4

Profit and loss statement for month of February

	February			Year to date		
	Estimated	Actual	Difference	Estimated	Actual	Difference
	£	£	£	£	£	£
Opening stocks	37,000	37,000	—	37,000	37,000	—
Closing stocks	38,000	38,000	—	38,000	38,000	—
Alteration in levels of stock	(1,000)	(1,000)	—	(1,000)	(1,000)	—
Add Purchases	13,000	13,500	+ 500	26,000	26,400	+ 400
Carriage inwards	300	400	+ 100	600	700	+ 100
Factory wages and salaries	4,000	4,000	—	8,000	8,000	—
Factory overheads	3,700	4,000	+ 300	6,700	6,900	+ 200
Depreciation of machinery	2,000	2,000	—	4,000	4,000	—
Cost of sales	£22,000	£22,900	+ £900	£44,300	£45,000	+ £700
Sales	36,000	35,000	−1,000	73,000	72,000	−1,000
Less Cost of sales	22,000	22,900	+ 900	44,300	45,000	+ 700
Gross profit	£14,000	£12,100	−£1,900	£28,700	£27,000	−£1,700
Less Wages and salaries – administration staff	3,300	3,400	+ 100	6,600	6,700	+ 100
Wages and salaries – sales staff	4,000	3,800	− 200	8,000	7,800	− 200
Administration expenses	2,300	2,500	+ 200	4,600	4,800	+ 200
Distribution expenses	1,700	1,700	—	3,200	3,200	—
Finance charges	500	600	+ 100	1,000	1,100	+ 100
Sales commission	300	200	− 100	600	500	− 100
Depreciation of office equipment	300	300	—	600	600	—
Other expenses	1,000	1,200	+ 200	2,000	2,300	+ 300
Total expenditure	£13,400	£13,700	+£300	£26,600	£27,000	+£400
Net profit on ordinary activities before tax	600	(1,600)	−2,200	2,100	nil	−2,100
Tax	285	(690)	− 975	975	nil	− 975
Net profit on ordinary activities after tax	£315	(£910)	−£1,225	£1,125	nil	−£1,125

shown for February, so that February's loss has nullified January's profit, plus the expected profit for February. Tax will not be payable as there are no profits in the year to date, and the tax provided on the January profits can be written back in the figures for February (for the sake of simplicity the figure of £690 estimated tax for January has been used in this example). In practice the tax figures are sometimes not included in the comparison of actual to estimated figures. This is because the tax computation can be very complicated and the figures can change if capital equipment is purchased and tax allowances claimed. Some companies include both corporation tax and deferred tax to provide some consistency. If the tax figures are not included a separate statement on taxation should be presented to the board of directors.

Monthly cash statements

The results for February are not at all satisfactory, but to complete the picture we must have a cash statement for the month of February and this is shown as Example 5.

EXAMPLE 5

Cash statement for month of February

	Estimated	Actual	Difference
	£	£	£
Bank balance at start of month	(11,700)	(12,300)	– 600
Add RECEIPTS			
Cash sales	500	500	—
Debtors	36,000	35,500	– 500
Sub total	24,800	23,700	–1,100
Less PAYMENTS			
Cash purchases	1,000	1,000	—
Creditors	10,000	11,000	+1,000
Factory wages and salaries	3,500	3,700	+ 200
Factory overheads	2,500	2,500	—
Wages and salaries – administration staff .	3,000	3,000	—
Wages and salaries – sales staff . .	3,500	3,500	—
Administration expenses	2,000	2,000	—
Distribution expenses	1,300	1,300	—
Finance charges	—	—	—
Sales commission	—	—	—
Tax	—	—	—
Capital expenditure	20,000	22,000	+2,000
Other expenses	500	1,000	+ 500
Total payments	47,300	51,000	+3,700
Bank balance at end of month	(£22,500)	(£27,300)	–£4,800

These figures show that the bank overdraft at the start of the month was £600 greater than estimated and instead of collecting £36,000 of debtors only £35,500 was received. As for the creditors, it appears that £10,000 was insufficient to satisfy them, and £11,000 had to be paid out. There were certain other increases in expenditure, and also the capital expenditure came to £22,000 instead of £20,000, with the result that at the end of the month the bank overdraft was £4,800 greater than forecast. At this stage, of course, a banker would ask questions because the bank account is so different from that predicted, but a careful look at the outset at the estimated profit and loss account and cash projection would have given prior warning.

To give further point to this, it is often found in practice that when losses are being made financial statements are late in being produced to the bank, further delaying remedial action as far as the bank is concerned. The bank will be aware of the increased overdraft, but will be anxious to know the reason.

At this point it would be as well to digress, and deal with one aspect of cash management which must be understood by bankers. All bankers realize that the management of cash is important, and in the last example it has been shown that if care had been taken at the outset, when the original estimated profit and loss account and cash projection were produced, the trouble with the eventual shortage of cash would have been anticipated.

Management of cash

Management of cash is only one aspect of a company's business as all the assets and liabilities should be properly managed. The following example will show that a concentration on cash management alone can lead a banker astray, and that it is necessary to view the whole position of a company. In Example 6 the balance sheet figures for company 'A' have been set out for three successive years with a few extra details at the foot of each column. The directors' fees are quoted merely as a note and will have been debited in the profit and loss account. By specifying them, however, it does show how much the directors are taking out of the business. The net current assets are the current assets less the current liabilities, and the net worth is the amount of the proprietors' stake in the business. In this case it consists of the capital, plus the profit and loss account.

In the first year there was a bank overdraft of £14,000 which was reduced to £2,000 in the second year, and eliminated entirely in the third year, and replaced by a credit balance of £3,000. There seems nothing for a banker to worry about and, in fact, by the third year he might not have an opportunity of seeing the company's accounts.

However, a detailed examination of the figures will show that all is not well with the company. The creditors are increasing annually, but losses are being made. The company has had to raise additional loans and there has been an increase in capital, although the profit and loss balance has reduced from £19,000 to only £2,000.

The assets figures in the balance sheet show that the debtors have decreased annually in line with the reduced turnover. Stock, however, has

EXAMPLE 6

Company 'A'

	1st year	2nd year	3rd year	
	£	£	£	
CURRENT LIABILITIES				
Bank	14,000	2,000	—	Reducing
Creditors	22,000	28,000	30,000	Increasing
Current taxation	17,000	4,000	—	Eliminated
Total current liabilities	53,000	34,000	30,000	
Future taxation	7,000	—	—	Eliminated
Loans	—	4,000	8,000	Increased
	60,000	38,000	38,000	
Capital	40,000	50,000	50,000	Increased
Profit and loss account	19,000	10,000	2,000	Reducing
Totals	£119,000	£98,000	£90,000	
CURRENT ASSETS				
Cash	—	—	3,000	Now in credit
Debtors	24,000	20,000	18,000	Decreasing
Stock	20,000	24,000	30,000	Increasing
Marketable investments	20,000	2,000	—	Sold
Total current assets	64,000	46,000	51,000	
Freeholds	40,000	40,000	30,000	Reduced
Plant and machinery	12,000	10,000	8,000	Reducing
Fixtures and fittings	3,000	2,000	1,000	Reducing
Totals	£119,000	£98,000	£90,000	
Turnover	£250,000	£230,000	£200,000	Reducing
Net profit on ordinary activities before tax	(2,000)	(9,000)	(8,000)	
Tax	—	—	—	
Net profit on ordinary activities after tax	(£2,000)	(£9,000)	(£8,000)	Losses
Directors' fees	20,000	20,000	20,000	Steady
Net current assets	11,000	12,000	21,000	Good
Net worth	59,000	60,000	52,000	Covers fixed assets

increased, and marketable investments, which were £20,000 in the first year, have now been sold. Freeholds have also been reduced in the third year, and it looks as if plant and machinery, and fixtures and fittings, have not been replaced but have depreciated annually.

If we look at the net current assets, and a banker is very interested in this figure, we see an increase annually which reflects the fact that the company is managing its liquidity in a satisfactory way.

The new worth, although reduced in the third year, is not much different from that in the first year. However, this is after an injection of £10,000 of additional capital.

The company, although managing its liquidity well, is in a poor state with annual losses, and possibly with old plant and machinery and little in the way of assets which can now be sold.

To emphasize the error in judging a company by its cash management alone another illustration (Example 7) is given opposite.

In this instance the bank overdraft has increased from £4,000 to £26,000 over the three years. Creditors are also increasing, as also is taxation, and the total current liabilities reflect this trend. There is also a substantial amount due for future taxation, and the capital of the company is small at £15,000 when considered in relation to a turnover of £400,000. Nevertheless, this is a very good company, as can be seen by the profits produced each year and the substantial plough back of this profit after paying dividends. The profit and loss account balance has increased by £20,000 to £100,000 in the three years.

In looking at the assets figure we see that the debtors have increased in line with turnover, as also has the stock. The company has been able to buy additional freeholds, plant and machinery, and fixtures and fittings. The net current assets have reduced each year, but the net worth has had a rapid increase. Although the cash position does not look too good and the net current assets have fallen to only a small figure, the company should have no difficulty at all in putting its finances on a sound basis. If it delays further investments in freeholds for a year, or cuts down its purchases of plant and machinery and fixtures and fittings, it will be able to control its bank overdraft without trouble. In fact, a company making the profits shown would have no difficulty in raising loans or extra capital.

After this digression let us turn again to management accounts, and see what other financial statements are necessary to see the results of a full trading period in perspective.

Estimated balance sheets

So far we have examined the estimated profit and loss account and have translated the figures into an estimated monthly profit and loss statement, and then followed this with a comparison of the estimates with the actual figures. Similarly a cash projection has been prepared on a monthly basis,

EXAMPLE 7

	Company 'B'			
	1st year	2nd year	3rd year	
	£	£	£	
CURRENT LIABILITIES				
Bank	4,000	20,000	26,000	Large increase
Creditors . . .	25,000	28,000	32,000	Increasing
Current taxation . .	14,000	12,000	20,000	Increasing
Total current liabilities .	43,000	60,000	78,000	
Future taxation . .	12,000	20,000	22,000	Increasing
	55,000	80,000	100,000	
Capital	15,000	15,000	15,000	Static
Profit and loss account .	20,000	60,000	100,000	Large increase
Totals	£90,000	£155,000	£215,000	
CURRENT ASSETS				
Debtors	27,000	30,000	35,000	Increasing
Stock	30,000	40,000	50,000	Increasing
Total current assets . .	57,000	70,000	85,000	
Freeholds . . .	—	30,000	60,000	Purchases in two years
Plant and machinery .	30,000	50,000	60,000	More machinery bought
Fixtures and fittings .	3,000	5,000	10,000	More bought
Totals	£90,000	£155,000	£215,000	
Turnover	£320,000	£360,000	£400,000	Increasing
Net profit on ordinary activities before tax .	34,000	66,000	70,000	Good increases
Tax	12,000	20,000	22,000	
Net profit on ordinary activities after tax . . .	£22,000	£46,000	£48,000	
Directors' fees . . .	15,000	25,000	35,000	Large increases
Dividends	4,000	6,000	8,000	Shareholders are benefiting
Net current assets . .	14,000	10,000	7,000	Reduced and insufficient
Net worth	35,000	75,000	115,000	Rapid increase

and a comparison has been made between the estimated and the actual figures.

It can be seen, therefore, that if we start with a balance sheet at the beginning of a trading period and then use the estimated profit and loss account it will be possible to prepare an estimated balance sheet for the end of the trading period. However, this is not quite so easy in practice. To prepare estimated figures all departments of a business must be involved, and to have full consultation between departments and agreement on a feasible programme it will probably be necessary to start the estimating procedure say three months before the end of a trading period.

On the other hand actual profit and loss and balance sheet figures cannot be prepared until the end of a trading period, and with all the complicated adjustments and tax considerations it will probably be three months after the end of the trading period before the profit and loss account and balance sheet are ready. So when the estimated profit and loss account and cash budget are presented to a banker to discuss banking facilities for the coming trading period an estimated balance sheet, as at the end of the trading period, will not be available.

Sources and application of funds

Liquidity is very important when considering company accounts and many businesses have failed through paying too little attention to liquidity. With this in mind accountants are now supplementing balance sheet figures by producing an additional statement showing the sources from which funds have been acquired during a trading period and how these funds have been used. Statement of Standard Accounting Practice No. 10 (SSAP 10) stipulates that this is a requirement for all companies with a turnover of £25,000 or over. By examining the account for two successive years it is possible to construct such a statement and an illustration of how these figures are prepared appears in Examples 8, 9 and 10.

It will be seen in Example 8 that the differences between the two years are shown in the final column. If all the increases in the liabilities and the capital section of the balance sheet are extracted together with the decreases on the assets this will show items from which funds emanated. Additionally there must be taken into account any adjustments (such as depreciation) which do not involve the movement of funds.

Example 9 lists the differences as per the balance sheet and then shows the adjustment for depreciation. From these figures a final statement of Sources and Application of Funds has been produced (Example 10).

A look at a statement of this kind quickly brings the salient points to view. In the Example it can be seen that the cash liquidity of the company is better as a bank overdraft has been repaid and there is an increase in the cash balance. This is in spite of spending more money on plant and machinery and stock and also making a loss in the year. How it has managed

EXAMPLE 8

	1st year £	2nd year £	Difference £
CURRENT LIABILITIES			
Bank	4,000		−4,000
Creditors	56,000	60,000	+4,000
Current taxation	8,000		−8,000
Total current liabilities	68,000	60,000	
Loans	8,000	16,000	+8,000
	76,000	76,000	
Capital	100,000	100,000	
Profit and loss account	20,000	4,000	−16,000
Totals	196,000	180,000	

	1st year £	2nd year £	Difference £
CURRENT ASSETS			
Cash		6,000	+6,000
Debtors	40,000	36,000	−4,000
Stock	48,000	60,000	+12,000
Marketable investments	4,000		−4,000
Total current assets	92,000	102,000	
Freeholds	80,000	60,000	−20,000
Plant and machinery	20,000	16,000	−4,000
Fixtures and fittings	4,000	2,000	−2,000
Totals	196,000	180,000	

The profit and loss account shows the following adjustments not involving the use of funds:

Depreciation of plant and machinery	£18,000
Depreciation of fixtures and fittings	£2,000

EXAMPLE 9

List of differences in balance sheet

SOURCES	£
Additional creditors	4,000
Increase in loans	8,000
Reduction in debtors	4,000
Sale of marketable investments	4,000
Sale of freeholds	20,000
Reduction in value of plant and machinery	4,000
Reduction in value of fixtures and fittings	2,000
	46,000

APPLICATION	
Repayment of bank overdraft	4,000
Tax paid on previous year's profits	8,000
Loss for year	16,000
Increase in cash balance	6,000
Increase in stock	12,000
	46,000

ADJUSTMENT NECESSARY FOR DEPRECIATION

Plant and machinery has reduced by £4,000 but depreciation was £18,000. Therefore £14,000 of additional plant and machinery was purchased.

Fixtures and fittings reduced by £2,000 but this was the same amount as the depreciation.

EXAMPLE 10

Statement of Source and Application of Funds

SOURCES OF FUNDS	£
Funds generated by operations	
Loss before taxation	(16,000)
Adjustment for items not involving the movement of funds:	
Depreciation	20,000
	4,000
Taxation paid	8,000
Total funds generated from operations	(4,000)
Increase in creditors	4,000
Increase in loan	8,000
Decrease in debtors	4,000
Sale of marketable investments	4,000
Sale of freeholds	20,000
	£36,000

APPLICATION OF FUNDS	
Purchases less disposals of plant and machinery	14,000
Repayment of bank overdraft	4,000
Increase in cash in hand	6,000
Increase in stock	12,000
	£36,000

to do this is shown clearly in the items listed under the source of funds. Sales of assets have been necessary and the company has stretched its creditors, squeezed its debtors and taken out a loan.

This type of statement is also useful when forecasting. The current year's balance sheet can be projected forward and an estimated statement can be prepared for sources and application of funds. This can be very useful and will show the areas in which funds are expected to be generated and how they will be used.

Care re Forecasts

Obviously care should be exercised by bankers when examining forecasts. In all forecasts it is necessary to see that the forecasts are worked in the correct manner as set out in this chapter. It is not correct to start with a figure of possible bank overdraft and then work out what volume of sales can be achieved. Unfortunately, this is how some forecasts are produced. The correct method is to estimate the market and the capacity of the enterprise. A sales figure which is capable of achievement can then be used as the starting point for devising a forecast.

A simple enquiry will soon elucidate whether the forecasting has been done the right way round.

The banker's skill

The financial statements discussed are those normally available to bankers, but the financial statements available to businesses will, in most cases, be far more detailed. Each department of the company will have its specific detailed figures, and there is a variety of methods of compiling figures dependent on the costing methods used. When a banker is dealing with a company which has serious financial difficulties it may well be that an examination of the detailed figures available to the company will be required.

This book cannot describe management accounting fully as this is a separate subject on its own. Naturally many companies do not use management accounting methods and unfortunately bankers will, in many instances, still have to make up their minds about lending propositions, and to help them in their decisions all they will have will be out of date and inexact information.

The banker's skill is derived from his judgement in lending propositions in both sets of circumstances:

1. when full information is available; and
2. when little information is available.

It is only through a knowledge of interpreting financial statements and the interrelation of items in profit and loss accounts and balance sheets, that a banker gains the experience to make reasonable assumptions when dealing with cases where full information is not available, and also gains the confidence in dealing with customers who produce their estimated forward figures. If a banker, through his interpretation of profit and loss accounts and balance sheets, has confidence in the ability of his customer he will be more likely to accept his customer's forward projections.

Many groups of people examine company accounts. Shareholders wish to protect their capital and look at the prospect of increasing income, creditors wish to see the worth of a company and to see how much credit can be granted. Employees are anxious about the wealth of their employer and the prospect of employment continuing. Management look at accounts to plan and monitor their activities. The Government is interested in accounts of many companies, and investment analysts make judgments for use by other people. All these groups have their particular requirements when looking at accounts, but in this book we shall be considering the particular requirements of bankers.

The figures which appear in balance sheets cannot be regarded as absolute. Some figures can be objective, such as the actual cost of items bought, but other figures will be based on the subjective view of directors and managers. Also, of course, the figures are being measured as if by an instrument that is constantly changing its length. The value of money varies from year to year, and in times of high inflation comparison of annual figures can be meaningless unless adjustments are made. This certainly does not mean that accounts of business customers are useless, but rather that the accounts must be scrutinized intelligently, and with greater skill.

Monthly figures to compare with estimates are now being called for more often by bankers. They are a means of exercising closer borrowing control and need not be confined only to companies going through difficult periods. The use of such figures can enable bankers to see when troubles might be looming and when corrective action is necessary.

This is far better than being alerted to troubles only when the balance sheet is produced many months after the end of the financial year. It is generally much harder to put matters right at this stage as the problem can then be more difficult to solve.

A banker should seek to get his customer's figures as often as possible, and extract the utmost information from them. It should be his aim to discuss the implications of the figures with his customers not merely from the banker's point of view, but with the object of getting to know the customer and his business in more detail. This way confidence will be built up, and this should be of benefit both to the customer and the banker.

CHAPTER 2

The Balance Sheet

Distinction between the balance sheets of sole trader, firm and corporation – Basic structure of balance sheet – Different connotations of 'capital' – Net worth and surplus – Current assets – Liquid capital – Working capital – A percentage balance sheet – Liability ratios – Assets ratios

It is essential to understand clearly the differences between the balance sheets of a sole trader, a partnership and a corporation, the most common of which is a company limited by shares and registered under the Companies Acts. To a lender these differences are important.

Sole trader

It is customary for the business balance sheet of a sole trader to include only those assets which are actually employed in the business, and to disclose only those liabilities which arise directly out of it. Obviously, therefore, his balance sheet may give an incomplete picture, and one on which a banker can rely only to a very limited extent. Moreover, it must be remembered that a sole trader is under no obligation either as to the production of a balance sheet at all, or as to its form and content where one is prepared. The same lack of legal obligation exists in relation to the auditor, if any. He does not often certify the balance sheet of a sole trader, but merely signs it, and has no duty to disclose any reservations which may exist strongly in his mind. If, as is usually the case, the accounts have been prepared mainly with an eye to the taxation liabilities of the trader, the position, as far as the actual trading results are concerned, may sometimes be presented in the least favourable light possible. Furthermore, the banker, when he examines the accounts of a prospective borrower, usually does not know if the profit disclosed has actually been agreed by the Inspector of Taxes. A direct enquiry from the accountant, with the customer's consent, will often reveal that substantial adjustments have been made. This indeed is true of all kinds of accounts.

On the capital side, too, the balance sheet of a sole trader may present a misleading picture. His overall position may be much better than the figures indicate, by reason of substantial personal assets apart from the business. On the other hand, there may be outside liabilities so large as to cancel out the apparent balance on capital account, or even to create a serious deficiency. The main value of a sole trader's accounts to a banker will therefore lie in the trading and profit and loss accounts, rather than in the balance sheet itself; for those accounts will at least disclose the scale of operations, whether profits are being earned in excess of drawings, and generally whether the business is making progress or not. But most bankers will be able to recall cases where, according to his audited accounts, a trader had been doing very well, but in fact, unknown to his bank manager until it was too late, he had been running a side-line which was losing money so heavily as to undermine the whole position. It should never be forgotten that behind the figures is a living person, with his share of human qualities and weaknesses. This fact the banker can ignore only at his peril.

Partnership

The balance sheet of a partnership, on the other hand, will, if properly drawn up, show all the liabilities of the firm and the assets which appear will all be available to meet such liabilities. In other words, the position should not be worse than the balance sheet shows: from the point of view of a lender it may very well be much stronger; for, in addition to the partnership assets, a creditor of the firm has recourse (subject to the prior satisfaction of each partner's private debts) to the private means of all the partners (other than limited partners, if any) until he is paid in full.

Limited company

The balance sheets of a limited company will show its complete position: its finances are entirely self-contained; the full liabilities will be disclosed, and equally the total assets available to meet them. Only in the case of a company limited by guarantee, or where the balance sheet indicates that some of the share capital is not fully paid-up, can a creditor look beyond the assets shown for repayment of his debt. In the case of companies, too, a substantial minimum of information is obligatory, and the protection of the certificate of a qualified auditor is of real value.

To sum up, a company balance sheet is the most exact; that of a firm the most conservative; and that of a sole trader the least complete and reliable. Subject to these fundamental differences, which must always be kept in mind, nothing will be lost if the rest of this book concerns itself mainly with company accounts. *Mutatis mutandis*, the same principles of interpretation apply to all three types, and all balance sheets have the same essential structure.

The formats of published accounts for limited companies are laid down in the Companies Act 1985 which consolidated the Companies Acts 1948–1983 with effect from 1st July 1985. The various formats first appeared in the Companies Act 1981 which implemented proposals in the

EEC Fourth Directive designed to harmonise accounting practices and the content of accounts in the member states of the Common Market. Companies may choose between two balance sheet formats and four profit and loss formats and these are reproduced in Chapter 21. Once a format has been chosen it must be used each year subsequently, unless in the opinion of the directors there is a special reason for a change. In such circumstances the reason must be specified in a note to the accounts.

In essence, the formats for the balance sheet are either for a columnar type or for a double sided type. The profit and loss account formats are concerned with analysis either by type of expense or by function. There are four varieties because these also can be set in a columnar form or a double sided form.

Most Public Liability Companies (P.L.C.s) are using columnar figures and, for the most part columnar figures will be used in this book. It should be noted that the double sided form of balance sheet set down in the Companies Act 1985 reversed the sides on which, traditionally, have been shown in the United Kingdom the items for assets and liabilities. Also, by statute, the fixed assets appear before the current assets and the long term liabilities appear before the short term liabilities. A banker, however, except when term lending is being considered, is particularly interested in current liabilities and current assets and the examples in this book will, at times, give prominence to these items regardless of the statutory forms which, of course, must be used for full balance sheets and profit and loss accounts.

The joint accountancy bodies in the United Kingdom produce Statements of Standard Accountancy Practice (SSAPs) designed to produce uniformity of practice in the preparation of accounts and in an endeavour to reduce the subjective approach to valuations of assets which hitherto had produced wide variations between companies.

It could be thought that with statutory control for harmonisation between countries and with the accountancy profession laying down standards between companies that all figures in balance sheets could be taken at their face value. This, however, is far from true and has been evidenced by the collapse of companies only short times after issues of satisfactory audited accounts. There is still a large measure of subjective judgement available to directors apart from variations which can occur in the normal order of events; these points will have attention when we deal with the individual items of assets and liabilities.

The basic structure of a balance sheet

As a direct result of the fact that in double entry bookkeeping—and for our present purpose we can ignore anything else—every debit has its countervailing credit somewhere in the books, a balance sheet is a statement ultimately presenting a twofold view of the fund of assets controlled by the business. Details vary with the special requirements of differing types of business, but in essence all balance sheets are constructed on the framework set out below:

Balance sheet 31st December 19—

	£		£
1. Fixed assets . . .	2,000	4. Proprietors Capital .	2,000
2. Current assets . .	1,500	5. Long term liabilities .	1,000
3. Intangible assets . .	500	6. Current liabilities . .	1,000
	£4,000		£4,000

Both sides of the balance sheet are a representation of the same total of funds. There are certain assets in the company represented by the left-hand side of the balance sheet, and claims against these funds which are set out on the right-hand side. Items 1, 2 and 3 represent the assets of the company, and items 5 and 6 the claims by outside parties against the assets. Any sum remaining belongs to the proprietors.

The figures shown in balance sheets can be arranged in many different ways, and it is common now to see a vertical or narrative form which is possibly easier to understand by those who do not have a detailed knowledge of accountancy. A narrative form is shown below:

Balance sheet 31st December 19—

	£	£
Fixed assets		2,000
Intangible assets		500
		2,500
Current assets	1,500	
Less Current liabilities . . .	1,000	
Working capital		500
		3,000
Less Long-term debt . . .		1,000
Proprietors' capital . . .		£2,000

The relationship of the balance sheet items to each other is elementary but important, because it explains the different and apparently contradictory uses of the word 'capital'. As the capital fund of a company is exactly the same fund whether regarded from the angle of accountability or of make-up, there is nothing illogical in referring to certain items as 'proprietors' capital' and 'loan capital', while at the same time referring to certain groups of assets as 'fixed capital', 'circulating capital' and 'liquid capital'. The first two indicate the *source* of part of the capital fund, the next three the *nature* of certain parts of the fund. Nor indeed is there anything unsound in combining certain items from both sides of the balance sheet to ascertain the 'working capital'.

As will have been seen in the vertical form, the combination of two items, one a debit and the other a credit, has produced a figure for working capital which is the excess of current assets over current liabilities. Example 11 will make this clear. This is a simple balance sheet of a manufacturing company. There is, of course, no particular merit in using the accounts of a manufacturing company for the purpose of illustration. This book is concerned with basic principles: the figures of any other type of business would serve equally well. Placed opposite to it, for convenience of comparison, is a simple and exceedingly useful form of analysis, Example 12, which has extracted the essentials of the balance sheet, and at the same time serves to clarify the various uses of the word 'capital' to which reference has been made. Such analysis applied to any balance sheet will bring out the cardinal points: share capital, surplus, 'net worth', fixed capital, loan capital, net fixed assets, floating capital, circulating assets, working capital, most of which are discussed in detail in this and following chapters.

A point to note particularly is the fact that the total net assets exactly equal in amount the 'net worth' items. This truism will be found helpful when the mechanics of consolidating accounts are considered in Chapter 12.

Surplus and 'net worth'

The SURPLUS in the present case comprises retained (or 'ploughed back') profits, whether especially set aside by way of reserve or provision, or left unallocated in the profit and loss appropriation account. It may also include capital reserves and any other items which, had the business been wound up at the balance sheet date, would not have involved accountability to outside persons. In other words, the SURPLUS is the amount[1] which would have been returnable to the shareholders, *in addition to their capital*, had the assets all realized their book value. 'NET WORTH', which is the real total proprietors' interest in the company, is thus made up of the paid-up share capital, plus the SURPLUS. In estimating net worth in his assessment of creditworthiness, a banker will make a deduction for intangible assets which most certainly would not realize their book values if the company became unsuccessful. In the present instance £540 (discount on debentures) has been subtracted from the nominal net worth figure ascertained as above, to arrive at the true figure. The usual intangible assets deductible in this way are:

1. preliminary (or formation) expenses;
2. expenses or discount in connection with the issue of capital or debentures;
3. suspense accounts, used to spread large revenue expenditure over several years (e.g. the cost of an advertising campaign or a major programme of re-fertilization on a farm);
4. adverse profit and loss balance, representing accumulated losses.

[1] Disregarding liquidation expenses, which in practice would probably be heavy.

EXAMPLE 11

Petrangle P.L.C.

	£	£	£
FIXED ASSETS			
Intangible assets			
Discount on debentures		900	
less written off		360	540
Tangible assets			
Freeholds			79,589
	cost	amounts written off	
Long leases (over 50 years unexpired)	9,183	1,958	7,225
Short leases	10,017	3,377	6,640
Plant and machinery	124,876	70,561	54,315
Fixtures, fittings, tools and equipment	21,145	8,000	13,145
Motor vehicles	7,719	3,885	3,834
Total fixed assets			165,288
CURRENT ASSETS			
Stocks			
Raw materials and consumables		21,582	
Work in progress		37,759	
Finished goods and goods for resale		100,000	
Debtors			
Trade debtors		105,247	
Investments			
Listed investments at cost (market value £6,118)		6,234	
Cash at bank and in hand		21,139	
		291,961	
CREDITORS: AMOUNTS FALLING DUE WITHIN ONE YEAR			
Bank loans		46,164	
Trade creditors		70,408	
Taxation, payable 1st January next		18,148	
Proposed dividend		15,945	
		150,665	
Net current assets			141,296
Total assets less current liabilities			306,584
CREDITORS: AMOUNTS FALLING DUE AFTER MORE THAN ONE YEAR			
7% debentures (secured) repayable in 10 years		30,000	
9% debentures repayable in 4 years		12,894	42,894
			£263,690
CAPITAL AND RESERVES			
Called up share capital			159,449
Capital reserve			18,257
Other reserves – general			48,668
Profit and loss account			37,316
			£263,690

He will also make a deduction for intangible assets such as goodwill and trade marks. These can be very valuable and can contribute greatly to a company's success—but if the company is unsuccessful its goodwill will be valueless and its trade marks are likely to fetch little if anything.

Intangible assets for accountancy purposes, as specified in the Companies Act 1985, comprise development costs (in specified circumstances), concessions, patents, licences, trademarks and similar rights and goodwill. Apart from goodwill the amounts concerned are normally relatively small and are written off over a few years. Goodwill can only be included to the extent that it is acquired for valuable consideration and it must be depreciated over not longer than its useful economic life. The period chosen must be disclosed in a note to the accounts.

EXAMPLE 12

Petrangle P.L.C.

ANALYSIS OF BALANCE SHEET AS AT 31ST MAY 19—

(£000's omitted)

		£	£	£
Share capital	Share capital			159
Surplus	Reserves	67		
	Profit and loss account . . .	37		
			104	
	Less Intangible assets		1	104*
	Amount of capital contributed or 'Net worth'			263
	Represented by			
Fixed capital	Fixed assets		165	
Loan capital	*Less* Long term liabilities . .		43	
	Net fixed assets			122
Floating capital	CURRENT ASSETS			
Circulating assets	Stocks – raw materials	22		
	Work in progress. . . .	38		
	Stocks – finished goods	100		
	Debtors	105		
	Cash	21		
			286	
	Quoted investments		6	
	Total current assets.		292	
Current liabilities	*Less* Current liabilities		151	
	Net current assets or 'working capital'			141
	Total net assets			£263

*This kind of error is inevitable when the nearest significant figure is taken, but in this sort of analysis, exactness is not necessary.

Current assets

Current assets are also known as floating assets or circulating assets and consist of items which, apart from cash or near cash (such as short term investments) are in stages of conversion into cash. Stock is bought, work is done with the stock which, when completed, is sold and debtors are generated. When debtors pay their accounts cash is produced and the cycle starts again. The usual current assets are therefore cash, short term investments, bills receivable, debtors, work in progress and stock. It is by the turnover of these assets (i.e. the circulation of them) that profits and losses are made. Liquid assets are a sub-division of current assets and consist of the items which are the equivalent of cash, or can quickly be turned into cash. The actual items can vary between businesses, but normally liquid assets are the current assets minus stock and work in progress. Naturally if debtors are bad, or are poor payers, their liquidity is somewhat doubtful and bills receivable from unsound acceptors will be difficult to discount. The liquidity of liquid assets can be accurately assessed only by a detailed knowledge of each business.

The basic difference between a debt on open account and a bill receivable must be appreciated. Should doubts arise as to the safety of the first, legal action for the recovery of the debt can be taken quickly, even though no preliminary demand has been made: for, in law, it is the duty of the debtor to seek out and pay his creditor. But when it is known that the parties liable under a bill are in difficulties, no effective action can be taken against them until the bill matures, perhaps months ahead, and is dishonoured.

Working capital

Example 12 clearly shows the nature of working capital, or net current assets, and the method of ascertainment from the balance sheet. The amount of the working capital is the excess of current assets over current liabilities. The net fixed assets, after satisfying the fixed liabilities, plus the working capital, will equal the net worth. This will be true even where either net fixed assets or working capital is a minus quantity; or even both, in which case the 'net worth' would be a minus quantity, too, indicating a position where all the proprietors' stake and some of the creditors' money has been lost. Such book loss might be increased or decreased on realization. The net worth of Petrangle P.L.C. (Examples 11 and 12) on 31st May 19— was represented by £121,854 of net fixed capital and £141,296 of working capital, the remainder of the tangible assets being notionally appropriated to offset the amounts due to the loan and current creditors.

The question of working capital is of such importance to lending bankers that it will be dealt with in a separate chapter, with a detailed consideration of the whole current positon.

At this stage it will suffice to point out that the term 'working capital' is often mis-applied. A banker is frequently asked for overdraft facilities 'for working capital purposes'. But overdrafts are repayable on demand. So, even if all the overdraft were used towards building up net current assets, the overdraft itself would be a current liability, and the amount of working capital would be unchanged. In these special circumstances (although the overdraft does allow more freedom in the timing of receipts and payments, thus supplementing working capital) it would be better to call it an overdraft 'for normal trading purposes'.

Percentage balance sheet

Much useful information can be extracted from a single balance sheet, an operation which can be greatly helped by adding against each figure its percentage of the balance sheet total. This makes easier the comparison of one item with another, whether on the same side or on opposite sides, and simplifies the working out of various financial ratios. A percentage balance sheet, based on Example 11, is set out below:

EXAMPLE 13

Balance sheet ratios
(£000's omitted)

	£	%		£	%
Fixed assets	165	*36*	Capital	159	*35*
Circulating assets	292	*64*	Surplus	104	*23*
			Loan creditors	43	*9*
			Current liabilities	151	*33*
	£457	*100*		£457	*100*

Here we have in easily assimilable form the liability ratios and those for the different classes of assets. It will be noted that capital surplus and long-term loans amply cover the fixed assets and provide a substantial portion of the current assets, the balance of which has been provided by the current creditors. Reliance on creditor finance is reasonably small at 33% and capital and surplus have supplied 58% of total resources. Only just over one-third of the capital fund of the company is represented by fixed assets, but no inference can be drawn from this fact without a close knowledge of the business itself.

Liability ratios

Full liability percentages will bring out clearly the respective investments in the business of the proprietors, the loan creditors, the bank (under the Companies Acts bank loans and overdrafts must be shown separately from other creditors) and the other current creditors. Variations in these different interests from year to year are important indications of changes in the business and in its financial strength. An increasing reliance on the bank or outside creditors is a danger signal, and the banker will especially watch that his stake does not become disproportionate to that of the shareholders. In the case of a private company where it is customary to insist on the personal guarantees of the directors, with or without supporting security, for any bank accommodation, it will be recognized that the whole position, and not merely the balance sheet, must be taken into account. The 'net worth' of the proprietors, as shareholders, plus their backing as individuals, may warrant an extent of bank assistance far beyond what would be justified by the net worth alone.

Assets ratios

Current assets constitute the vital, organic part of the business; indeed, they are, in a very real sense, the business itself. The fixed assets correspond to the stage setting and properties in a theatrical production, but 'The play's the thing'. All the action and achievement of the business leading to progress and profits (other than capital profits) take place in the movement or turning over of the circulating assets. Against a lavish background a flimsy play, with poor direction and an ineffective cast, looks ridiculous. In business a similar disproportion between fixed and floating capital may well be disastrous. For it must not be forgotten that only the circulating assets can earn profits to provide an adequate return on the capital employed, and a sufficient surplus for amortization.

A business overloaded by fixed assets is like an overbodied car. It is sluggish instead of lively, unresponsive instead of flexible, and expensive to operate. The current/fixed assets ratio has for the financial director the same significance as the power/weight ratio has for the automobile engineer. And that business will progress fastest and farthest which has only the necessary minimum of fixed asset deadweight to carry.

Clearly the proportion of fixed to current assets will vary with businesses of different types, and in the same business in different stages in its development. Often in the case of manufacturing business an initial overplus of fixed assets will gradually be corrected by a build-up of current assets as profits are earned and ploughed back into the business. The balance sheet of a retail business which holds its shop on lease will show little more in the way of fixed assets than fixtures and fittings, and perhaps delivery vans. On the other hand, a retailer who sells exclusively for cash will, in the absence of debtors, carry circulating assets much lower than those disclosed in the balance sheet of a similar business which sells on long credit; but might well carry higher cash balances. A manufacturer, in addition to his buildings, must carry heavy fixed assets in the form of plant and machinery, which may or may not be accompanied by substantial current assets under the headings of raw materials, stores and work in progress.

Many undertakings require nothing in the way of fixed assets beyond a few pieces of office furniture. The permutations of the different asset relationships in business balance sheets are limitless.

Nevertheless the ratios between the classes of assets (fixed, current, and intangible) is important. No universally applicable rules can be given for these ratios. Each business must be considered on its merits. But a comparison of shifting ratios over several years is a useful exercise. Often imbalances, usually between fixed and current assets, will be the first indication of financial difficulties.

Comparison of debit and credit items in a balance sheet will be equally suggestive. Even if we ignore the more significant relationships which are dealt with in some detail in the pages which follow, thoughtful and intelligent comparisons of the figures on either side of the percentage balance sheet are often fruitful in practice. Comparison of the changes in items year by year is also useful. It is common now to see in published accounts a statement showing these comparisons for the current year and the preceding year as a statement of sources and application of funds on the lines set out in Chapter 1. If this is extended to show the changes over several years trends can be seen which are helpful for a full understanding of each company's business. Time spent in brooding over figures is seldom wasted.

CHAPTER 3

The Balance Sheet: Reserves

Reserves: capital reserves, revenue reserves – Provisions – Hidden and secret reserves – Bills payable – Bills receivable – Balance sheet notes – The valuation element – The auditor's report

Reserves

The demonstration of the make-up of net worth in Example 12 emphasizes the true nature of reserves and will help to remove certain popular misconceptions of their significance. For the accountant reserves are of two main kinds: capital reserves arising from exceptional capital transactions and revenue reserves built up by transfers from profit and loss account. Each forms part of the surplus, but the main distinction arises in their disposal. Capital reserves cannot be regarded as available for distribution by way of dividend, whereas all other reserves are revenue reserves, and can be re-transferred to the appropriation account and distributed. In the light of the nature of a balance sheet as explained in the previous chapter, it must be appreciated that, strictly speaking, reserves and profits cannot be distributed. It is cash, *an asset,* which is distributed and the reserve or profit and loss balance on the accountability side of the balance sheet is reduced accordingly.

Capital reserves are accumulated in various ways, and may include premiums on shares or debentures issued; capital profits arising from the sale of fixed assets at a figure in excess of their book valuation; increase of value of fixed assets over book values, on revaluation, and the 'capital redemption reserve fund' created out of revenue in connection with the redemption of redeemable preference shares.

Revenue reserves, on the other hand, are the result of one or more book entries between two credit accounts which, of course, figure on the liabilities side of the balance sheet. *They do not reflect any change whatever in the total or make-up of the assets.* Example 11 shows:

Reserve . . .	£48,668
Profit and loss . .	£37,316

If the £48,668 were re-transferred to profit and loss account, the balance sheet would not be weakened, or indeed altered, in any material way. The surplus and net worth remain exactly the same. There is no more merit or significance in a transfer of profits to reserve than in the transfer of a 50p piece from a man's trouser pocket to his coat pocket. He still has exactly the same amount of cash available. It is true that prudent directors like to reduce the apparently distributable balance on profit and loss account to discourage shareholders from looking for higher dividends. Properly regarded, this is merely a benevolent deception; for the amount on revenue reserve is still available for distribution. The point is stressed because many people are more impressed by a balance sheet showing £30,000 on reserve and a carry forward of £10,000 only, than by one showing no reserve, and a carry forward of £40,000. In so far as the creation of a revenue reserve indicates the intention to conserve working capital by curtailing dividends, it is an admirable gesture and psychologically sound. It is not, and cannot be, anything more.

Also there is misunderstanding of the effectiveness of setting aside profits to meet either specific future liabilities or unknown contingencies. Contra entries between credit accounts in the company's books cannot affect the assets. In common with all the other items making up the liabilities side of a double sided balance sheet, reserves and provisions are represented in common with all the other items on the liabilities side of the balance sheet by the changing assets as they are from day to day. If, when cash is needed, there is no cash, it is not the slightest help if a large figure appears on the other side of the balance sheet against 'reserves'. A business with no reserves and plenty of cash or other liquid assets is far better able to meet payments than one with large reserves and no liquid assets. The following skeleton balance sheets show the position of two companies at a date when each requires £15,000 to replace machinery or renew a lease:

Company A.

	£		£
Fixed assets	40,000	Capital	50,000
Stock	53,900	Reserves	20,000
Debtors	15,000	Profit and loss account	5,000
Cash	100	Mortgage	30,000
		Creditors	4,000
	£109,000		£109,000

Company B.

	£		£
Fixed assets	40,000	Capital	50,000
Stock	15,000	Reserves	nil
Debtors	17,000	Profit and loss account	5,000
3½% War Stock	10,000	Mortgage	30,000
Cash	10,000	Creditors	7,000
	£92,000		£92,000

Company A has large reserves but negligible cash; it could find the £15,000 only with the greatest difficulty unless it resorted to borrowing; Company B has the necessary liquid resources all ready.

Reserve fund

The term 'reserve fund' should be used only for reserves which are specifically represented by earmarked assets outside the business. Investments being built up for repayment of loans and insurance policies to replace assets are examples of the assets which constitute true reserve funds. Unfortunately there is an exception in the case of the redemption of fully paid redeemable preference shares. When such shares are redeemed out of distributable profits (instead of out of proceeds of a fresh issue of shares) there must be a sum, equal to the nominal value of the shares redeemed, transferred from profit and loss account or revenue reserves to a 'capital redemption reserve fund'. What happens to a reserve fund built up out of profits which has served its purpose? For instance, a company has created by transfer from profits a true factory extension reserve fund, thus:

Factory extension reserve fund	£10,000	Factory extension reserve fund investments: £10,000 4% Funding stock at cost . .	£10,000

In due time the stock is sold for £10,000 cash and the cash is spent on a new factory wing. The books will now show:

Factory extension reserve fund	£10,000	Additions to freehold factory	£10,000

But there is no longer any reason for retaining the reserve fund item in the balance sheet; and it is no longer a true reserve *fund.* It would therefore, as a matter of accounting practice, be transferred to general reserve: as it was accumulated out of revenue, it *could* equally well be re-transferred to profit and loss appropriation account. *It will be self-evident that the investments could equally well have been bought and later used in this way whether the reserve fund had been set up or not.*

Provisions

We have seen that the creation of revenue reserves for general purposes merely changes the make-up of the surplus without affecting its total. Provisions for specific *future* liabilities have a similar effect. All other provisions fall into two main classes: provisions for depreciation in value of fixed assets; and, in the working capital sphere, provisions for diminution in value of current assets, or for current liabilities: and provisions of both classes *decrease net worth.*

Provisions for depreciation of fixed assets will be shown in the balance sheet as deductions from the respective asset values. The effect is to decrease net worth (by reason of the reduced profit and loss account balance) and fixed asset values, by equal amounts. Working capital is not affected.

Provisions for liabilities such as current taxation or proposed dividends, increase current liabilities and therefore decrease working capital in step with a decrease in net worth.

Provision for bad and doubtful debts will normally be deducted from debtors, thus reducing current assets and therefore working capital in step with the reduction in net worth.

The point that provisions for depreciation of fixed assets do not reduce working capital or cash should be especially noted for future reference.

Hidden and secret reserves

So far attention has been given only to reserves created by normal open accounting procedure and visible in the accounts. There is, however, a whole range of reserves which are not disclosed in the accounts and it is important to consider them both in relation to the method of their creation and their use. Classified according to their method of creation they are:

1. HIDDEN RESERVES

These are normal reserves or provisions created in the ordinary way by transfers from the appropriation account, but hidden as to amount (if not as to their existence) under some such heading among the liabilities in the balance sheet as 'sundry creditors, and other credit balances' or 'creditors, including provision for contingencies'. This is now only permissible under the Companies Act for banks and other exempted companies.

2. SECRET RESERVES

These have been created freely in the past in the following ways:

(a) by charging capital expenditure on fixed assets to revenue, which is particularly easy when a company creates a fixed asset (e.g. a factory extension) with its own labour. This has the effect of understating the value of the fixed asset in the balance sheet. Strictly, this method is not permissible even for exempted companies;

(b) by making excessive provision for wear and tear or for the diminution in the value of fixed assets or for bad and doubtful debts, which similarly reduce the balance sheet figures for the relative asset items;

(c) by undervaluation of stock, work in progress and similar circulating assets. As auditors have to accept valuations by the company's officers, this method is still available in practice to all companies.

Exceptionally, these three methods create not only secret reserves, but a corresponding and quite deliberate understatement of profits.

Hidden and secret reserves can also arise by:

1. showing fixed assets in the balance sheet at historic cost or an old valuation, even though, because of inflation or otherwise, the true value is much greater. Where it is decided to write up the value of an asset in the balance sheet, contra entries for the amount of the increase will have to be credited partly to capital reserve and a note concerning the contingency for deferred taxation in respect of capital gains tax should be appended to the balance sheet. Such tax will not have to be paid unless and until the asset is sold later, when the actual liability may differ widely from the amount reserved;
2. including reserves and provisions, undisclosed, with other grouped liabilities;
3. diverting from the profit and loss account exceptional items of profit direct to a contingency reserve, which is hidden as in (2) above;
4. overstating the liabilities;
5. omitting, as is usual, such valuable items as goodwill, patents, trade marks, exclusive agencies and concessions.

Successful companies do, of course, have considerable goodwill as going concerns. Goodwill is never written up in accounts. Indeed it appears only when another business is bought and in such cases is usually written off immediately or over a period, which in itself creates a secret reserve.

Whenever hidden and secret reserves are created, the balance sheet and sometimes the profit and loss account will be distorted. The accounts will then fail to present a true and fair view of the company's affairs. Where an incorrect profit is shown serious questions as to the dividend which can properly be paid could arise. Everyone looking to the accounts for information can be seriously misled. For most companies the deliberate creation of such reserves is now prohibited by the Companies Acts which require all reserves and provisions to be specifically disclosed. Where assets are deliberately written down by excessive amounts, reserves must be created. This is not very easy to enforce. Opinions on values can vary even among specialist valuers. In practice, undervaluations of assets and overvaluation of liabilities can still occur.

For certain companies such as banks and insurance companies (whose stability is a matter of national importance) there is a case for permitting hidden reserves. These enable such companies to even out large fluctuations and to absorb exceptional losses without causing uneasiness to people who do not have deep understanding of accountancy matters. Recognizing this, the Companies Acts have allowed a measure of exemption to certain companies.

Balance sheet notes

Some items (besides the contingent liability on bills discounted) which must be disclosed in all company balance sheets laid before its general meeting, by footnote or otherwise, are:

1. details of arrears of fixed cumulative dividends;
2. the existence of any charge on the company's assets to secure the liabilities of third parties;
3. other contingent liabilities; e.g. guarantee liabilities and liabilities under endorsements;
4. liabilities on contracts for capital expenditure;
5. prospective commitments for capital expenditure authorized by the directors, but not yet contracted for.

All or any of these may be of vital importance to a lending banker. Unless an authentic copy of the balance sheet, *as circulated to the shareholders,* is supplied to him, the banker should always bear in mind that there are no penalties laid on the company or its directors if the copy supplied to him fails to comply with the requirements of the Companies Act. There would therefore be no obligation for the copy to be signed by the directors or to be accompanied by a profit and loss account, or the auditor's certificate or report and the director's report. A banker should be especially on his guard against the omission (or suppression) of the last two. In all cases of doubt, the only safe course is to insist on receiving copies of the balance sheet, profit and loss account and reports exactly as required to be laid before the company in general meeting.

For details of other items to be specified in the notes see Chapter 21. Notes to balance sheets contain a wealth of information and the custom is now to restrict the actual balance sheet to a minimum of figures with the details being given in the notes. It is therefore important that the notes should be read thoroughly.

The valuation element

This aspect will be dealt with more fully in following chapters but some general remarks would be appropriate now.

It is obvious that assets and liabilities of all kinds can be represented in the accounts only in terms of money. This at once introduces the question of valuation. In Example 11 every one of the items making up the circulating assets represents someone's estimate of value; raw materials, work in progress and stock figures are actual valuations; while the value of debtors and bills receivable will have been reviewed to fix amount of the provision, if any, necessary for bad or doubtful debts. The same thing is true of fixed assets. The proper amount of provision for depreciation is a matter of opinion and may quite honestly vary between wide extremes, according to the judgment of those responsible. The amount of provision may be determined from a revenue angle: that is to say, by estimating the actual loss in value resulting from the year's working, and properly chargeable as an expense. Or an attempt may be made to adjust the book value of an asset to its existing value at the balance sheet date; and existing value itself may be estimated at the lower of cost or – according to the directors' preference – saleable value, replacement value, or value to the business as a going concern.

Normally the annual provisions for the depreciation of fixed assets can be settled only by estimating:

1. the length of the remaining useful life of the asset;
2. its residual value at the end of that life;
3. selecting the appropriate accounting method, e.g. 'straight-line', fixed percentage of diminishing value, or annuity method, etc.

If full provision for replacement is wanted, a further estimate of the cost of replacement at the end of the estimated period will also have to be made. All or any of these estimates may be falsified in the event.

On the liabilities or 'source' side of a double sided balance sheet, on the other hand, practically every item is a record of historic fact, and estimation hardly features. Apart from the profit and loss balance which, indirectly, rests on many of the estimates referred to above, and probably the provision for taxation, all the liability items shown in Example 11 record precise facts. But on the assets side it is important to bear in mind always that certain items in every balance sheet represent, not statements of fact, but expressions of opinion. Furthermore, no inference as to quantities of circulating assets is valid, since the basis of valuation is unknown. Stock is normally valued at the lower of cost or market selling price, but in time of fluctuating prices it is extremely difficult, if not impossible, to apply this cost basis correctly to stock, for the stock will include items bought at different times and prices. Work in progress may be valued at:

1. prime cost only;
or 2. prime cost plus estimated proportion of overheads;
or 3. prime cost, plus overheads, plus part of the ultimate profit.

In view of the accounting canon that no profit should be brought into the accounts until it is actually earned, method 3 is justified only in the case of partly completed work under long-term contracts which straddle two or more account years. In such cases, if no credit for part of the profit were taken in intermediate end-account valuations of work in progress, no profit at all could be shown for any one contract until the account year in which the contract is completed. If his lending is 'near the bone', and the work in progress item is of significant size in relation to the total of current assets, the banker will be well advised to make searching enquiries into the basis of valuation adopted.

The auditor's report

Under the Companies Acts auditors are 'placed in a powerful, independent position, free to do their duty fearlessly, without risk of losing their appointment if they resist pressure from the directors of the company on any occasion when there is a divergence of views between the board and the auditor as to the form of the accounts, or the auditor feels it incumbent upon him to qualify his certificate'. Careful attention to what the auditor says is of immense value to the banker.

It is therefore important for bankers to insist on seeing the auditor's certificate and/or report, and to be on their guard against any deliberate suppression of adverse comments.

Any departure from the usual form of words should be viewed with caution. An auditor's qualified certificate must be taken seriously and the reasons for the qualification adequately probed. There are some qualifications such as statements that the auditors have been unable to verify documents of title to the company's land or investments, or statements that full explanations have not been obtained, which a banker must regard as danger signals. It is unfortunate, however, that qualified statements are now seen more often, and that some qualified statements are not danger signals. This is because the mass of legislation has brought forth many regulations and standards and at the same time has provided scope for different methods of accountancy. The result has been to generate debate on fundamental issues of accountancy within the profession and there is not universal acceptance of the methods to be used. Sometimes, therefore, companies are prepared to have their accounts qualified in ways which they consider to be minor, or to be on points of accounting principle. From a banker's point of view any qualification must be carefully read and an adequate explanation sought. If this is not forthcoming a banker has no alternative than to regard the accounts with suspicion.

CHAPTER 4

Current Assets

Stock, general considerations – Raw materials – Work in progress – Finished stock – Stock control – Debtors – Debtor control – Cash – Cash Control

A lending banker provides funds either on overdraft or on loan. The funds which are available for lending relate to the amounts which are deposited with the bank and, as it is normal to allow deposits to be withdrawn either immediately or on short notice, a large proportion of banker's lending must also be kept on short repayment terms. Overdrafts are repayable on demand but of course it would be impossible to obtain immediate repayment of all overdrafts if all depositors demanded their money back. However, it is unlikely for all depositors to take this action if a bank conducts its business on sound lines and lends the bulk of its funds on short term. Nevertheless, some loans are fixed for longer terms. With loans fixed in this way it is often prudent for bankers also to borrow on fixed term to match the lending, or to make some arrangements with the borrower which will have the same effect. This can be achieved by fixing the rate of interest at a margin above the inter-bank rate for wholesale funds and placing the responsibility for variations with the borrower. For example, if a borrower requires £100,000 for five years the bank might agree to 2% over inter-bank rate as the interest rate and with annual roll overs. This would mean that the bank would borrow for twelve months £100,000 on the money market and on-lend it with a 2% margin. After twelve months the bank would repay the £100,000 it had borrowed on the money market and borrow this sum again for a further twelve months and the customer would then pay 2% over and above the rate the bank paid to pick up the funds again. The effect would be to match the borrowing with the lending, as if the interest rate increased too much the customer would endeavour to repay.

Banks with widespread businesses and numerous depositors can lend some of their deposits on term loans without matching, but this can be done only with caution. Otherwise a situation develops of lending long and borrowing short, and there are numerous examples of disaster occurring through such circumstances. Confidence is a fragile asset which can quickly be destroyed.

It can be seen that apart from matching term loans the bulk of bank lending to companies is done with an eye to having overdrafts which swing well, or loans on relatively short terms, and that the bank will, in the main, be looking for the swing in the overdrafts to come from normal trading, and repayments of loans or hardcore borrowing to come from profits. The current assets circulate and are available for normal trading and any profits or losses come through increases or decreases in the net current assets. For a banker dealing in advances of this type the current assets of companies are of prime importance. Organizations which lend on long term have a different approach. The company must be sound and the asset base strong to provide for the greater risk involved in longer term lending, but the current assets must still generate sufficient surplus funds to provide for interest as it becomes due and the agreed programme of repayments.

In either event the current assets are vital and bankers pay particular attention to them. We will therefore consider the main circulating assets in detail. They are:

1. stock, under various sub-headings;
2. debtors;
3. cash.

Stock generally

For limited companies the Companies Act lays down that in published accounts in the balance sheet figures stocks shall be sub-divided under four headings.

1. Raw materials and consumables.
2. Work in progress.
3. Finished goods and goods for resale.
4. Payments on account.

For management accounts and when detailed analysis is required it may be desirable to have separate figures prepared for:

1. raw materials;
2. works sundries: oil, fuel, etc.;
3. loose tools;
4. bought-in components;
5. work in progress;
6. complete and saleable stock;
7. crates, containers and packaging materials;
8. by-products.

It should always be borne in mind that the inventory gives scope for imagination, and it is just at this point where it is most required that the 'protection' of an auditor's certificate is of least value. For the auditor is not an appraiser and in final accounts, as in interim figures, must accept both the taking and valuing of stock of all kinds by the company's staff. This is particularly true where work in progress is concerned. The auditor may advise on the proper basis of valuation, but is powerless to ensure that his advice is followed. Where full stock accounts are kept, reinforced by a system of regular internal checks, the position may be a little more satisfactory. Generally, however, a banker is very much in his customer's hands as far as stock figures are concerned, and here the question of character and integrity is of the highest importance. If a real check is considered essential in a particular case, it is a job for an expert in that particular line of business; in cases of real doubt a banker should put in his own nominee to investigate and report.

Special attention should be paid to the valuation of stock which has been acquired by 'trading-in' – for example, second-hand cars which have been taken in part payment for new ones – often brought into the accounts at the figure allowed to the customer, as being the cost price. This cost figure is obviously an arbitrary one and may have no relation to the true figure which should be re-assessed in the light of market conditions. This error is perhaps more likely to occur in interim figures than in the annual stock-taking at the end of the account year, but is no less dangerous on that account.

Particularly in connection with interim figures, but at other times as well, attention should also be paid to fashion goods, which, if they miss their market, may be almost valueless; to lines which are hanging fire perhaps in the face of the competition of a superior product; to special lines such as cheap government surplus which the trader may be tempted to write up to a figure based on current prices (thus improperly anticipating a profit yet to be earned); and to by-products, which may have been valued at the expected selling price in a market which no longer exists.

Finally the banker should satisfy himself (and in so doing help to protect his customer's interests as well) that all stock is fully covered by insurance against fire, burglary, flood and other risks appropriate to its nature. It is the easiest thing in the world for a busy trader to overlook this essential protection: and so many, even in a large way of business, fail to realize the impact of an average clause if they are under-insured and suffer only a partial loss. The average clause provides that where property is insured for less than its true value the insured and the insurance company shall share all losses, total or partial, in the same proportion that the sum insured bears to the value of the property. If property valued at £1,000 is insured for only £750 the owner is deemed to be carrying a quarter of the risk himself. When loss or damage to the value of e.g. £400 is sustained, the insurer will be liable to pay £300 only.

A loss of profits (or consequential loss) policy is a useful safeguard against loss of earnings during the period of dislocation which will follow a serious fire, or other hazard for which cover is available.

Raw materials

This item appears only in the accounts of manufacturing and processing concerns. The end product of one industry will often be the raw material of another. For example, the cloth is the weaver's finished product, but the maker-up's raw material. It may vary from a basic raw material like raw cotton to highly specialized bought-in components. Most basic raw materials will readily find a buyer, but specialized components are often completely valueless except to the business and for the product for which they were designed. So before a banker can estimate either the absorbability into normal production of raw materials, or their saleability, he must know the business. Absorbability involves consideration of the ease with which the materials can be processed or incorporated into finished stock: anything from simple assembly to the most intricate operations may be involved. Familiarity with the process of manufacture is accordingly important in measuring the risk that the channels of normal production may be clogged. Where several types of material or component have to be incorporated into the final product, the shortage of only one item may for a time 'freeze' all the remaining stocks of raw materials, as well as a large amount of work in progress.

Work in progress

This type of stock wants especially close watching. If it is larger in relation to the other circulating assets than previous records of the same business and of similar businesses have shown to be normal, bottle-necks, or other important difficulties affecting production may be suspected, and the matter should be fully probed. An excessive figure for work in progress indicates serious clogging in the circulation which is detrimental to the health and efficiency of the business as a living organism. Furthermore, when it is necessary to put in a receiver to turn work in progress into cash, heavy expenditure is often necessary to complete the work in hand before it can be turned into cash, and often the completion of the work can be achieved only at a loss. This is because the company is already in difficulties financially and the more experienced and efficient staff may well have left to seek better opportunities.

Where, as is frequently the case, progress payments are received, it is now a statutory duty to show separate figure for work in progress and for payments on account. If this was not the case distortion could occur, as the following will show:

	£	£
Work in progress, as valued by the Managing Director	17,500	
Less Amounts received on account .	10,000	7,500

The quoting of work in progress at £17,500 and the inclusion of the £10,000 with other creditors would be open to the following objections:

(a) the total of effective current assets would be overstated by £10,000 – a very material thing where a banker is lending an agreed proportion of current assets as valued in monthly or quarterly certificates;
(b) the total creditors would be similarly overstated: yet the £10,000 will not, like other creditors, have to be paid out by the company in cash, unless the company falls down on the contract or, in special cases, refunds are due;
(c) the normal relationship between current assets and current liabilities will be distorted.

Finished stock and goods for resale

Finished stock may be difficult to sell when the banker has appointed a receiver: and the more specialized the product, the greater the difficulty. It may well be that for an exclusive commodity, a separate selling organization has had to be created. If this has broken up before the receiver has assumed control his task will be unenviable indeed: low prices and high expenses are to be expected. Moreover, time is important. If stocks are to be sold quickly, especially when buyers are aware that the seller is in financial trouble, the stocks will fetch very little. Receivers and bankers have often tried to recover their money quickly with the inevitable result that the amounts realized from sales of stock have been small. The tendency now is not to be too hasty, but this means delay and consequent expense.

Any excessive accumulation of stocks must be regarded as a danger signal. It probably means that demand has fallen and sales have dwindled or that requirements have been overestimated and the business is overstocked. Stock in trade will not pay pressing debts. If cash is urgently required, therefore, sales must be forced by reducing prices, perhaps drastically, and this is not the way to run a profitable business. Example 14 indicates the effect of successive additions of £5,000 of stock bought on credit, and shows the percentage of the book valuation of stock which must be realized on break-up to satisfy the creditors; a 100% collection of debtors is assumed.

In actual liquidation it might be possible to realize stock at 22% (a) of its book value, or even 55% (b) under favourable conditions: but it would be a very optimistic liquidator or receiver who expected to collect 68% or 75%, *after allowing for the expenses of realization.*

Stock control

Whether the administration of a business is efficient or not can often be judged by knowing if a good stock control system is maintained. It is easy to see that to make profits one must sell at a higher price than one buys and that the difference must cover all expenses and profit but, although good buyers, a good product and good salesmen can be effective, the benefit they generate can be dissipated by poor control of assets and liabilities. This is particularly important in the control of stocks.

Money tied up in stock is not immediately generating profit and, at times of high interest rates, keeping large amounts of stock is expensive. Yet most businesses cannot continue without holding stock. It is important, therefore, not to keep too much stock and entail unnecessary expense, and not to keep too little which could be even more costly in lost orders or lost productive capacity. Pilfering must not be permitted by lack of control.

How then can these objectives be achieved?

The most important aspect is to see that someone senior has the responsibilities for all matters relating to stock including documentation, security, control systems, ordering, issuing and checking. This person must have a knowledge of production requirements and forward planning to establish minimum and maximum holdings of individual items of stock, must lay down the requirements for ordering and chasing late deliveries and see that goods received are properly checked into the stores. He must also see that there is a proper system for issues from the stores, records kept up to date, and spot checks by an independent person are made frequently. Proper control must relate to all types of stock, not just raw materials. Work in progress and finished goods must also be properly controlled. Adequate security systems must be instituted to prevent pilfering.

One of the simplest methods of stock control is the 'two bin' system. One bin is full and the other bin is used until empty when re-ordering takes place. This system can be used throughout the whole process of stores to operations. The use of stock by operatives can then be compared with output. Any system, however, must be looked at from time to time to see if it matches the requirements of the business, and to see if maximum and minimum amounts need revising, or delivery times updating.

It is management responsibility to ensure that the system meets its purpose and to cost it in relation to the benefits achieved. Naturally, for small inexpensive items, the cost of keeping a very tight system would outweigh the benefits achieved.

Stock costing

Price, in a good market, is determined by demand and supply and the marginal costs of production. Government legislation, monopolies and price controls tend to upset this determinant of price. In any event, it is important for businesses to know the costs of their products and the relationship of such costs to sale prices. Manufacturing, trading, and profit and loss accounts give totals of expenses, but unless these figures are broken down into departments, or related to products, the cost of individual items cannot be determined. It is essential in all but the very small businesses to have a proper costing system to determine, not only the split of expenses as to past costs, but also as a guide for future estimates. There should also be a method of checking costs and comparing them with estimates in order to take quick remedial action if this is necessary.

EXAMPLE 14

		£	£	
(a) Creditors £5,000	Cash	500		
	Debtors	3,000		
			3,500	
	Stock at cost £7,000 must produce		1,500	=21.4%
			£5,000	
(b) Creditors £10,000	Cash and debtors		3,500	
	Stock £12,000 must produce		6,500	=54.2%
			£10,000	
(c) Creditors £15,000	Cash and debtors		3,500	
	Stock £17,000 must produce		11,500	=67.6%
			£15,000	
(d) Creditors £20,000	Cash and debtors		3,500	
	Stock £22,000 must produce		16,500	=75%
			£20,000	

Costing is a subject on its own but a banker should know about some of the methods used to appreciate the variations which can occur in stock figures when different costing systems are used.

In simple terms costs can be divided into direct and indirect costs. Direct costs are those which have a direct relationship with the work in hand, and are incurred only because of such work. Therefore, the raw materials used and the costs of labour are direct costs and, as can be appreciated, direct costs vary with the amount of work on hand. Indirect costs can be subdivided into fixed costs which do not vary greatly in relation to the volume of work (such as insurance, depreciation, supervisory salaries), and general overheads which are incurred for the general running of the business (such as works overheads and head office administration expenses). It is possible to allocate all costs to the products produced and, by so doing, a business can compare its products costs with sale proceeds. Allocation can be made to products or departments and several ways can be used. The overheads can be spread according to area used, or man-hours worked, or value of production, etc., and a combination of ways is probably best in the interests of providing an equitable solution, and gaining the co-operation of the work force in giving full support to cost control methods. This method of allocating all the costs to the products is known as the full costing or absorption costing method. It is not a perfect system as the allocation of overheads can be done in differing ways, but it is widely used and adequate for many businesses.

Another method favoured by some accountants is the marginal costing method. This recognizes that it is not easy to allocate accurately the indirect costs and it calculates only the direct costs of the various products and compares these with the income receivable from sales of those products. The surplus income is referred to as the contribution as it is, of course, a contribution towards covering the indirect costs. The argument put forward for supporting this method is that in absorption costing the product can be shown to be making a loss, and its production may, therefore, be curtailed whereas marginal costing may show that the product is making a contribution towards payment of the overheads, and its production should be continued until some other products can be found which will make a bigger contribution. Marginal costs can also help in the evaluation of different products to see which one makes the greatest contribution towards indirect costs.

This method also is not the perfect solution as a product making a relatively small contribution which uses only a small space and needs little attention can be more worthwhile than a product making a bigger contribution which takes up vast space, and needs considerable control. As with all decision-making, the decision based on one aspect alone can be wrong.

The best method of costing so far devised is known as standard costing. With this method considerable record keeping is necessary to provide the evidence to start the system, and to continue it. Costs of labour, materials and overheads are allocated to each product and a standard cost of each product is calculated. Subsequently the actual costs incurred are calculated and compared with the standard. It will be appreciated that if sufficient detail is provided when devising the standard it will be possible to see where differences from the standard occur. These differences are called variances, and it should be possible to see if, for example, more time was taken on production than was estimated, whether more expensive labour was used, if the cost of raw materials differed, or if specific overheads cost more or less than estimated. If alerted in good time management should be able to take remedial action, or possibly alter the standard if circumstances have changed. However, a good costing system matters little if it is not operated in an efficient manner and management ability is one of the qualities which bankers must assess when dealing with their customers.

With this knowledge of costing systems it will be seen that the stock figure in balance sheets can be affected by the costing methods used and the proportions of the overall costs which are used to enhance the basic cost of the raw materials bought. The balance sheet figure for stock is traditionally quoted at the lower of cost or market value, but the cost can be assumed to be the initial basic cost of the raw materials, or can include an element of direct costs (say 50% at one stage and 75% at another stage of manufacture), or elements of both direct and indirect costs.

Stock valuation

The difficulties of putting a correct value on stock have been highlighted in recent years by rapid inflation. If, for example, stock costing £1,000 is sold for £2,000 a profit of £1,000 is made, on which tax has to be paid. However, if in the meantime with inflation the same volume of stock costs £2,000 instead of £1,000 a businessman would consider that he had been unjustly treated by having to pay tax on the profit of £1,000. All that has happened is that the business has stood still and merely replaced its stock.

The fact is that by using the historic cost in times of high inflation a fictitious profit is made and many businesses have found themselves under strain in trying to keep up their volumes of stock at rapidly increasing prices and, at the same time, having their liquid resources reduced by payments of tax on unreal profits. Considerable thought has, therefore, been given to the methods which have been used for valuing stock. A simple method of valuation is used in businesses which deal with slow selling units such as antiques, or valuable paintings. Each item has a cost price, and the sale price can be related to it. This method, which is known as unit costing, is unsuitable for most businesses. Another method used is the average costing method. Uniform items of stock are bought in quantities throughout the year and when stock is received the cost of the new stock, plus the stock in hand, is averaged to give the cost of individual items.

The most popular method in the UK is known as 'first in first out' (FIFO) which in times of stable prices would seem to be a sensible way of accounting for stock. It is assumed that the old stock is used first and, therefore, stock in hand at balance sheet dates is valued according to the prices paid for the later stock receipts. The method, however, is not suitable for use in times of high inflation unless a corrective element is introduced to mitigate against the fictitious profit made.

The method which has a reverse effect is the 'last in first out' method (LIFO) which assumes that the later items bought are used first and stock in hand is priced according to the prices paid for the earlier goods received. In many businesses this does not accord with reality, but the advantage claimed for this method is that fictitious profits caused by inflation are to a large extent eliminated. It will be appreciated that after using this method for a few years the figure shown for stock in a balance sheet is quite meaningless unless the stock is revalued in line with current prices.

A further method which endeavours to overcome the difficulties caused by inflation is the base stock method. This is suitable for companies which deal in large quantities of goods which can be easily classified, such as basic raw materials. A minimum holding of stock which is not reduced afterwards is decided on and that stock is valued at the price paid, and appears in subsequent balance sheets at the same price. Purchases during any accounting period are matched as far as possible with sales and, therefore, the profit shown for the accounting period is the actual profit made. If there are any temporary surpluses of stock at balance sheet dates over the base (or minimum) stock it is generally valued at its purchase price. This system gives an accurate representation of reality, but it is suitable only for a relatively small number of companies. There are a number of other methods of valuation but the ones described are the main ones. A note must be included in the notes to the accounts if there is any material difference between the amounts shown in the balance sheet and the replacement costs.

The difficulties over the inflation aspect were, for some years, recognized by the Government and some relief from taxation was granted to businesses for their apparent increases in stock.

A further hazard which must be taken into account by bankers when considering stock is the ownership of the stock. Ownership depends on legal considerations, not on accounting ones, and companies can show stock in balance sheets which in a receivership or liquidation can be proved to belong to their suppliers. This is because some suppliers reserve the title to the goods to themselves until payment. This is not a new concept, but was given considerable publicity in 1976 by the Romalpa case. In this case a Dutch company supplied goods to Romalpa, an English company, which subsequently went into liquidation. The Dutch company had reserved title to the goods until payment in full, and the Courts decided in favour of the Dutch company. The effect of the judgment and subsequent judgments is that a supplier of goods in some circumstances can claim the return of the goods, or the proceeds of sale of such goods, and may also have rights against any article into which his goods have been incorporated. Since this case many suppliers have imposed similar conditions particularly when supplies have been dealing with companies which are not financially strong. It would appear to be sensible to treat stock supplied on these conditions as stock on consignment. Where amounts are material attention should be drawn to this in a note to the accounts.

Altogether, it will be appreciated that the figures for stock which appear in balance sheets can vary considerably, dependent on the valuation method used, and the costing system in force for work in progress, and finished goods. The Romalpa case decision can also affect the ownership of goods shown in balance sheets. The experience of receivers and liquidators shows that when a company is in trouble it is very difficult to dispose of stock at anything like book price, and forced sales produce low returns.

It is little wonder, therefore, that normally bankers are loath to take into account as security for advances more than a small fraction of the stock valuation. A knowledge of a company's methods concerning stocks can help a banker in his assessment, and it can also help him to understand how the profit and loss account reflects these methods.

Nevertheless, in adversity the fact is that stock generally fetches only knock-down prices.

Debtors

The term is used here to include normal trade debtors, whether on open account or represented by bills receivable. The usually insignificant amounts representing deposits and payments in advance may be excluded for our present purpose, as they will not produce any future inflow of cash while the business is in being, and very little if it is wound up. In a business which sells wholly on credit, debtors are the only current asset which produce cash, and in most businesses are the sole source of the cash receipts.

In the building and similar trades it is not unusual for contracts to provide for retentions up to as high as 25% of the contract price, deductible *pro rata* from interim payments, and retained by the builder's customer for three to twelve months after completion. This is to meet counter-claims, or to cover latent defects which may appear after the work is finished: the retentions will usually be lost if, for any reason, the work is not completed. Retention moneys being thus vulnerable in many ways, the prudent banker will deduct the amount so retained from the debtors' figure in estimating the value of current assets. The clogging effect of retentions of the inflow of cash will be obvious.

It may not be out of place to add here that local authorities and government departments often require indemnity bonds for perhaps 10% or 15% of the amount of the contract from the contractor's banker, or other surety of standing. If the contractor defaults on his contract he may not only lose his retention moneys, but also have to face a claim from the surety under the usual counter-indemnity. This will certainly arise if the retentions are insufficient to pay some other contractor to complete the work.

To the extent of retentions, debtors cannot be regarded as a liquid asset: and its liquidity will often vary seasonally and geographically in different industries and trades, and even in the same business. For example, the book debts of an agricultural engineer or merchant will be very much more liquid in November than in April: and if a tradesman cannot collect the amounts due from his seaside hotel and boarding-house customers before October, he may very well have to wait until the following summer. The flow of book debts is extremely sensitive to changes in general financial conditions. Often one of the first signs of tightness of money is not falling off in retail sales, but an increase in debtors, accompanied by a slowing down in collections. The increase in debtors in such circumstances is, of course, due to the switch-over of certain buyers from cash purchase to credit purchase. It is obvious that when an inflow of cash is most essential, the collection of debtors is generally most difficult: and when times are bad, book debts are anything but liquid. It is true that certain financial houses are prepared to purchase book debts, though only after minute investigation and at a discount large enough to cover the risk and costs of collection and yield a profit. But this merely emphasizes that sometimes debtors are not liquid in the true sense of the word.

It may be appropriate here to sound a note of warning about the possible existence of trading set-offs. Where the same person appears both in the bought ledger and the sold ledger of the same business, e.g.

Creditors include	*Debtors* include
Merchant Supplies Ltd. £10,000	Merchant Supplies Ltd. £30,000

the debtors figure, on which the holder of a floating charge can rely, may be overstated by £10,000 if a true legal set-off exists. If the lending banker relies on the full £30,000, he will be disappointed to find that only £20,000 can be collected by his receiver. The undisclosed credit for £10,000, previously regarded as unsecured, will thus, in effect, rank as preferential in front of the bank's floating charge.

There is a further danger that debtors may not be well spread. Where a large amount appears against one name, or as due from a subsidiary company (as a separate entry in the balance sheet), enquiry should be made as to whether the debt is 100% good.

With these two points in mind the banker's prudence will, in suitable cases, suggest calling periodically for full lists of both debtors and creditors.

Debtor control

Control of debtors is an important management function, but very often little control is exercised. Similar considerations apply as for the control of stock in that the amount of debtors should be neither too large nor too small. The amount of credit given should be in line with the normal terms applying in the particular trade. If debtors are allowed to get too large the company will have unnecessary expense by depriving it of cash, and if debtors have become unduly depressed by harsh measures to restrict credit terms this will have the effect of curtailing future trading activities. What, therefore, are the aspects which a business should take into account in devising a debtor control system?

Firstly, the length of credit to be allowed must be established. To maintain a competitive position the length must be near the normal period allowed in the particular trade. It could, of course, be established at a longer period than normal, giving the business a competitive edge, but the additional credit granted must be costed at an interest rate (either on borrowed funds, or on the rate available to the business for use of its own funds) plus a margin to compensate for the additional risk. A business may be able to insist on shorter credit terms than normal, if the demand for its product is high, and still not damage its trading position. Also, it is not necessary for the same length of credit to be given to all customers, as it may be worthwhile to grant longer credit for the better customers, and curtail the length of credit for the poorer customers. Any extension of the length of credit should, however, be costed.

Secondly, the limit of the credit granted to each customer must be established, and to do this a system of status reports must be introduced. A trade agency is the best source for these reports as the information is much fuller than the brief replies to enquiries given by banks. Naturally the initial status reports alone will be insufficient to support a continuing trading relationship, and regular reviews of the credit granted should be made, and further reports obtained, as considered necessary.

Thirdly, a business will have to consider how much credit it can afford to give. Deciding on the amount of credit justified for each customer, and length of time for payment which it would be prudent to allow, will not be sufficient if the business cannot afford to grant as much credit. It may well be that to increase turnover the amount of credit granted must be curtailed. To calculate the total amount of debtors which can be allowed, a business will have to take into account its circulating assets and liabilities. The creditors will have to be assessed on the amount of credit it will be prudent to take; the turnover will have to be analysed between cash and credit receipts; the cash available, or the limit of borrowing, must be known. It will then be possible to set an overall limit to the total of debtors, and to devise a system of expansion or contraction of debtors, dependent on the level of business.

After this stage has been reached a checking system must be devised to ensure that full control is exercised. Sales personnel must not arrange transactions which will take individual debtors over their credit limits without reference, and ledger clerks must report excesses both as to time and amount. At regular intervals lists must be provided for senior management showing the length of time for which debts are outstanding. This can be in groups of, say, one month, two months, three months, etc., with individual names and amounts specified for the long-outstanding debtors. A chasing procedure will then be required for poor payers, and then consideration will have to be given for curtailing further supplies if the debtors do not co-operate. Should there be any debtors whose debts do not fall for payment within one year the amounts must be separately disclosed in company published balance sheets.

Valuation of debtors

What is the worth of the figure for debtors which appears in a balance sheet? Should a banker look at it and take it at its face value, and expect that the full amount will, in due course, be received? Obviously not. The value will depend on the individual items as some items will be bad debts which will be irrecoverable, there will be some doubtful debts, and some items could well be set off against creditors. Also retentions are often included in the debtor figures, and sometimes these prove irrecoverable, and if inter-group transactions are included the true value of the debtor figure is difficult to estimate. Knowledge of the make-up of the debtor figure helps to get nearer to estimating the value, and when bankers are relying particularly on the debtors regular lists of debtors should be produced and explained by the customer. Quality of management is often reflected in the quality of debtors.

It is little wonder, therefore, that a banker, even when dealing with a first-class company, is reluctant to lend more than 50% against debtors. A factoring company is often prepared to lend 75% to 80% and this is easy to understand as the factor will have examined the books of the company, extracted lists of debtors, eliminated some of the entries, know which ones are old outstanding amounts, and will have obtained status reports on the important debtors in the list. Its experience in collecting, and knowledge of similar businesses and, in many cases, knowledge of the debtors concerned, will enable it to come to a more accurate estimate of the value.

If factoring is involved a lending banker will want to know the details of the arrangement as this can affect the amount of the debtors due.

Factoring can take several forms. It can be purely administrative or can involve the sale of book debts or arrangements similar in some ways to borrowing against book debts.

If it is purely administrative the factoring company takes over the job of collecting the debts due and the customer need not then employ staff for this purpose. The other types of factoring can be tailored to the requirements of the customer, but the main ones are as follows:

1. Without recourse. The customer's debts are purchased by the factor on the basis that if the debtor is unable to pay, the factor bears the loss. Payment from the factor can be at an agreed maturity date (generally the average time, judged from experience, of when the debtors settle) or some other prior date. If the average maturity date method is used, all that happens is that cash is substituted for debtors and would be, in some respects, similar to the collection of debts without the involvement of the factor. However, if a prior payment date is involved, cash will have been received into the customer's account and in these circumstances a banker would be misled if he considered the bank overdraft in relation to the current assets without making a deduction from the debtors to cover the cash paid by the factor.
2. With recourse. Similar arrangements are made as in 1. but with the customer bearing the responsibility for bad debts. As the debts are purchased by the factor the customer will have a contingent liability for bad debts and this should appear as a note to the balance sheet.
3. Confidential factoring. In this case the factoring company does not notify the debtor of its interest and the collection of the debts is continued by the customer. The factor will have paid the customer for the debts and will expect reimbursement on specified dates. It will be readily appreciated that as the debts will have been sold to the factor and the same debts are being collected by the customer that the bank account can be credited twice for the amount of the debts prior to reimbursement to the factor.

In all these cases payments for debts can be 100% of the agreed sum on initial payment or some lesser proportion with the balance to follow later.

Invoice discounting can also be used in order to anticipate the receipt of payment from debtors. This is similar to confidential factoring but does not cover the whole of the sales ledger but deals with individual transactions.

With so many different ways of dealing with debtors through factoring and finance companies a lending banker must obtain full details of the factoring or invoice discounting arrangements with any customer to whom he is lending and, in doing so, is placing some reliance on the customer's current assets.

Bills receivable

An unexplained decrease in the amount of bills receivable, or in the absence of the item from the balance sheet of a customer in whose business the use of bills is customary is a warning. It may be that the trader is borrowing from tomorrow's collections to meet today's payments, by discounting—sometimes one of the early signs of financial stringency, though often sound business if it enables good discounts for prompt payment to be secured, or borrowings at higher rates of interest to be reduced.

The balance sheet of the company which is laid before the company in general meeting must disclose the contingent liability on bills discounted, whether by way of a footnote or otherwise. But no penalties are imposed if such a footnote is omitted from the copy of the balance sheet provided to its bankers in connection with an overdraft. Apart from this possibility, where a banker is comparing figures in the last audited balance sheet with interim current asset figures, the latter will probably not be accompanied by any similar warning note. The only indication of new or increased discounting will then be a fall in the aggregate of debtors and bills receivable inconsistent with the trend of recent sales, and other related figures.

There is some justification for the view that the worst unsecured lending can be to a customer with a fixed and regular income, whether an employee or an annuitant. If he cannot live on his income this month or quarter, how can he live on the same income during the next period, and in addition, repay what he overspent in this period? Like all general principles it can quite easily be modified in special cases. Borrowing can be quite justified to enable a salaried man of sound character and thrifty habits to spread a large item of exceptional expenditure over a reasonable period, but the principle is clear enough and it applies with equal force to a large company. Borrowing from the future is an expedient to be used with reluctance; in any case, while it may be done progressively, it can only be done fully, once.

Cash

Cash may appear to be the most desirable current asset for a business as it can be used in many ways, unlike debtors and stock. Also the object of having stock is to turn it into debtors, and then turn the debtors into cash. However, circulating assets circulate and the flow does not stop when cash is obtained as the cash has to be used for buying more stock as well as for the payment of wages, overhead expenses and financial charges. An excess of cash could indicate the management is inefficient, and that the assets of the business are not being properly used. Excess cash can, of course, be invested on the stock market, but a business should be able to make more profit by using its cash than investing in this way; otherwise there seems little point in continuing in business.

Cash loses its value in times of inflation and so it is not desirable to retain large quantities for a long time. It should be put to work. When dealing with the control of stock and of debtors it was shown that for proper control not too much and not too little of either type of asset should be held. The same applies to cash. If too little is held the business cannot function properly (unless a reserve can be called on, such as a bank overdraft), and if too much is held proper use of the asset is not being made.

The control aspect has been demonstrated in Chapter 1 in which it was shown how the various activities of a business are brought together through their respective estimated budgets from which a cash projection is produced. Actual results are then compared with the projection. A shortage of cash is normal, at times, for an efficient business, as it then uses a trading overdraft and does not have to keep cash idle but can put it to work in the business. Whether or not an overdraft is available to the business there will come times when additional funds are required, and a business must plan accordingly. Additional overdraft facilities must be obtained, or cash provided. It can often happen that cash must be provided, and by forward planning a good financial controller will see that sufficient cash is retained from the flow of cash into the business via the circulating assets to provide for these occasions. When surpluses are held temporarily, they should be invested in safe securities so that some return is obtained on the funds. Cash budgeting is, therefore, vital in order to get the best out of cash resources.

Cash, of course, also has to be available for capital investments and withdrawals from the business such as dividends, but it is a mistake to use cash for these purposes if by so doing the necessary working capital of the business is depleted. If dividends cannot be afforded they should not be paid, and if capital investments are required which cannot adequately be paid for from an excess of working capital then a loan for the purchase should be obtained, or additional proprietors' funds should be introduced. Any loan obtained should be related to what the business can afford, and hardship is the result of trying to borrow short term when a longer term is better suited to the earnings of the business.

Often a bank manager is asked by customers for an overdraft to help with normal trading, whereas the working capital has been depleted by a capital purchase. The proper way to deal with the request is to examine it as a loan for a capital investment, and not for a normal trading overdraft.

When a business has several branches full control can be exercised by having all receipts and payments centralized, but this must be set against any disadvantages which might result in the particular business by having such strict control. In any event, branches should not be permitted to keep large sums idle. When overseas branches or subsidiaries are concerned the control of cash can be very complicated, as exchange control regulations must be taken into account as well as fluctuating rates of exchange. Centralized amalgamation of receipts in one country may not then be advantageous, but detailed research should be made to devise the best method of control for the particular circumstances.

In short, therefore, cash needs to be controlled just as much as other assets, and not just left to chance or dealt with in a haphazard way.

CHAPTER 5

Fixed Assets

Land and buildings – Valuation – Plant and machinery – Depreciation – Fixtures and fittings

It may be wondered why this chapter on fixed assets does not appear before the one on floating assets, because fixed assets normally appear ahead of floating assets in balance sheets. The point is that floating assets are far more important to a banker. It is from the use of floating assets in trading conditions that profits are generated, and it is from the increase in floating assets that bankers look for repayment of overdrafts. Lending on overdraft is primarily for use for normal trading and the repayment, therefore, comes from the normal trade of the business.

A banker looks first of all at the proposition and decides whether it is viable. It is only after he has decided if the proposition is viable that he has to look at the safety of the advance, and fixed assets often come into the picture here as they provide stability and security to which a banker can look. A balance sheet without much in the way of fixed assets is a poor one to present to a banker to support a lending proposition for any substantial amount, as in times of trouble current assets can quickly disappear. Also, of course, long term lenders have to look closely at fixed assets for their security. Naturally they also have to look at the trading position of the business to see if sufficient profits are being generated to service the borrowing, but it is not possible to look many years ahead and estimate what the trading position will be then. Long term lenders, therefore, have to look to the fixed assets to see them safe. Fixed assets should not be bought in a haphazard way, or according to some whim, and the fixed assets which appear in balance sheets should have been the result of investment decisions and appraisal, as set out in Chapter 13.

The main types of fixed assets are:

(a) land and buildings;
(b) plant and machinery;
(c) fixtures, fittings, tools and equipment;
(d) investments.

Land and buildings

Land and buildings can be divided into freeholds and leaseholds and it is not usual to find that freeholds are depreciated in accounts. Normally all property depreciates over a period of time, and this must apply to freeholds as well as leaseholds. Usually, however, freeholds are valued at their historic cost, and repairs and renovations are debited to profit and loss account. Leaseholds depreciate even if it is a long leasehold as eventually the property will revert to the freeholder. Although it is normal accountancy practice to value assets at the lower of cost or market price, there have been some changes in recent years over the historic cost valuations of freeholds and leaseholds, and quite often these accounts have been valued upwards after a professional valuation. The cause of this change of attitude is rapid inflation. Properties have kept their real values whereas money has depreciated, and many businesses have felt that an inaccurate picture is given if freeholds and leaseholds are quoted merely at cost price. Strictly, in book-keeping terms, it is not right merely to value one type of asset and not, at the same time, to value all the other assets, and all the liabilities too. Nevertheless bankers are faced with the fact that sometimes freeholds and leaseholds are revalued, and sometimes put in at their historic cost price. Even without revaluation a banker can look at the freeholds and, if he knows the particular properties and values in the area generally, will be able to estimate a new value for such properties. The increase in value in this case would, in fact, be a secret reserve. There is, however, a snag both in the revaluation of properties and in mentally estimating a secret reserve: taxation provisions. When a property is sold capital gains tax has to be paid on any profit, unless in some instances a new property is bought with the proceeds. This will be dealt with more fully in the chapter on taxation, but if a banker is mentally taking into account the enhanced value of a property he must also take into account the tax that might have to be paid; if the banker is looking to the sale of the property to provide repayment of an advance he must also realize that there could be a liability for tax. The value of a property in a balance sheet, whether at historic cost value or at a professional valuation, is not satisfactory from a banker's point of view. The historic cost is merely the price paid, and possibly reflected the open market price at that time. A professional valuation will probably be made at an existing use value to the business, whereas a banker requires to know the forced sale value of a property because it is only when difficulties have occurred that the banker has to insist on a sale. It is usual, therefore, for bankers to disregard whatever values are put on properties in balance sheets, and either to make their own valuations or to get professional valuations on a forced sale basis. Normally this is the only item in a balance sheet specifically valued by bankers.

Where a banker is considering the forced sale valuation of factory premises the following considerations are important:

1. is it specialized in layout and construction, or is it widely adaptable to many types of industry? For instance, are the upper floors capable of carrying heavy machinery? Are heavy duty elevators installed or installable?
2. is it well served by railway, road, river or canal or do the available transport facilities confine their use to light industry?
3. do planning restrictions limit its possible user?
4. what are the available supplies of labour: skilled and unskilled, male and female? In times of housing shortage which exacerbate the natural immobility of labour this is vital. In practice the range of the market will be severely limited if the available labour force is not flexible in character.

All these factors bear on the adaptability of a particular property. The less the adaptability the narrower the market and the lower the price obtainable.

Short leaseholds are generally put into the balance sheet at the cost price of obtaining the lease, and then depreciated fairly rapidly over the term of the lease as at the end of the term they are worth nothing. Often, from the banker's point of view, they are worth nothing from the outset because there are generally clauses in the leases which restrict the trade which can be carried on in the properties, and enable the landlord to retake possession on failure to pay rent, or on the bankruptcy or insolvency of the leaseholder.

Plant and machinery

This item can often be very large in the balance sheets of manufacturing companies, but when a banker considers such plant and machinery as security he can take into account only a very small proportion of the stated value. Should he ever wish to rely on it for repayment of his advance he will be lucky to realize anything other than a relatively small amount. Among the many other relevant factors which a banker cannot know except after the closest inspection and enquiry are:

1. how much of the plant is fixed and immovable (e.g. furnaces, tanks, stills, driers and the like) and therefore virtually unsaleable. Moreover such plant will often 'run with the land' and be caught up by mortgages or mortgage debentures;
2. how much of the machinery (e.g. drills, lathes, boring machines, presses, etc.) is of general utility and therefore reasonably saleable, and how much is specialized and useless except for the production of that particular factory or industry. Purpose-designed machinery may be virtually useless if the industry itself is in the doldrums;
3. the proportion of slow-moving, long-lasting machinery to fast-moving machines with a high rate of wear and a short life;
4. the extent to which both plant and machinery are modern, obsolescent or out of date. New inventions may quickly reduce much of even new

machinery to little more than scrap value: a marked shift in the direction of customer demand may have the same effect;

5. the adequacy or otherwise of the past depreciation provisions which obviously affect the starting figure for any estimate of break-up value;
6. the extent to which the machinery is subject to hire purchase or pledged as security. This will certainly be a very real factor when an attempt is made to assess what will be available from the liquidation for a debenture holder and an unsecured creditor.

Although the same pieces of machinery can often be used in different factories the fact remains that once machinery is brought into use it is very difficult to resell it at anything near the purchase price. This is particularly so when a company gets into financial trouble as then any possible buyers will always hold back in the hope of picking up the machinery at a knock-down price. Plant and machinery wears out and therefore an item for depreciation must be written off the value of the plant and machinery annually, and similarly debited to the profit and loss account. There are several ways in which the depreciation can be calculated and two main methods are:

1. the straight line method by which an equal amount is written off the plant and machinery annually; and
2. the reducing balance method on which a proportion of the value is written off each year. This percentage is calculated on the annual reducing balance.

There are other methods more suitable to particular trades and industries and in fact any method can be used which is prudent and consistent and satisfies the auditors. An important point which must be kept in mind is that depreciation, although written off in the profit and loss account, cannot be taken into account when calculating the profit for tax purposes. The depreciation written off in the accounts has, therefore, to be added back to the profit figure before a calculation is made concerning the tax payable. Capital allowances or writing down allowances are substituted for annual amounts of depreciation and these allowances are deducted from the profit figure before the tax is calculated. When capital allowances were at the rate of 100% the entire cost of the asset was written off in the first year. In other words, the whole of the depreciation of the asset which is accounted for over the life of the asset is, for tax purposes, deducted in the first year. It will be appreciated that the benefit from such accelerated capital allowances is in the question of timing. The same amount of depreciation is written off. It is merely that the capital allowances permit this depreciation to be written off in the first year instead of over several years and, therefore, the business has the advantage of a delay in the payment of tax. Such money can, of course, be put to use until it is required to meet the eventual tax bill, and this can be of considerable advantage.

Replacement of plant and machinery in times of inflation can cause a great deal of concern to businesses. When machinery needs replacing it is often found that the cost is very much higher than the original price of the machinery to be replaced. The object of writing off depreciation in the accounts is to write off the value of the plant and machinery which has been consumed in the business during the accounting period, and the whole cost price of the machinery, less the price for which it is disposed of at the end of its useful life, should be written off as depreciation over the period of time for which the machinery is in use. This has the effect of conserving in the business the resources which, theoretically, should provide for the replacement machinery in due course. However, because of inflation, this does not occur and additional sums have to be found.

Several attempts have been made to try to overcome this problem. One method suggested is to revalue the machinery annually, and then to re-calculate the depreciation on the new figure. This, of course, does not go the whole way; it provides depreciation annually on the figure increased by inflation but it does not, of course, take into account extra depreciation or backlog depreciation which should have been accounted for in the past. It does, however, go part-way to providing the funds required for the replacement machinery.

Businesses can, of course, provide for replacement by taking the amount of the depreciation out of the working capital of the company and investing it in a separate fund. The fund will eventually be of use when the new machinery is bought. However, it is not necessary to withdraw the depreciation money into a separate fund, and a business can quite often use the resources to better advantage in its own business than it can by investing in a separate fund. Naturally the resources will not then be available when replacement machinery is necessary. If this is the case it will then have the problem of providing for the replacement machinery either out of additional proprietors' funds, or from borrowing. Borrowing is quite often the solution and, if the working capital is generating sufficient profit to finance replacement over a relatively short time, a banker should be quite happy to assist with the necessary loan.

Fixtures, fittings, tools and equipment

Generally only small amounts are involved, which a company tries to write off quickly. They are not of much value if a resale is expected, and a banker would put little reliance on the sum quoted in a balance sheet if considering fixtures, fittings, tools and equipment as security.

Investments

Substantial amounts often appear under this heading. The investments may be in listed companies which are dealt with on the stock exchanges, or in companies which do not have such ease of dealing in their shares. Should the investment be merely a temporary one the asset should be shown among the current assets, but if it is of a more permanent nature it is probably a fixed asset. This applies whether or not the investment could be sold at a moment's notice. It is the intention which is important.

It may well be that there are good trade reasons for holding the investment with a sale not normally being contemplated. Obviously, in these circumstances, it may not be of advantage also for receivers to dispose quickly of such investments and a banker would be reluctant to rely fully upon the values quoted in balance sheets for these investments.

The banker's view

It will be seen that the figures shown in balance sheets for fixed assets are not relied on by bankers for security. Fixtures and fittings are generally regarded as valueless, plant and machinery can fetch only a knock-down value in times of difficulty, and property must be considered at forced sale values, and not at balance sheet values. Nevertheless, a banker is reluctant to lend large sums to companies which do not have fixed assets. It is relatively easy for floating assets to be moved, or to be run down quickly by unscrupulous people, but fixed assets give more permanence to a business.

One of the difficulties facing bankers relates to interest on overdrafts. This is normally the cheapest method of borrowing and borrowers naturally wish to use overdraft financing in preference to other methods. Overdrafts, however, are suitable for normal trading and for use in overcoming the uneven inflow of amounts due, and the outflow of payments. When fixed assets are bought it may be possible to contain the cost within an overdraft arrangement if the swing in the banking account is a wide one, and adequate receipts are expected over a relatively short period. When any substantial amount is involved, however, the price can probably only be repaid over a period of several years, and an overdraft is not usually the most suitable method of finance. A loan (for a short or a long period, dependent on the expected cash flow), or the provision of proprietors' funds, is more likely to be the correct way of financing. There is not much point in straining the liquid resources of a business to buy fixed assets out of working capital as this can cause a restriction on the trading capacity of the business. Unsophisticated borrowers, however, will not see that there are different methods of financing for different purposes, while sophisticated borrowers will often try to force overdraft facilities out of bankers for unsuitable purposes because of their relative cheapness.

CHAPTER 6

Liabilities and Proprietors' Funds

Debentures – Mortgage bonds and unsecured loans – Convertible loans – Inter company lending – Deferred taxation – Share capital – Reserves – Profit and loss account – Minority interests – Financing by share capital or borrowing – Planning of fund raising – Current liabilities – Creditors – Bills payable – Directors' loans and current accounts – Taxation – Dividends – Preferential liabilities – Off balance sheet liabilities

This chapter deals with the items which appear on the right-hand side of a double sided balance sheet with the assets appearing on the left-hand side. The liabilities and the proprietors' funds are, in effect, claims against the assets, and if we take the current liabilities away from the assets we are left with the net assets. The funds which provide the net assets are long-term liabilities and proprietors' funds. It is popular nowadays to call these items claims as they are, in effect, claims against the net assets and there is, therefore, a similarity between long-term liabilities and proprietors' funds.

Long-term liabilities can be repayable or can be permanently lent to the company and would then be paid only on a winding up. Share capital, represented by proprietors' funds, would likewise not be repayable until there was a winding up unless permission of the court was received beforehand, but a company can distribute to shareholders the amounts represented by the revenue reserves and the profit and loss account. This distribution will, of course, come out of the assets of the company and both the assets and the claims against the assets will be reduced by the amount of the distribution. When a company becomes insolvent and is wound up the shareholders lose part or all of their funds. Lenders can also suffer in these circumstances if there are insufficient assets to repay what is owed to them.

We therefore see that both long-term liabilities and proprietors' funds have some similarities, but there are also differences in that the proprietors take the ultimate risk for running the business and gain appropriately if the company is successful, or come last in the queue of claimants if the company fails. We will not go into full detail about all claims against a company as this is outside the scope of this book, but will deal only with the claims which appear in balance sheets, and will consider how variations between these claims can affect the lending banker.

Long-term liabilities

Firstly, let us deal with long-term liabilities. The usual ones, as seen in accounts, are as follows:

- debentures
- mortgages
- bonds
- unsecured loans
- convertible loans
- loans from parents, subsidiaries and associates
- deferred taxation
- provisions for liabilities and charges.

Debentures

Debentures can be of two main types. They can either be issued to lenders of the funds and would then appear in a balance sheet as debenture stock; money would be received and would be used in the company's business. Generally debentures are issued with a date for repayment, but occasionally they are issued on a permanent basis. They can be repaid also by such methods as annual drawings, or can be bought in the market by the company itself and cancelled, or held for re-issue. This, of course, can be very profitable to a company as when interest rates rise the price of fixed interest bonds and stocks tend to fall, and a company may, with advantage, then seize an opportunity to redeem some of its debenture stock. Debentures can also be issued as a security for money lent by a bank or, indeed, by some other lender, in which case the balance sheet will merely show the amount of the borrowing, and will indicate that it is secured. Debentures can be issued giving security over some of the assets of a company, but normally they cover all the assets of the undertaking.

Often when debenture stock is issued trustees are appointed to look after the interests of the debenture stock holders, and sometimes a company is required to set up a sinking fund to repay the debentures in due course. Such a sinking fund would appear in a company's balance sheet. The banker should not be misled by seeing such an item among the assets of a company. A sinking fund is, in effect, held in trust for the trustees of the debenture stock holders and in a winding-up would be claimed by the trustees.

Mortgages, bonds and unsecured loans

These items describe liabilities of a company which are either secured on the fixed assets of the company, or are unsecured. In the same way as debentures they can be repayable at a fixed date, or from time to time, or they can be permanently lent to the company. Also, in the same way as debentures, mortgages could be given as security for a bank loan, in which case the bank loan would then be annotated in the balance sheet of the company as being secured.

Bonds have been included in this section because it is not unusual nowadays to find that a company borrows from the Eurobond market in which case it would have a liability for borrowing in a foreign currency. When this happens the company is taking on an additional risk because the rate of exchange between a foreign currency and sterling can fluctuate widely. It is as well, also, to note the terms of such loans and not only when they are repayable, but if there are roll-over provisions. This means there may be terms in the agreement for the bonds to be rolled over annually, or at some other interval, and the interest rate would therefore be subject to alteration according to market rates on the roll-over dates. Not only is there a risk as far as the exchange rate is concerned, but there is, in addition, a risk concerning fluctuations in the interest rate.

Convertible loans

These are loans which have certain options for conversion into shares at specified times. It will be appreciated that with convertible loans there is not a definite liability for repayment, and if terms are favourable to holders of such loans there is a possibility that they will take the option to convert into shares and, as a result, money will not have to be provided by the company for repayment.

Loans from parents, subsidiaries and associates

Loans of this type can be semi-permanent capital, or can, in fact, be current liabilities, and a banker will not be able to decide in which category such loans fall without the detailed knowledge of the company's affairs and its relationship with its parent, subsidiaries or associates, and also the banker will have to have knowledge of the finances of the company which provided the loan.

Very often parent companies provide very little in the way of share capital for their subsidiaries, which they prefer to finance by loans. In this way the parents have a claim against the assets of the subsidiaries which is a prior claim to the one which it would have if it provided funds by way of share capital. Bankers when faced with subsidiaries financed in this way must see that any lending which should be secured is secured with a claim prior to that of the proprietors.

Deferred taxation

There are differences in the profit calculated for accountancy purposes and the profit calculated for taxation. There are some receipts which are tax free, and there are certain amounts of expenditure which are disallowed for calculating tax. There are also items included in accounts which will be dealt with for taxation in different periods. When these timing differences occur between the accounting entries and the taxation requirements a deferred taxation account is set up to cover the differences.

This aspect is dealt with more fully in the chapter on taxation.

Provision for liabilities and charges

The items covered by this description will be such things as pension liabilities whereby the liabilities will be spread over a long period. However, each case must be examined by a banker because there may be occasions when such liabilities could be payable rather more quickly than originally expected. Also included would be any other provisions, and particulars of any material ones would have to be shown.

Proprietors' funds

We will now turn to proprietors' funds. The normal headings seen in balance sheets for proprietors' funds are as follows:

called up share capital
share premium account
revaluation reserves
capital reserves
revenue reserves
profit and loss account
minority interests.

Called up share capital

For practical purposes the authorized share capital has no significance. It is the issued capital which is important. This issued capital cannot be repaid except in a winding-up or by permission from the Court. Both the authorized capital and the issued capital must be shown.

Preference share capital is not popular now because of the taxation, a very important aspect. Dividends are paid out of net profits after tax, whereas interest on loans and debentures is an expense which is deducted before the net profit is deduced and, therefore, before the tax liability is calculated. If companies are looking for funds on which they will pay a fixed rate of return they will be more inclined to borrow the money, or issue debentures, than to issue preference stock. Investors, too, are happier to have debenture stock than preference stock because they have some security for the money they have invested.

Share premium account, revaluation reserves and capital reserves

These are reserves which cannot be used for distribution to shareholders and they consist of such items as the excess over the share price when the shares are issued at a premium, or when assets are revalued. Although they cannot be used for distribution to the shareholders in the way of cash, capital reserves can be distributed in the form of bonus shares. This, in effect, has little significance because the amount of funds represented by the share capital and the reserves remains the same.

It has in the past been possible for a company to purchase from shareholders its own issued redeemable preference shares, and the Companies Act 1981 extended this right of purchase to equity shares. It is, of course, necessary for the company to be solvent, not just on an asset basis, but as a going concern also, and a special resolution is required from shareholders which will expire in no more than 18 months and will specify the maximum number of shares which may be purchased and stipulate maximum and minimum purchase prices.

If the purchase consideration comes out of profits the contra entry will be to a Capital Redemption Reserve Account. If the consideration is partly from a fresh issue at less than the nominal value of the shares being purchased the difference must be credited to the Capital Redemption Reserve Account. This reserve cannot be distributed except as a bonus issue.

Revenue reserves

These are the reserves which have been built up by the company out of profits and are claims (which are, of course, represented by part of the total assets) which are freely available for distribution to shareholders if it is the company's wish to do so. The distribution, as previously mentioned, must be made from the assets and both the assets and the claims against the assets will then be reduced by the same amount. However, companies like to build up their reserves because if they are expanding their businesses they require more money to do so, and by ploughing back profits instead of distributing them the companies are able to use these profits as one method of providing for expansion. When the reserves build up to a substantial amount proportionately to share capital it often happens that the reserves, or part of them, are capitalized in some way by an issue of bonus shares. This then prevents that part of the revenue reserves being available for distribution to shareholders (with, of course, a corresponding reduction in the assets). Sometimes the revenue reserves are specifically designated to cover projects or contingencies such as premises, replacement reserve, or repairs reserve. The designation, however, makes no difference and the assets which are the contra to the reserve can be used in whichever way the company wishes.

Profit and loss account

This consists of the profits a company has made and retained and which it has not transferred to reserves or capitalized. It must be kept in mind that reserves are not cash. People with a non-financial background often make the mistake of looking at a balance sheet and, seeing an amount under reserves, think that it is a reserve fund which can be used for specific expenses, but a reserve fund would be shown among the assets in a balance sheet, whereas the reserves in a balance sheet are merely part of the proprietors' funds and have been used in the general financing of the company.

Minority interests

Items under this heading occur when one company owns the bulk of the shares in another company. Naturally it cannot take the profit of the other company into its own accounts as part of it belongs to the outside shareholders. Similarly a proportion of the reserves and the appropriate amount of capital also belong to the outside shareholders. The total of these claims against the assets is entered under the term minority interests. The claim of minority shareholders is similar to that of the other shareholders in that repayment can be obtained only in a winding-up or by a Court order, except for dividends and payments out of revenue reserves and profit and loss accounts.

Relationship between long-term liabilities and proprietors' funds

The amount of the long-term liabilities is a specific sum which can be read from a balance sheet, but the proprietors' funds consist of the excess of the net assets after deduction of long-term liabilities. The amount of proprietors' funds shown in a balance sheet is therefore only correct if the assets are shown at correct values. Of course in a winding-up the assets are turned into cash, but the amount realized is equivalent to the forced sale value of the assets, whereas a balance sheet shows assets valued under varying conventions. Some of the assets are valued at the lower of cost or market value, and some assets are put in at written down values. Also properties are sometimes revalued at market price, or at a proportion below market price. It is obvious, therefore, that the amount of the proprietors' funds cannot be accurately determined. For example, if fixed assets are grossly undervalued a hidden reserve exists, and this increases the proprietors' funds, but is not shown in the balance sheet.

We therefore have several figures which could be considered as the amount of proprietors' funds, one being that shown in the balance sheet, another being the value with best estimates being made of the assets of the company, while a banker will be cautious and deduct from both these figures some intangible items such as goodwill, patents and trade marks. It will be appreciated that the amount of the proprietors' funds is not a static amount, but varies continuously with the success, or otherwise, of the company. As profits are made and retained so the amount of the proprietors' funds increases and vice versa.

There are companies which have financed themselves with relatively large amounts of long-term liabilities compared with the proprietors' funds, and other companies which have done the reverse and whose proprietors have provided most of the funds. There are advantages and disadvantages in both methods. Financing by long-term liabilities gives stability to a company. It is known in advance what the cost of servicing the liabilities will be for years ahead and the company is able to plan accordingly. On the other hand, proprietors lose flexibility with this method. The company is, to a large extent, working for its creditors and until the requirements of creditors have been satisfied the company will not be getting the benefit of its work for itself. However, when profits are high the proprietors will share the excess profits over a relatively small amount of proprietors' funds and will therefore obtain high rewards. When profits are low the proprietors suffer and their reward is cut drastically. The relationship between the amount of long-term liabilities and proprietors' funds is known as the gearing (or leverage) of the company, and if a relatively high proportion of the finance is provided by long-term liabilities in relation to proprietors' funds the company is said to be highly geared. Many entrepreneurs like to aim for high profits and are prepared to take the risk of high gearing.

Taxation, too, plays a large part in the decision of whether to borrow or provide funds. As far as a company is concerned the interest which it pays on its liabilities is charged to its profit before the profit is assessed for taxation, whereas dividends are paid out of profits after tax. As far as an individual is concerned it does not matter whether he receives interest on money advanced or dividends on his shares if the net amount after tax is the same in both instances. Where interest is received taxation at the standard rate is deducted before it is paid to the investor, but when a dividend is received a net amount is paid by the company and the amount of the tax deducted is imputed to the shareholder.

There is, therefore, a tendency towards borrowing for a company's business but, of course, there is a limit to the amount of borrowing which a company can obtain. This will depend on the amount of its assets, and on the company's record of success or failure. Weak companies will have difficulty in obtaining such finance and will have to depend more on proprietors' funds. Unquoted companies also will not be able to raise money so easily as they cannot approach the stock market for their requirements. They, too, will have to depend on raising more funds from proprietors or by making profits and retaining them, or by approaching long-term lenders such as insurance companies, pension funds, or organizations such as Investors in Industry. Finance directors and officials of companies should have a knowledge of the capital markets, and where and how they can raise money in all its various forms.

Although the raising of large sums generally occurs infrequently in the life of a company the effect can have a large impact on the company's affairs for many years thereafter, and mismanagement of this aspect can weigh heavily against a company. Proper planning is therefore necessary and long-term plans should be made on the basis of the requirements of the company for its assets and for its future projects, and then by assessing such requirements in relation to internally generated funds, and the amounts in their various forms which it would be possible to raise either from proprietors, or from outside lenders.

Over recent years interest rates have fluctuated widely, and it is now generally accepted that waiting until the money is required and then raising it is not the proper way to plan a company's finances. It is better to look at long-term requirements and to make regular reviews of interest rates and the market for funds. When the time looks right as far as the cost of raising funds is concerned it must also be considered if the company should then obtain its requirements. Certainly it may not be able to use the funds in the business immediately, and keeping the funds on one side in an investment could well entail the company in a short-term loss. However, the advantages would outweigh this if interest rates rose sharply, and a company when it needed the funds had to go to the market and pay dearly for them.

Proper planning is necessary, not only the planning of raising funds, but also the planning of repayment of liabilities. A company will know when its liabilities are due and should make the necessary provision. If no proper plan is made the bank is likely to feel the effect. If funds have not been raised in time then the company will no doubt wish the bank to come to the rescue until the time is right to approach the market. Such funds are in fact equivalent to long-term liabilities or proprietors' funds although they are requested from the bank on a temporary basis only, but a banker will find that he will have difficulty in charging a rate of interest appropriate to long-term borrowing because the company really requires a short-term bridge. Having obtained a short-term bridge at fine rates the company will then be reluctant to go to the market and pay higher rates to obtain its long-term requirements. The message is that long-term planning is essential, not only from the point of view of the company, but also from the effect of lack of planning upon the bank.

Current liabilities

It has been shown how long-term liabilities have an effect on a banking account but, of course, current liabilities have a more immediate effect. There are some current liabilities which are necessary for the normal trading of a business, and liabilities of this nature are those such as trade creditors. There are other liabilities, however, which when paid, deplete the working capital; they cause resources to be lost to the business. These items are those such as tax and dividends.

The normal current liabilities which are seen in accounts and falling due within one year are:

bank overdrafts and loans
short-term loans
trade creditors
bills payable
amounts owed to group companies and to related companies
directors' loans and current accounts
taxation and social security
dividends.

Bank overdrafts and short-term loans

Overdrafts are usually provided for normal trading and the banking account should swing widely and ideally have no hardcore borrowing. If there is a solid portion of borrowing the cash generation should be sufficient to repay this hardcore over a relatively short number of years. Alternatively, if a loan is needed it can either be subject to annual review, or taken for a fixed term. In the latter case a separate arrangement is made with the bank, or the other lender of funds, when all the terms and conditions are set down. Accountants include in balance sheets under current liabilities the amounts of any payments due in the coming twelve months. Anything over this length of time is included among the longer term liabilities.

A company's management of its banking accounts has already been dealt with in Chapter 1, and the only point now to emphasize is the theme running through this book that all assets and liabilities must have proper planning and control.

Creditors

The term creditors does, of course, cover all the liabilities of a company, but we have already dealt with longer term liabilities and now we will turn to the shorter term ones. The most important creditors are the trade creditors. A business prospers by buying and selling at a profit and although both aspects are important quite often successful buying enables sales to be made at an appropriate price to generate a good turnover. The buying policy must, of course, be an efficient one, and the correct goods both as to type and quality must be bought. The quantity must also be appropriate for the needs of the business and if good stock control procedures, as already described, are operated the correct quantities to buy should be known.

The next point which a company will want to decide is the amount of creditors it should have outstanding and the length of credit periods which it can take. If a company pays its accounts immediately on receipt of the relevant invoices it will undoubtedly obtain a good name in the trade, and in times of shortage should be able to obtain priority from its suppliers, but it may unnecessarily be draining its business of essential cash. Alternatively, a company which takes very long credit will, in effect, be using the creditors' money for running its business. Against this advantage it will have to set the reluctance of suppliers to deliver quickly, and the probable loss of discounts. The loss of discounts is a serious matter. For example, if the normal terms of settlement are within one month, but discount of 2½% is given for settlement within one week, a company which takes the discount will have the advantage of saving £2.50 on 97.50% of the price over a period of three weeks. This works out to approximately 38% per annum and, of course, is well above the interest rate which would be payable for a bank overdraft. A company offering discount should, of course, be aware of the large amount of interest which it is granting. Naturally if the discounted price is really the price the supplier wishes to obtain the larger invoiced amount incorporates a surcharge for not paying promptly.

In most trades there are normal terms for settlement and if a company takes the normal amount of credit by paying promptly on the due date it will obtain a good reputation, and the advantages which go with this. It will also have the use of creditors' money for the time of the term of credit given. It is wise also for a company to have, if possible, a wide spread of its creditors as then the company is not dependent on a few suppliers and vulnerable to any troubles which may beset its supplies.

A good system for payment of creditors should, therefore, be instituted. A simple system would be to file invoices in the order of the dates when they are due for payment, not overlooking dates for claiming discounts. Naturally creditors cannot be paid if there is no money or credit available, and an examination of the cash book will be necessary before the issue of cheques. However, if the overall plan for the company has been properly devised, as described in Chapter 1, and there are good planning systems for the individual items of debtor control, stock control, cash control, fixed assets control and fund raising, then the payment of creditors should fall neatly into place. There is nothing more worrying and time consuming than to be harassed by creditors, and the effect of this soon tells on the ability of the officials or proprietors who are running a business. Naturally there will be times when businesses require additional banking facilities outside what has already been arranged in order to settle creditors, and provided there are good reasons a banker need not be greatly concerned because of such requests, but if it happens frequently it shows that the customer's planning has not been good, or that control has been weak.

Where there are liabilities which do not fall due until after more than one year these liabilities are not current liabilities.

Bills payable

In some trades it is normal to settle accounts by means of bills, and in such cases an item for bills payable will appear in the accounts. This amount should be treated by a banker as equivalent to creditors and grouped with them. However, if it is not normal practice in the trade, and an item for bills payable appears in the accounts, the banker should consider the significance of the item. Is it an isolated transaction and of no consequence, or does it indicate that the customer cannot meet his liabilities on time? Has the customer stretched his credit by issuing bills, and probably accepted some penalty for being allowed to settle in this way? Or, more seriously, are the bills mere accommodation paper which have been issued not for the settlement of a trading transaction, but to obtain cash to tide the company over for a period?

This is not to say that bills issued to obtain credit is always wrong. It may well occur that an acceptance credit line has been agreed with a merchant banker and bills are accepted under this credit to provide finance. Such bills should be in respect of underlying transactions, the settlement of which should provide funds to pay the bills when presented. If an acceptance credit line is in existence other bankers lending to a customer should know of its existence and its terms to assess the effect of this credit line on the overall financing of the company, and its effect on other overdrafts and credit facilities which have been provided.

Directors' loans and current accounts

These can often be seen in the accounts of the smaller private companies, and although in many cases such amounts are left with the companies for long periods and act, in effect, as additional proprietors' capital, they cannot be classed as such by a lending banker unless the directors have undertaken not to withdraw the sums involved. In practice, however, these undertakings are of doubtful value as after a short time they are often forgotten and then ignored by the directors. The methods by which a banker can protect his own interests are further discussed in Chapter 18.

Taxation and social security

Another item among the current liabilities is the tax due. Generally this consists of corporation tax on the profits of the company as assessed for tax, but there can also be amounts of income tax (such as deductions of tax from debenture interest payments) if they have not been remitted to the tax authorities. Corporation tax is often shown with the date quoted by which the tax should be paid, and for companies formed before April, 1965, this would mean that two amounts are shown with separate dates. Companies formed after April, 1965, do not have the same concessions for delay in payment of tax and have to settle within nine months from the end of their financial years. It is very useful for a lending banker to know the dates when these sometimes substantial liabilities are due for payment and, as it is now unusual for payment to be delayed because of the heavy penalties, the effect on the banking account can be gauged.

A banker will expect a company to take payment of tax into account when devising the cash budget. The tax, of course, is part of the profit made and although the funds should be put to use in the company's business before payment of the tax, the sum must be withdrawn from these activities, or otherwise provided, to meet the tax at the proper time. It must be kept in mind that tax paid is lost to the company and a sudden request to a banker for additional overdraft facilities to meet tax payments could well be an indication of poor planning.

The subject of taxation is a complicated one and it has, therefore, been dealt with more fully in a separate chapter.

Social security payments can now be for substantial amounts and failure to pay these amounts to the authorities at the correct time is a serious matter.

Dividends

Dividend payments are also current liabilities and in some respects, from a company's point of view, similar to tax payments. The money is lost to the business although, of course, if shareholders are well treated they will be more likely at some future time to put up fresh funds in response to a company's call for additional capital. In the annual accounts the final dividends are designated as proposed dividends because the accounts are issued to shareholders before the annual general meeting at which approval for the payment of the dividends is given. Payment then follows soon afterwards.

Preferential liabilities

Included in the overall total of creditors there are some items which are of vital importance in a winding-up or a receivership. These are preferential liabilities and the items are set out in Schedule 19 of the Companies Act 1985. Preferential liabilities take priority over any part of a bank's advance which is secured only by a floating charge over the assets of a company and in order to calculate the amount of the preferential liabilities reference has to be made to a relevant date. In the case of voluntary liquidation this is the date of the passing of the resolution for winding-up. If subsequently a compulsory winding-up order is made this does not change the relevant date but if voluntary winding-up has not commenced the relevant date will be the date of appointment of the provisional liquidator or, if an appointment has not been made, it is the date of the winding-up order. In the case of a receivership the relevant date is the date of the appointment of the receiver. The preferential liabilities are as follows:

1. All taxes assessed on the company up to the 5th April next before the relevant date and not exceeding in whole one year's assessment;
2. All sums due for the twelve months before the relevant date for deduction of income tax from emoluments and any similar deductions made from payments to construction industry contract workers;
3. V.A.T. due in the twelve months up to the relevant date;
4. Any car tax due in the twelve months up to the relevant date;
5. Any betting or gaming duty or licence fee due in the twelve months up to the relevant date;
6. Rates due in the twelve months up to the relevant date;
7. All Social Security debts;
8. All wages and salaries for four months before the relevant date, with an overall limit of £800 per employee. There is an exception here whereby a labourer in husbandry who has contracted to have his wages paid as a lump sum at the end of the year may apply to the court for priority;
9. Accrued holiday remuneration.

It will be seen that this is a formidable list and the amount involved can be a substantial sum. A banker should be able to make a fair estimate of many of the items involved if close attention is given to the company's accounts. This is very necessary when a bank is relying on floating assets and there is a possibility of the company getting into difficulties, as a banker will want to know how his own estimate of the amount of preferential liabilities compares with the amount quoted by the company when giving its periodical statement of current assets and liabilities.

Other liabilities

There are some liabilities of companies which do not figure in the accounts at all, and there are some liabilities which appear only as footnotes to the accounts. Some claims against a company are not liabilities in the accountancy sense. A number of legal liabilities to third parties are in this category. For example, if an employee has a contract of service the company has a liability under this contract, or if a contract has been given for future services the company has, of course, a future liability. The same applies to interest which is accruing, and also to any warranties or guarantees which a company has given when selling its products. These items are, of course, all legal obligations to outside parties, but they are not liabilities for which accountancy entries are passed.

There is another class of liabilities known as contingent liabilities. Quite often a firm figure cannot be put on such a liability, and the types of liability under this heading are such matters as law cases where possible damages could be granted against the company, or extra assessments for tax which the company is disputing. Also, if the company has guaranteed the debts of another party, this becomes a contingency liability. When such liabilities are for material amounts a note should be added to the balance sheet.

One form of off balance sheet financing is where it is hidden in contingent liabilities. This occurs when company A forms another company B with a nominal capital but company A subscribes none of the capital and takes no part in the management, and has no representative on the board. Company B is, therefore, neither a subsidiary nor an associate of company A. Borrowing arrangements for a specific project are then made, and the borrowing is then taken in the name of company B with repayment of the borrowing to come from the income generated by the project. As security for the borrowing company A gives its guarantee. As far as the lender is concerned this is equivalent to lending direct to company A but the balance sheet of company A will show no reference to this transaction in the figures in the balance sheet, but will only mention the liability under the guarantee in the notes attached to the accounts.

The balance sheet and the notes should also be scrutinized for details of leasing and hire purchase commitments. Fortunately, SSAP21 now requires full disclosure of these transactions and as they are continuing commitments they will affect the cash outflow from the enterprise. For further explanation of these types of transaction and the method of disclosure see Chapter 22.

The lesson to learn is that the notes accompanying annual accounts must be studied thoroughly.

CHAPTER 7

Working Capital

A business in slow motion – Circulation of assets – Working capital reconciliation – Estimating current profit – Factors affecting working capital – Importance of current assets make-up – Control of working capital

Circulating capital is aptly so-called because, in the normal process of daily business, it circulates; and working capital, as it works, changes in make-up and amount. It will be instructive to follow such changes during the first nine weeks' operations of an imaginary manufacturing company. The figures given have no pretensions to probability in a real business, but will help to demonstrate 'how the wheels go round'.

EXAMPLE 15.

Start (1st January 19—)

(a) Cash	£2,000	Capital	£2,000
(b) Fixed assets	1,000	Capital	2,000
Cash	1,000		
	£2,000		£2,000

1st week. *Wages paid £200: Materials bought on credit £280: Power, etc., on credit £30: Overheads £30 cash, £70 on credit: Materials consumed £140: Production (all unfinished work) £370.*

End-week balance sheet

	£		£
Fixed assets	1,000	Capital	2,000
Materials	140	Trade creditors	280
Work in progress	370	Expense creditors	100
Cash	770		
Profit and loss account	100		
	£2,380		£2,380

Note: In this, and the following eight weekly balance sheets, the fixed and all the circulating assets are brought in at prime cost.

There has been a considerable change in the make-up of the current assets, which have increased along with the current liabilities. Working capital has fallen by the amount of the loss (overheads £100).

2nd week. *Wages £200: materials bought on credit £70: Works expenses on credit £30: overheads £30 cash, £70 credit: materials consumed £70: production £300.*

Balance Sheet

	£		£
Fixed Assets	1,000	Capital	2,000
Materials	140	Trade creditors	350
Work in progress	550	Expense creditors	200
Finished stock	120		
Cash	540		
Profit and loss account	200		
	£2,550		£2,550
Working capital	£800		

3rd week. *All items as second week, AND sale on credit for £500 of goods costing £250 to produce.*

Balance Sheet

	£		£
Fixed assets	1,000	Capital	2,000
Materials	140	Trade creditors	420
Work in progress	450	Expense creditors	300
Stock	270		
Debtors	500		
Cash	310		
Profit and loss account	50		
	£2,720		£2,720
Working capital	£950		

In this week we have finished with merely exchanging certain assets for others of equal aggregate value, or acquiring assets and compensating liabilities, and have, for the first time, exchanged an asset stock, £250, for another asset, debtors, of greater value, *viz.* £500, and the element of profit, £250, is for the first time introduced. Exactly the same result would have followed had all or any of the £500 sales been for cash; the aggregate of debtors and cash would have been the same. Working capital has been increased by the amount of the selling profit, £250, less £100 overheads.

4th week. *As 2nd week, AND stock costing £280 sold for £560.*

Balance Sheet

	£		£
Fixed assets	1,000	Capital	2,000
Materials	140	Trade creditors . . .	490
Work in progress . .	400	Expense creditors . .	400
Stock	340	Profit and loss account .	130
Debtors	1,060		
Cash	80		
	£3,020		£3,020
Working capital . . .	£1,130		

As a result of further profitable sales, the adverse balance on the profit and loss account has been converted into a a credit balance. The balance sheet totals continue to grow.

5th week. *As 2nd week, AND stock costing £310 sold for £620: 1st week's creditors £380 paid: £500 borrowed on a debenture.*

Balance Sheet

	£		£
Fixed assets	1,000	Capital	2,000
Materials	140	Debenture	500
Work in progress . .	350	Trade creditors . . .	280
Stock	380	Expense creditors . .	400
Debtors	1,680	Bank overdraft . . .	30
		Profit and loss account .	340
	£3,550		£3,550
Working capital . . .	£1,840		

The working capital has been increased by a further week's net profit, £210, and also by the long-term loan of £500. The latter has increased the current assets (cash) without increasing the *current* liabilities. In spite of the substantial net profit made, and the 84% increase in working capital, compared with the start (b), a very unliquid position has developed, necessitating a temporary borrowing from the bank. With creditors at £680 only, debtors at £1,680 and other current assets at £870, the £30 overdraft would be covered by imminent debtor collections.

6th week, *As 2nd week, AND stock costing £350 sold for £700: 3rd week's sales £500 collected: 2nd week's creditors £170 paid.*

	£		£
Fixed assets	1,000	Capital	2,000
Materials	140	Debenture	500
Work in progress	400	Trade creditors	280
Stock	280	Expense creditors	400
Debtors	1,880	Profit and loss account	590
Cash	70		
	£3,770		£3,770
Working capital	£2,090		

With debtors now being collected the business may be said to have reached normal working during this week. The cash position has improved accordingly.

7th week. *As 2nd week, AND stock costing £300 sold for £600: 4th week's sales £560 collected: 3rd week's creditors £170 paid.*

Balance Sheet

	£		£
Fixed assets	1,000	Capital	2,000
Materials	140	Debenture	500
Work in progress	400	Trade creditors	280
Stock	280	Expense creditors	400
Debtors	1,920	Profit and loss account	790
Cash	230		
	£3,970		£3,970
Working capital	£2,290		

8th week. *As 2nd week, AND stock costing £340 sold for £680: 4th week's creditors £170 paid: 5th week's sales £560 collected: new machinery bought £400.*

Balance Sheet

	£		£
Fixed assets	1,400	Capital	2,000
Materials	140	Debenture	500
Work in progress	380	Trade creditors	280
Stock	260	Expense creditors	400
Debtors	2,040	Bank overdraft	10
		Profit and loss account	1,030
	£4,220		£4,220
Working capital	£2,130		

Working capital has been increased by the week's net profit £240 and decreased by the purchase of fixed assets for £400: recourse to the bank is again necessary.

9th week. *As 2nd week, AND stock costing £330 sold for £660: 5th week's creditors paid: 6th week's sales collected.*

Balance Sheet

	£		£
Fixed assets	1,400	Capital	2,000
Materials	140	Debenture	500
Work in progress	420	Trade creditors	280
Stock	190	Expense creditors	400
Debtors	2,000	Profit and loss account	1,260
Cash	290		
	£4,440		£4,440
Working capital	£2,360		

The directors now decide to close the accounts after:

(a) providing £225 for depreciation of fixed assets;
(b) paying £100 directors' fees in cash;
(c) providing £390 for taxation;
(d) providing £10 for accrued debenture interest.

The resulting final accounts are set out in Example 16. The business has been running soundly and successfully. The frequent balance sheets make it possible to see the action of the business in slow motion, and we have already quite unconsciously fallen into the way of picking out changes in the individual balance sheet items and considering how they have come about: this is always one of the most profitable ways of extracting information from a balance sheet. The following points deserve special notice:

1. in the nine weeks the bank account has swung from Cr. £1,000 at the start (b), to ovedraft £30 (week 5), finally closing at Cr. £190. A wide swing in the bank account is a healthy sign, and should always be expected. The banker is in a specially favourable position for watching this important aspect of his customer's business.
2. the initial working capital was barely enough to see the business through to satisfactory production; but had half the sales been for cash, the bank balance would never have fallen below £560; and £500 initial working capital would have sufficed without recourse to the bank.

EXAMPLE 16

TRADING ACCOUNT, 9 weeks ended 3rd March 19—

	£		£
Purchases	840	Sales	4,320
Less Closing stock materials	140		
Materials used	700		
Wages	1,800		
Works expenses	270		
Cost of production	2,770		
Less Work in progress	420		
Cost of finished goods	2,350		
Less Closing stock	190		
Cost of goods sold	2,160		
Gross profit (50%)	2,160		
	£4,320		£4,320

PROFIT AND LOSS ACCOUNT

Overheads	900	Gross profit	2,160
Director's fees	100		
Depreciation	225		
Debenture interest	10		
Net profit	925		
	£2,160		£2,160

APPROPRIATION ACCOUNT

Provision for taxation	390	Net profit	
Balance	535	for period	925
	£925		£925

BALANCE SHEET as at 3rd March 19—

(after adjustments)		£	£	£
Capital				2,000
Balance of profit and loss account				535
				£2,535
Represented by				
Fixed assets at cost		1,400		
Less Depreciation		225		
			1,175	
Less Loan, secured by debenture			500	
Net fixed assets				675
CURRENT ASSETS				
Raw materials		140		
Work in progress		420		
Stock		190		
Debtors		2,000		
Total circulating assets		2,750		
Cash in hand		190		
			2,940	
Less Current liabilities:				
Trade creditors		280		
Expense creditors		400		
Provisions:				
Taxation	390			
Debenture interest	10			
		400		
		1,080		
Working capital			1,860	
Total net assets			£2,535	

3. although progressive profits were made after the second week, at no time were they realized *in cash*, but represented by a mixture of current assets, with debtors predominating (fourth week onwards). The company is carrying forward undistributed profits of £535, but at the final balance sheet date, the cash in hand was £190 only.
4. the changes in the make-up of the current assets illustrate the extraordinarily fluid nature of a business, and emphasize the danger of relying on out of date balance sheets. The percentage analysis set out below shows how rapidly the current asset position can change in the ordinary course of business, even from week to week.

Percentage analysis of current assets

			End of week								
		Start (b)	1	2	3	4	5	6	7	8	9
			%	%	%	%	%	%	%	%	%
Materials		—	11	10	8	7	5	5	5	5	5
Work in progress		—	29	41	27	20	14	14	13	14	14
Stock		—	—	9	16	17	15	10	9	9	6
Debtors		—	—	—	30	52	66	68	65	72	66
Cash		100	60	40	19	4	—	3	8	—	9
Total current assets	%	100	100	100	100	100	100	100	100	100	100
	£	1,000	1,280	1,350	1,670	2,020	1,550	2,770	2,970	2,820	3,040

It will also be profitable to extract a reconciliation statement showing how the changes in the amount of working capital during the nine-week period were brought about:

	£	£
Opening working capital (Start (b))		1,000
Add Net profit after tax provision	535	
Depreciation	225	
Loan	500	
		1,260
		2,260
Deduct Capital expenditure		400
Closing working capital as per final balance sheet		£1,860

It will be seen that depreciation has been added back to the net profit figure because it did not involve a cash disbursement, nor any other diminution of current assets. Depreciation of fixed assets merely reduces by an identical amount the net worth and the fixed assets.

The bearing of this analysis in a banker's control of a balance sheet advance will be clear from the following calculation, based on the same figures. It is assumed that he is supplied with periodical figures of current assets and current liabilities.

EXAMPLE 17

1st January — Working capital £1,000

5th March (interim figures, *not* final balance sheet):

Creditors	£	*Current assets*	£	£
Trade	280	Materials	140	
Expense	400	Work in progress	420	
		Stock	190	
	£680	Debtors	2,000	
		Cash	290	
				£3,040

Deduct creditors	680
Working capital	£2,360
Increase in working capital	£1,360
Adjust for non-revenue items:	
Add Capital expenditure	400
	1,760
Deduct Loan raised	500
Increase in working capital, attributable to PROFIT for the period	£1,260

Such profit will, of course, be subject to provisions for taxation, and depreciation, and also for accrued expenses which may not have been recorded in the books, as for instance, directors' fees and debenture interest. Where such amounts are likely to be material, a notional figure based on the last audited accounts can be deducted. In any case the profit figure so deduced is only an approximation. It is however, invaluable as an up-to-date indication of current trends, and of *non-revenue* receipts and payments for the period since the last figures were furnished.

The surprisingly few ways in which the amount of the working capital can be increased or decreased are tabulated below for convenience of reference.

Fluctuations of working capital

	Increases	*Decreases*
Cash transactions	Fresh capital raised. Long-term borrowing. Sale of fixed assets.	Capital repaid. Loans repaid, or made. Purchase of fixed assets. Dividends, drawings and taxation.
Credit transactions	Sale of fixed assets on credit.	Purchase of fixed assets on credit. Provisions for dividends and *current* taxation.

	Increases	*Decreases*
Profit and loss	Undistributed net profits (adding back depreciation of *fixed* assets).	Net losses (deducting depreciation of *fixed* assets).
	[1]Profits represented by increased circulating assets or decreased current liabilities in any combination.	[1]Losses represented by reduced circulating assets or increased current liabilities in any combination.

[1]Though cash must be found to pay dividends or taxation, profits will not necessarily be represented by increased cash; nor will losses necessarily be accompanied by a fall in cash.

The make-up of working capital is not less important than its amount. The point is well brought out by the following analysis of the working capital shown in three consecutive balance sheets of 'Manufacturers Limited', set out in Appendix I.

EXAMPLE 18

'Manufacturers Limited'

Analysis of working capital position, 31st March
(£000)

	Year A	Year B	Year C
CURRENT ASSETS			
Raw materials	5	10	10
Work in progress	7.5	15	50
Finished stock	20	40	50
Trade debtors	24.5	17	17
Bills receivable	7.5	5	—
Liquid assets	12.5	10	—
Total	77	97	127
Current Liabilities (Details below)	22	42	72
Working capital	£55	£55	£55
CURRENT LIABILITIES			
Trade creditors	5	17	43
Bank overdraft	—	—	5
Taxation	12	10	14
Proposed dividend	5	15	10
	£22	£42	£72

The following points should be noted:

1. the working capital is the same in each case.

   Possible explanations:

   (a) no profits have been earned;

   (b) profits have been earned and paid away, or expended on fixed assets, etc.;

   (c) losses have been sustained, but made good by non-revenue receipts;

2. debtors have not moved in step with stock and work in progress, which suggests that there has been over-production and a fall in sales;
3. creditors have increased faster than debtors;
4. liquid assets have disappeared;
5. bills receivable have disappeared. Discounted?
6. had the business been closed down on the balance date in:
   (a) Year A, the creditors could have been met from liquid assets and only 80% of debtors;
   (b) Year B, the cash and all the debtors were insufficient, and 25% of the stock would have had to be realized at book value to clear the creditors;
   (c) Year C, creditors exceeded the whole of the debtors and finished stock, and recourse to raw materials and/or work in progress would have been necessary.

Numbers 2 to 6 inclusive are consistent with progressive over trading, a subject which will be examined fully at a later stage in this book. It will suffice at this point if it is realized that the make-up of current assets and their cash-producing potential is what really matters in a going concern. The quality of the individual items is therefore vital.

Control of working capital

In the previous chapter it was shown how the individual items making up the current assets have to be controlled, and it is also necessary for liabilities to be controlled. However, it is insufficient for individual items to be controlled without fitting this control into the overall plan for the business. Thus, when current assets and current liabilities are concerned the control of the individual items must link into the control of working capital.

If a business is making a profit the working capital should increase through the cycle of purchases, production, sales, and collection of proceeds. It will be necessary to decide how much working capital is necessary for the business at the start of the accounting period, and whether the same amount will be required for the trade envisaged during the accounting period. Perhaps more working capital will be necessary to support the increased turnover.

The profit made (ignoring capital gains) increases working capital but can be used for buying capital equipment, for distribution to the proprietors, or left to augment the existing working capital. Use of the increased working capital should be planned and not just left in a haphazard way. To do this an estimate must be made of the profit likely to be made, and this must be broken down and related to a cash projection as shown in Chapter 1, and then followed through to a statement of sources and application of funds.

CHAPTER 8

Profit and Loss Accounts

Profit and loss accounts – Percentage profit and loss accounts – The relation between profit and loss accounts and the balance sheet – Break even analysis

So far consideration has been given to the balance sheet alone; but no reader with a working knowledge of accounts will need to be reminded that a balance sheet by itself can give only limited information. To shed fuller light on the state of any undertaking *the balance sheet must be read in conjunction with the profit and loss accounts.*

To illustrate this, two widely differing, but quite possible, sets of profit and loss accounts of 'Manufacturers Limited' – *A* and *B* – are given in Example 19. As far as form is concerned, it will be noticed that a separate manufacturing profit is shown – always an advantage where a selling price can be determined based on sales or comparisons with similar products dealt with in the open market. In the absence of such price, the less useful alternative is to incorporate the manufacturing cost of the finished production as a credit to the manufacturing account, the same figure being debited as a quasi-purchase in the trading account. The gross selling profit will then include, for at least part of the goods handled, both manufacturing and merchanting profit. In the present instance the method adopted is doubly desirable, because the company also sells bought-in goods. In such a case the inclusion of certain purchases at manufacturing cost and others at wholesale prices, in proportions which may obviously vary from time to time, might well invalidate any comparisons of the gross profit rate from year to year.

Much more important than the form, however, is the fact that such varying financial and trading operations could have led to an identical balance sheet at the end of the year. In the X accounts both manufacturing and trading rates of gross profit are satisfactory at 46.5% and 24% respectively. The Y accounts show only a negligible manufacturing profit (5.5%) and the bulk of the profit shown was earned in the merchanting department (29% of sales). Y sales are more than double X and carry a far higher merchanting ingredient. Moreover, the balance sheet at the end of the year gives no inkling of the fact revealed by the Y appropriation account that in the past losses have been made. The low tax provision in the Y accounts is either inadequate in itself or, if correct, indicates that there are substantial

EXAMPLE 19 (to be read in conjunction with year A of the balance sheet in Appendix 1)

'Manufacturers Limited'

ALTERNATIVE PROFIT AND LOSS ACCOUNTS FOR YEAR ENDED 31ST MARCH 19—

FACTORY ACCOUNT

	X	Y
	£	*£*
Stock at beginning of year	2,000	*10,000*
Purchases	10,000	*100,000*
	12,000	*110,000*
Less Stock at end of year	5,000	*5,000*
Materials consumed	7,000	*105,000*
Wages, power and expenses	50,000	*10,000*
Work in progress at beginning of year	3,500	*12,500*
	60,500	*127,500*
Less Work in progress at end of year	7,500	*7,500*
Cost of finished goods	53,000	*120,000*
Factory profit	46,000	*7,000*
Percentage of amounts transferred	(46.5%)	*(5.5%)*
Transfer to trading account (100%)	£99,000	*£127,000*

TRADING ACCOUNT

	X	Y
	£	*£*
Stock at beginning of year	7,000	*25,000*
Own manufacture	99,000	*127,000*
Purchases	43,000	*185,000*
	149,000	*337,000*
Less Stock at end of year	20,000	*20,000*
Cost of goods sold	129,000	*317,000*
Wages	25,000	*5,000*
Expenses	7,000	*24,000*
Cost of sales	161,000	*346,000*
Profit	51,000	*140,000*
Percentage of sales	(24%)	*(29%)*
Sales (100%)	£212,000	*£486,000*

Note: Convenient narrative form. The credit side is represented by the grand total.

PROFIT AND LOSS ACCOUNT

	X	Y		X	Y
	£	£		£	£
Debenture interest (gross)	3,500	*3,500*	Factory profit	46,000	*7,000*
Directors' fees	5,000	*50,000*[1]	Trading profit	51,500	*140,000*
Overheads	10,000	*20,000*	Sundry receipts	1,500	—
Provision for depreciation	23,400	*23,400*			
Net profit	56,600	*50,100*			
	£98,500	*£147,000*		£98,500	*£147,000*

APPROPRIATION ACCOUNT

	X	Y		X	Y
	£	£		£	£
Balance forward from last year	—	*15,100*	Balance forward from last year	13,400	—
Provision for taxation	35,000	*20,000*	Profit for the year	56,600	*50,100*
Interim dividend paid	20,000	—			
Provision for final dividend	5,000	*5,000*			
Balance	10,000	*10,000*			
	£70,000	*£50,100*		£70,000	*£50,100*

[1] This figure for directors' drawings is, of course, highly improbable, but has been included expressly to illustrate that such an undesirable depletion of working capital could not have been discovered from the balance sheet alone—or even suspected.

past losses brought forward in the tax computation, to offset a large part of the current year's profit. Clearly the balance sheet must be read with the profit and loss account if the undertaking is to be seen in its true light. Where a holding company issues with its own balance sheet a consolidated balance sheet and a consolidated profit and loss account, it is not required to issue at the same time its own profit and loss account although it must disclose what portion of the consolidated profit and loss has been dealt with in its accounts. The banker could call for a full profit and loss account if the printed accounts do not give him all the information he requires.

The differences between the two sets of profit and loss accounts will be brought out further when we consider the balance sheet/profit and loss relationship discussed later in this chapter.

The value of a percentage balance sheet has already been noted. It is also illuminating to set out a trading and profit and loss account reduced to percentages of sales, Example 20.

It may certainly be useful for the banker and the business man to know that for every £100 of sales (Account X):

£15.00 goes in handling expenses;

£11.00 in mortgage interest;

£4.50 in overheads;

and so on.

But it will not be overlooked that variations in individual profit and loss percentages from year to year may be the result of changes in overhead expenses with a constant level of sales, constant overheads with a change in total sales or of a combination of both. Clearly, however, if sales fluctuate widely from year to year certain percentage figures in the profit and loss account, calculated with reference to the changing amount of sales to which they have no direct relation, can be downright misleading, and year-to-year

EXAMPLE 20

'Manufacturers Limited'

TRADING ACCOUNT FOR YEAR A

	X	Y		X	Y
Cost of goods sold	61%	*65%*	Sales	100%	*100%*
Expenses	15%	*6%*			
Gross profit	24%	*29%*			
	100%	*100%*		100%	*100%*

PROFIT AND LOSS ACCOUNT

	X	Y		X	Y
Debenture interest	1.5	*.7*	Trading profit	24	*29*
Director's fees	2.5	*10.4*	Manufacturing profit	22	*1.4*
Overheads	4.5	*4.1*			
Net profit	37.5	*15.2*			
	46	*30.4*		46	*30.4*

comparisons may be meaningless. Usually a direct comparison between the actual profit and loss figures is simpler, more informative and more reliable.

But when we have studied our profit and loss accounts and compared this figure with that, what does it all add up to? How much have we learnt about what actually happened in the business during the period covered by the accounts? What is the reality behind the figures? A simple illustration will supply part of the answer.

Suppose we are told that a schoolboy leaves his home at 8.45 and reaches the school, a mile away, just in time to beat the bell at 9.15. What can we safely infer about his mode of progress? Any of the following things may have happened:

1. he may have strolled at a steady two miles an hour;
2. he may have started off at a brisk trot and then stopped for breath before approaching the school gates at a sedate walk;
3. he may have set out at a normal pace as far as the cycle shop and have remained there with a covetous nose flattened against the window, dallying so long that he had to do even time to the school;
4. or he may have lost time by returning home for his forgotten homework, making it necessary for him to run hard all the way to school in the last few minutes.

Change the time from half an hour to a whole year and substitute a live business for a schoolboy: will your revenue accounts tell you any more about set-backs, changes of pace, the early spurt and the slow finish, than the bare statement that our schoolboy took half an hour to get to school? In a trading account or a profit and loss account the condensing of a year's transactions has the merit of simplicity but it effectively hides all the price and sales trends of the period. No indication will be given of seasonal fluctuations, good selling lines and bad, progress or recession in different areas and at different times; nor of any changes in rates of gross profit on different articles, or their causes.

The following example shows the trading accounts, for two consecutive years, of a business which retails one article only:

EXAMPLE 21

		Year I		Year II
		£		£
Opening stock		672		672
Purchases		4,704		6,670
		5,376		7,342
Less Closing stock		672		1,764
Cost of sales		4,704		5,578
Gross profit	33⅓%	2,352	30%	2,392
Total sales		£7,056		£7,970

What does comparison of these two trading accounts tell us?

1. the sales are up by 11.3%;
2. purchases are up by 42%;
3. rate of gross profit is down from 33⅓% to 30%, and – most significant of all – ;
4. the value of the stock on hand at the end of year II is 2.6 times that at the end of year I.

The last point may mean that business is booming and every available penny has been put into increased stocks in anticipation of harder prices and bigger profits. It may equally mean that severe consumer resistance has developed and sales have fallen off unexpectedly in the latter part of the year. A look at the order book, if possible, will show which is the true explanation. From the information given by the trading accounts no valid inferences can be drawn, either as to the prices paid or realized or to the quantity of goods sold. We have, in fact, the mathematician's despair, one equation with two unknowns. Supposing we could ascertain the number of articles bought, sold and left on hand, we could then easily calculate the prices.

We might find this for year II: or this:

	A			B		
	No. of items	@	£	No. of items	@	£
Opening stock	168	£4	672	168	£4	672
Purchases	1,334	£5	6,670	1,113	£6	6,670
	1,502		7,342	1,281		7,342
Less Closing stock	504	£3.50	1,764	252	£7	1,764
Cost of sales	998	£5.59	5,578	1,029	£5.42	5,578
Gross profit		(30%)	2,392		(30%)	2,392
Total sales	998	£7.99	£7,970	1,029	£7.74½	£7,970

The selling price in *B* is 24½p lower than in *A*, and the cost of sales per article is also lower, 17p, and there are trifling differences in the numbers of articles sold, but it should be noted that the purchase and selling prices are *average* prices only. It may be that in fact not one single article was bought or sold at those prices.

The startling and significant thing, however, is the figures for closing stock. *A* shows a large quantity of stock (three times the opening stock), but valued at a price 30% below the *average* purchase price. As stock is valued at cost or market selling price, whichever is the lower, it appears that in the last few months of the year cost prices have fallen markedly; or that there has been a break in the selling price to less than half the average for the year; or else that there has been a substantial and perhaps deliberate undervaluation of stock. *B*, on the other hand, shows that stock has been valued at a figure in excess of average cost, and as no one is likely to over-value closing stock (which would inflate his profit), this can only mean that in the closing part of the year the cost of the articles has risen steeply.

All these extremely diverse business experiences are equally consistent with the same trading account figures. And even with the added information as to quantities which, in practice, could never be made available in a business of any complexity, the banker still could not learn from the accounts which of the possible reasons already given for the increased number of articles unsold at the end of the year (200% increase in *A* and 50% in *B*) is the true one.

It may be rewarding to go one step further with this simple trading account and to see how account *A* might have actually moved quarter by quarter.

Year II Account A

					Articles	@	£
Opening stock					168	£4	672
PURCHASES							
1st Qr.	400	@	£4.50	1,800			
2nd Qr.	200	@	£6	1,200			
3rd Qr.	434	@	£6.05	2,620			
4th Qr.	300	@	£3.50	1,050			
				£6,670			
					1,334	£5	6,670
					1,502		7,342
Less Closing stock					504	£3.50	1,764
Articles sold and cost of sales					998	£5.59	5,578
Gross profit (30%)							2,392
SALES				£			
1st Qr.	300	@	£7	2,100			
2nd Qr.	350	@	£9	3,150			
3rd Qr.	250	@	£8.53	2,132			
4th Qr.	98	@	£6	588			
Sales	998			£7,970	998	£7.99	£7,970

Here then we have a position perfectly consistent with the trading account *A*, but which could not possibly have been inferred from it. All or any of the following explanations may apply:

1. a sudden change from scarcity conditions to plenty: i.e. a natural break in wholesale prices;

or 2. the introduction of controlled wholesale prices;

or 3. the introduction into the market of cheap competitive lines;

or 4. the imposition of a heavy tax on the articles, increasing prices to the consumer and creating or strengthening strong consumer resistance.

The sole clue to the significant recession in sales during the last quarter might be a marked falling off in debtors in the balance sheet: and if there were such a business – dealing in one article only – the branch manager might well be aware of the change in the market. In a more complex business, however, it would be almost impossible to read the trading account correctly: especially as the debtor figure in the balance sheet might be affected by heavier credit and lighter cash sales, as consumer resistance made itself felt, or by quicker or slower collections.

It can now be asserted that any valid comparison between related figures in profit and loss accounts and balance sheet is possible only on the assumptions that:

1. the trading proceeded evenly throughout the year;
2. the balance sheet – struck at the end of the year—gives a fair picture of the position which, subject to accruing profits, has obtained throughout the year.

The validity of the various financial ratios, and of inferences drawn from changes in them year by year, will have to be considered in the light of these two propositions.

The quarterly percentages for the value of purchases and sales are a sufficient commentary on the first assumption.

Year II Account A

	Purchases		Sales
	%		%
1st Qr.	27		26
2nd Qr.	18		40
3rd Qr.	39		27
4th Qr.	16		7
Total purchases	100	Total sales	100

The interrelation between balance sheet and profit and loss account

This survey of profit and loss accounts and some of their inadequacies as indicators of the course of the business during the year makes it possible to consider now the real nature of the relationship between the profit and loss accounts on the one hand and the balance sheet on the other. The first shows *the way* in which the main changes in the undertaking's position – those brought about by its normal trading operations—have come about during the year. The second shows the end-year position and, by comparison with the previous year's balance sheet, just what the results of those changes have been. If just weight is to be given to the correlation of items in the profit and loss account with balance sheet items which are expressed in so many of the accepted accounting ratios, it is important to realize that in many instances we are comparing things which are not parate at all.

How far, then, can figures in a balance sheet be said to be properly comparable with related figures in the profit and loss accounts?

The answer depends on a true appreciation of what a balance sheet really signifies. It has been likened to a snapshot taken of something in motion. There can be few readers who have not at some time looked over the snapshot album of a friend who explains, 'That's my father.' Then noticing the observer's silence and his quickly suppressed smile adds, 'But he is not really a bit like that.' How true that may often be for two quite opposite reasons. A single snapshot taken of an entirely unconscious subject may libellously show him to be cross-eyed, hunch-backed or otherwise grotesque; though if a series of pictures discloses the same peculiarity one's belief in the disclaimer falls as one's admiration for filial loyalty grows. On the other hand, every snapshot album will contain portraits which are stiff, self-conscious and posed. There is always a definite danger that in exceptional cases, balance sheets will fall in the 'posed' category, with the subject all dressed up and – as Macaulay scathingly wrote of Robert Montgomery – 'doing his very best to look like a man of sensibility and genius, though with less success than his strenuous efforts deserve'. The directors always know when the balance sheet is going to be taken, and happy the banker who can recognize window-dressing when he meets it.

It may be added that he gets most benefit from the snapshot album who knows the subjects well and has a clear idea what they are really like and can accept, with such mental reservations as may be necessary, the explanation 'He is not really like that'.

Like all analogies, however, the snapshot idea must not be pressed too far. The camera cannot lie, we are told, and a properly focused instrument will show with clear definition exactly what is seen by the eye of the camera. There can, however, be no such sharpness all over the picture presented by a balance sheet. It must be kept in mind that some of the figures shown in a balance sheet are not absolutely correct as they are based on personal opinions.

A much better analogy is that of a 'still' produced when the action of a film running through a lecture room projector is stopped for a moment to enable a particular position to be closely examined. It is then viewed instinctively as a matter of suspended motion in connection both with the movements which led up to that position and those into which it merges when the projector is started up again. Moreover, the 'still' has significance only in relation to the movements *immediately* before and after the position studied. This consideration must be kept in mind when the true interrelation between balance sheets and profit and loss accounts is discussed in Chapter 9.

To assess the soundness of any business the banker will want to examine its accounts over a period of years. The changes in certain single items can be revealing. Thus the banker will watch the following trends closely:

1. *Turnover.* Whether this is rising, holding steady or falling is a valuable indication of adaptability to a changing world.
2. *Gross profit/industry average.* Where an average rate of gross profit for an industry is available, deviations – and particularly any *irregular* deviations – from that norm in a particular business will prompt useful enquiries, though the banker will always be conscious that circumstances alter cases. If the profit rate of a particular business is falling while the general trend is upward, a banker who is involved as a lender will want to know why.
3. *Expenses.* Overheads rising faster than a business is expanding may suggest an enquiry into management effectiveness.
4. *Net worth.* Whether this is showing steady growth is an important indication of the soundness of financial management. Dividend policy is a significant factor here.

Apart from these single items, there are a number of business factors which are closely related. The relationships between the figures in the accounts recording those factors have given rise to a number of standard ratios, year to year changes in which are invaluable pointers for the student of accounts.

These ratios will be discussed in the next two chapters, but before doing so it would be as well to consider briefly an aspect of sales in relation to costs.

Break-even analysis

We have already considered costing systems in relation to valuation of stocks from basic raw materials to finished goods, and a businessman after costing his product should be able to determine his selling price to give him his expected return. However, the selling price can be fixed only in relation to market conditions, and a lower mark-up might have to be accepted.

When considering costing we saw that costs could be divided into fixed and variable costs. It is obvious that if sales do not cover fixed costs a loss will be made. Sales in excess of the amount required to cover fixed costs will make a contribution towards the variable costs until such time that all variable costs are covered and the business is breaking even on that product. Any further sales will produce a profit. Mathematically, it is easy to work out the break-even point given all the costing information, but it is easier and quicker to appreciate the results from various levels of sales if the information is presented in the form of a graph, as per Example 22.

Fixed costs for this particular product are £2,300. Variable costs are additional and therefore plotted from the base point of £2,300 to give a line for total costs. Sales are plotted from zero upwards. Until sales have reached point B the sales income will not cover the fixed costs, but sales from point B to the break-even point will make a contribution towards the variable costs. Sales from the break-even point along the plotted line to point C will cover both the fixed and variable costs, and also make a profit. The shaded area before the break-even point is reached shows the loss-making area, and the shaded area above the break-even point is the profit-making area.

This presentation is in a simple form for the purpose of illustration, and all the lines are straight ones. In practice this will not be so. Fixed costs can rise in steps if, at a certain level of production, more factory space is needed. Variable costs do not necessarily increase in the same direct relationship to production, as efficiency may be enhanced at a higher level of output by full use of available machinery. Subsequently, there may well come a level of production which calls for added amounts of capital and labour, and variable costs could increase more than proportionately to the added output. After a certain level resistance to sales could increase and the sale price of the product might have to be lowered.

EXAMPLE 22. Simple break-even point.

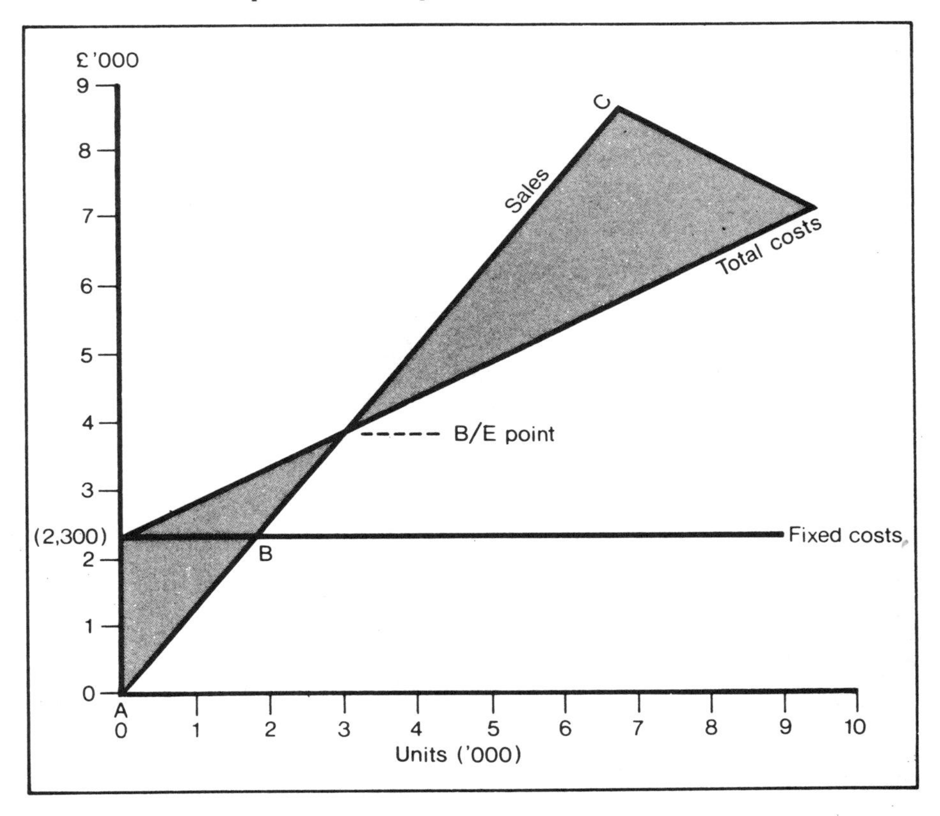

EXAMPLE 23. Two break-even points.

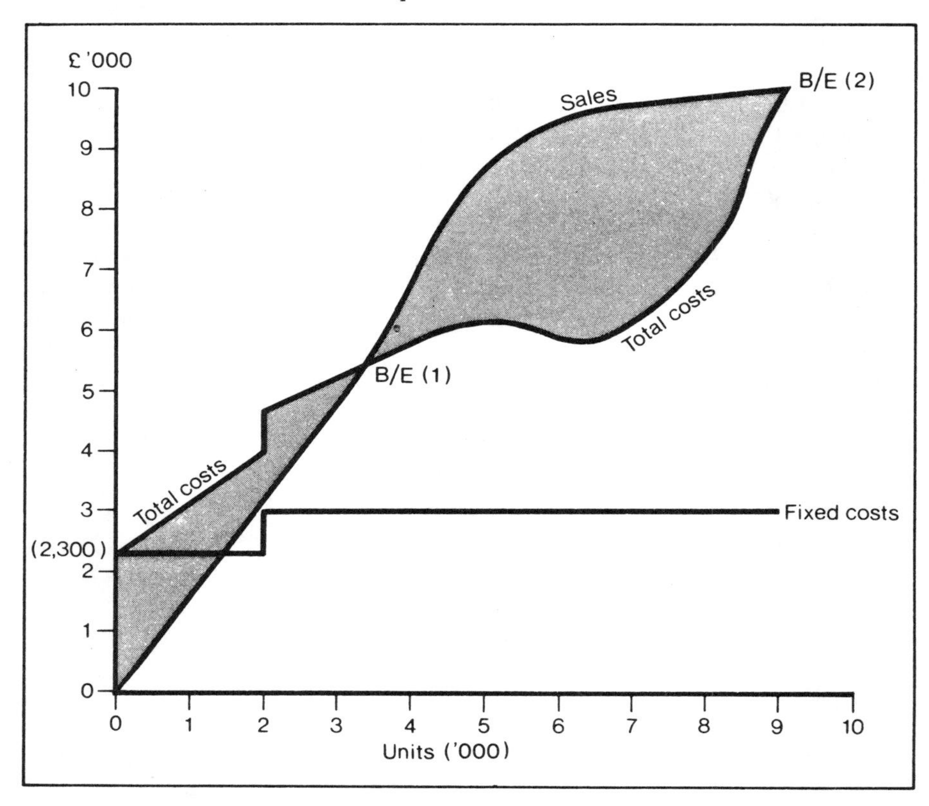

The appropriate assumptions must be taken into account, estimates made, and a break-even chart prepared according to the resulting figures. A chart such as shown in Example 23 could result. Although fixed costs start at £2,300 they increase to £3,000 when 2,000 units are produced, and likewise this £700 increase is reflected in the line for total costs (fixed costs, plus variable costs). Increased efficiency is reflected by the downward curve for total costs, but at an output of 6,000 units total costs start increasing disproportionately to output. As for sales at around 4,000 units the sale price has to be cut with a resulting downward curve for the line depicting sales. The result is that the two break-even points are shown. One is on the way up and is reached when sales revenue covers all costs, but break-even point number two occurs when costs are rising and income from sales is falling. At this stage there is no advantage in further production. Before B/E(2) is reached management should have considered whether relative costs can be brought down by, perhaps, modernizing machinery, or if a new marketing strategy should be adopted.

CHAPTER 9

Accounting ratios

Summary of ratios – The balance sheet ratios – Drs. crs. ratio – Current ratio – Liquid ratio – Revenue account ratios – Gross profit ratio – Net profit ratio – Sales purchases ratio

Accounting or financial ratios require detailed examination to test their validity and assess their value to the lending banker. He will want to know:

1. to what extent they are theoretically sound;
2. whether they are an essential part of his equipment or just academic frills of no use to the practical man;
3. how far they can help him to discover the reality behind the figures.

Investment analysts have carried out considerable research in comparing numerous ratios in an effort to forecast the results of companies. The ratios have enabled comparisons to be made between companies as a test of efficiency, and the trends seen in the ratios year by year have highlighted vital aspects. Some of the ratios used by investment analysts, however, are not of practical use to a banker. For example, a shareholder is interested in having a good return on his investment, and with his company being sound and having good growth prospects. If he did not feel that his requirements were being fulfilled he would consider his investment a poor one. The lending banker, however, could well take a different view of the company. If it was earning sufficient to service the bank borrowing the banker would be satisfied regardless of the fact that the dividend yield might be small, and the company's assets might not be fully used.

Therefore, the ratios used must be appropriate for the particular user, and in the following analysis the validity of four main types of ratio which could be of use to the lending banker is examined. For the sake of interest and to complete the picture a brief explanation of a few additional ratios used by investment analysts is added as a fifth group.

1. Balance sheet ratio:
   (a) liability ratio;
   (b) asset ratio;
   (c) the debtors/creditors ratio;
   (d) the current ratio;
   (e) the liquid ratio.

2. Profit and loss account ratios
   (a) rate of gross profit;
   (b) rate of net profit;
   (c) expenditure/sales ratio.

3. Balance sheet/profit and loss account ratios
   (a) rate of stock turnover (or stock/cost of sales ratio);
   (b) creditors/purchases ratio;
   (c) debtors/sales;
   (d) stock/sales;
   (e) working capital/sales;
   (f) net return ratio;
   (g) return on net assets.

4. Lending ratios

5. Additional investment ratios
   (a) return on equity;
   (b) earnings per share;
   (c) price/earnings ratio;
   (d) dividend yield;
   (e) dividend cover;
   (f) debt ratio;
   (g) interest cover.

Balance sheet ratios

(a) THE LIABILITY RATIO

This ratio has already been considered in Chapter 2 when it was shown that the percentages of the various claims against a company (i.e. proprietors', long-term lenders', banks', and creditors') bring out important relationships, and that variations from year to year can indicate changes in a company's financial strength. Generally speaking the liability figures are records of historical fact in that the total fund of assets was actually provided in the stated proportions by the owners, the loan and current creditors, and the bank. The liability ratio is, therefore, wholly valid, subject only to the proviso that the profits ingredient in the net worth figure is not entirely free from the 'opinion' element.

(b) THE ASSET RATIO

This ratio, which was also considered in Chapter 2 and deals with the relationship between fixed assets, circulating assets and fictitious assets, suffers from the fact that so many of the figures involve a high degree of estimation.

Moreover, while the current assets will be evaluated mainly on the basis of recent prices, many of the fixed assets may stand in the books at cost many years ago, which may have no relation to current values. Any comparison between fixed and current assets totals may therefore be distorted.

(c) THE DEBTORS/CREDITORS RATIO

Since selling and buying are closely associated features of day to day business, debtors and creditors logically based on and arising out of the operations have a definite and special association, crystallized in the suggestive debtors/creditors ratio. It is computed by dividing debtors and bills receivable by the figure for trade creditors including trade bills payable.

From *Example 18*

'Manufacturers Limited'

DEBTORS/CREDITORS RATIO, 31ST MARCH

Year A	$\frac{\text{Drs. and bills}}{\text{Creditors}}$	=	$\frac{32{,}000}{5{,}000}$	=	Ratio 6.4
Year B			$\frac{22{,}000}{17{,}000}$	=	Ratio 1.3
Year C			$\frac{17{,}000}{43{,}000}$	=	Ratio 0.4

It is clear that if a merchanting business sells only on credit and receives the same length of credit and a selling profit is being made, the debtors/creditors ratio should normally be greater than unity, except perhaps seasonally, when stocks are being built up. This is because the creditor figure is based on the value of goods at cost, while the debtor figure is based on such cost, *plus profit*. In a manufacturing business the ratio should be much higher, since the creditor figure will be represented mainly by the cost of materials, but the debtor figure will be based on cost of materials, the cost of processing (wages and works on-cost) and profits. On the other hand it may often be possible for the manufacturer to enjoy longer credit than he allows, when the ratio will be modified accordingly.

The three-year debtors/creditors ratios shown above reveal a marked and serious trend, and unless the fall can be off-set by a large increase in liquid resources, e.g. from cash sales or fresh capital, it is almost certain that disaster is not far off.

The foregoing is only the statement of a broad principle which, in the infinite variety of business, may be modified to almost any extent. For example, a retailer may buy on credit and sell mainly for cash. In such cases creditors would quite properly exceed debtors, and the ratio will be a small fraction only. The main point is to establish a ratio for a given business and note carefully the changes from year to year. The significance of such changes is classified in the table below.

Interpretation of variations in dr./cr. ratio

Favourable sign when due to:	*Unfavourable* sign when due to:
RISE	
1. Prompter payments of creditors and/or 2. Increased debtors following increased sales.	Increased debtors, owing to slower collections.
FALL	
Reduction in debtors due to more efficient collection or increased proportion of cash sales.	1. Making creditors wait for their money and/or 2. Increasing creditors and abnormal increase in stock without increasing debtors and/or 3. Decreasing debtors by reason of (a) falling sales; (b) pressing debtors with damage to goodwill. 4. Discounting bills receivable.

All or any of these factors may act together and indeed could cancel each other out. In bad times a trader might both take and have to allow longer credit without the ratio being affected at all. Like most ratios therefore the debtors/creditors ratio is suggestive rather than positive in the information it gives. But its value in assessing trends is greatly increased when it is considered in conjunction with other ratios.

In working out the debtors/creditors ratio the purpose of the comparison and the foregoing comments should be borne in mind, and only the correct items should be taken from the balance sheet. Broadly speaking the debtor figure should include only those items – trade debtors and bills receivable – directly associated with sales; and the creditors figure only those creditors directly associated with trade purchases. Expense creditors, bank overdrafts and taxation liabilities should be disregarded, as their inclusion will introduce arbitrary variations. These items will play their full part in connection with the current asset and current liabilities ratio, which will be considered later.

But even when accurately worked out, the reliability of this ratio must be suspect. If the business has been wound up at the balance sheet date, it would have been a fair indication of ability to meet trading liabilities. But it must be remembered that as soon as active trading ceases the natural relationship between debtors, as a main source of cash, and creditors, as one of the main calls for cash, ceases and current liabilities rank *pari passu* with long-term liabilities as claimants against the assets as a whole. On a 'going concern' basis its validity may be affected by the following considerations:

1. (a) the rate of debtors collections is not determined by the debtor figure in the balance sheet but by the amounts due month by month as determined by sales for the months immediately preceding the balance sheet date;

(b) similarly, the amounts payable to creditors month by month vary in step with recent purchases;

(c) there is thus no logical connection between the two figures unless there is – adventitiously – a close correspondence between purchases and sales in the relevant periods.

2. The ratio may be considerably affected by the extent to which purchases and sales are made for cash: and this will not be ascertainable from the accounts supplied.

Nevertheless, any marked fall in the debtors/creditors ratio should prompt enquiry. The answers may provide a satisfactory explanation: indicate a state of stringency in which debtors are being pressed and some creditors left unpaid: or, indeed, that for window-dressing purposes debtors have been 'whipped up' to improve the cash showing in the balance sheet.

This is a very sensitive ratio which can be influenced by diverse factors, and it may be thought that it should therefore be disregarded. In practice, however, the relationship between what a company owes and what is owed to it is of vital importance, and a banker faced with a balance sheet he has not seen before can easily make a rough judgment of this ratio during an interview without waiting for a full analysis of the balance sheet. Later on, the number of days of credit given and received can be calculated and compared, as will be explained when dealing with the debtors/sales and creditors/purchases ratios.

(d) THE CURRENT RATIO

This is one of the most commonly used ratios, obtained by dividing the current assets by current liabilities. It therefore deals with the items which make up working capital, and is particularly important to bankers. As it is important that short-term assets meet short-term liabilities this ratio is a measure of the liquidity of the business. Additionally, it is also a measure of safety, as a business is not sound unless it has sufficient liquidity to meet its obligations. However, the ratio itself cannot be accepted without looking at the individual items of assets and liabilities. The make-up must be appraised in order to see whether money coming in will be sufficient to meet current obligations. Stock will not pay creditors until it is sold and cash has been generated. A high current ratio would, therefore, not be a measure of solvency of a business if the current assets were made up mainly of stock which was not quickly saleable.

Obviously a business with a current ratio of less than unity will have a struggle, but with rapid turnover, and with longer credit taken than that given, many businesses are able to conduct their affairs with poor current ratios. It is not possible to lay down what ratio is correct for all businesses, as different trades need different ratios, dependent on the inflow of cash from their sales. Some trades deal in cash, or near cash, whereas others give long credit, and obviously the current ratios between these two extremes will vary greatly. Also some trades have, of necessity, to keep a wide range of stocks and this naturally brings down the ratio, if financed by an increase in creditors.

Generally a banker expects to see a ratio greater than unity and certainly there would be no justification for any unsecured lending to a company which has a current ratio of less than unity. A ratio of 2 to 1 gives comfort, and there are many examples of large companies with a ratio of around this proportion. The ratios of companies should be compared with other companies in the same trade, and the trend in the current ratio of a company should be watched year by year, together with the composition of the asset make-up.

In calculating the ratio there is sometimes difficulty over whether the bank debt should be included as a liability. Normally bank debts are repayable on demand and, as such, become current liabilities, but when a term loan has been arranged, or there is a hard core element in an overdraft, a banker will be able to make an appropriate adjustment. From this point of view a banker is in a much more fortunate position than a creditor, as a creditor would not have the knowledge to make the necessary adjustment.

In view of the importance of this ratio many companies try to improve it at balance sheet dates. For example, if current assets are £8,000 and current liabilities are £5,000 the current ratio would be 1.6 to 1. If just before the balance sheet date pressure was put on debtors and £2,000 was collected and the money used to pay creditors, or to repay a bank overdraft, the resultant current assets would be £6,000, and current liabilities £3,000, the ratio improving to 2 to 1. Naturally a business cannot continue to operate in this way other than for a short period, as it then has to revert to the normal terms of trade, but such efforts are made by many companies to impress bankers and creditors. This, of course, is one of the disadvantages of using published accounts, but if a banker is obtaining regular management figures from a company such devices will immediately be apparent.

It may be helpful to extract the current ratios from the nine weekly balance sheets in Example 15, set out in Chapter 7, and to see how the ratio moves within settled limits over an accounting period. (See diagram opposite.) Weeks 1 to 5 cover the build-up period during which financial movements were by no means normal; the payment of creditors, reducing both current liabilities and current assets, did not begin until the sixth week. Weeks 6 to 9 do, however, represent normal running, and in spite of the substantial profit build-up, the movement of the ratio between 4.07 and 4.47 is reasonably steady.

In an established business, changes in this ratio from year to year should be small, and for the purpose of comparison the ratio is of value. A fall may indicate an overbuying of stock on credit, an investment in fixed assets, or excessive dividend payments or drawings and may be caused by a fall in the rate of gross profit or a marked reduction in sales.

As an index of the *strength* of working capital the current ratio is valuable.

From *Example 15*

Week	Current ratios Fraction		Ratio	
1	$\frac{1,280}{380}$	=	3.4	
2	$\frac{1,350}{550}$	=	2.45	
3	$\frac{1,670}{720}$	=	2.3	(Profits start)
4	$\frac{2,020}{890}$	=	2.27	
5	$\frac{2,550}{710}$	=	3.6	
6	$\frac{2,770}{680}$	=	4.07	Normal working
7	$\frac{2,970}{680}$	=	4.37	Normal working
8	$\frac{2,820}{690}$	=	4.09	Normal working
9	$\frac{3,040}{680}$	=	4.47	Normal working

In Example 14 where the effect of successive purchases of stock on credit was examined, it will be remembered that the amount of the working capital remained unchanged throughout at £5,500. The obvious fall in the liquid strength of the working capital would have been clearly brought out by the changes in the current ratio:

From *Example 14*

			Current ratio
a	$\frac{10,500}{5,000}$	=	2.1
b	$\frac{15,500}{10,000}$	=	1.6
c	$\frac{20,500}{15,000}$	=	1.4
d	$\frac{25,500}{20,000}$	=	1.3

(e) THE LIQUID RATIO

This ratio is obtained by dividing the liquid assets by the current liabilities, and the liquid assets, as previously explained, are the current assets less stock and work in progress. This ratio, therefore, shows how much liquidity is available to meet current liabilities without reliance on stock sales. This ratio is also known as the 'acid test' as it is a test of whether a company can meet its liabilities if it stopped trading immediately. In normal circumstances, for a going concern, this ratio is not in touch with reality because most businesses do not stop suddenly, and this occurs only in the case of liquidation, receivership, or bankruptcy procedures.

As explained when dealing with the current ratio, it is necessary in a business to take into account the amount of money being generated from stock sales, but this ratio, when used in conjunction with the current ratio, highlights the stock and work in progress position and will show when these items are becoming too large for comfort. If the ratio comes out at one or greater than one then the company has, on the face of it, sufficient resources to meet its current obligations, but naturally the composition of the debtors' figure must be known for a full understanding. If bad debtors are included in the figure then obviously the calculations from the ratio will be invalid. This again emphasizes the need for care in looking at one ratio in isolation. Several ratios must be examined, and the trend year by year observed, or a wrong conclusion can be drawn.

Profit and loss account ratios

(a) RATE OF GROSS PROFIT

This is the oldest and most widely used financial ratio derived from the trading account, and expresses gross profit as a percentage of sales. In Example 19 the gross trading profit is 24% (*X*) and 29%(*Y*). It is of value for comparison between two similar businesses, or between different accounting periods of the same business. All, or any of the following factors may contribute to a change in the gross profit rate:

1. accounting factors
   (a) changes in the allocation of expense items between the trading and profit and loss accounts;
   (b) alterations in the basis of stock valuation (including work in progress) as the closing stock of one year is the opening stock of the next; any such change will affect the rate of gross profit for two years.
2. business factors:
   (a) stock losses due either to mark-downs or pilferage;
   (b) changes in buying and selling prices, i.e. in the rate of actual selling profit;
   (c) changes in the proportions of goods sold with differing profit margins, i.e. changes in the sales mix;
   (d) wage rate adjustments and other pay-roll additions and increases in social security payments;

(e) variations in rates of freight and delivery charges;
(f) improvements in productive efficiency: or the reverse, e.g. due to fuel cuts, bottle-necks, strikes, machinery breakdowns, and irregularity of supplies;
(g) fire or flood damage, in so far as it has not been made good by insurance, bringing about losses from interrupted trade as well as actual physical losses of stock.

It will be clear, therefore, that a variation in the gross profit rate gives very little information by itself. But the explanations which the banker will naturally seek can throw much light on the following questions:

1. are the factors which have produced a fall in the gross profit rate permanent or temporary?
2. must earlier estimates of future prospects be amended?
3. is the business meeting increasing competition?
4. should the banker's estimate of the quality of the management be revised?

The rate of gross profit rests on a comparison of figures which are logically comparable and, subject to the foregoing comments, is completely valid. It must be remembered, however, that the rate shown is an average for the whole year for all the departments of the business. In the light of the school-boy analogy in an earlier chapter, the profits being currently earned at the close of the financial year might have been higher or lower than the average for the year and the trend then may have been towards higher or lower rates of gross profit. An average rate of 25% gross profit for one year is therefore no warrant for assuming a similar experience in the following year. But the banker's contact with the accounts of businesses of all kinds and his awareness of current conditions and trends may enable him to forecast at least an order of magnitude for profits on a given turnover. If the ratio compares favourably with the norm for the particular type of business year after year, it is *prima facie* evidence of the soundness of the management. With the Companies Acts requiring the disclosure of turnover the growing tendency for individual corporations to supply their trade association with detailed figures is most welcome. These are collated into a composite account for the whole industry and circulated to all members who are thus provided with a standard set of accounts for comparison with their own.

As a steady build-up of net worth over a period is the best index of sound financial policy, so a steady and adequate rate of gross profit is the most reliable evidence of efficient management.

(b) RATE OF NET PROFIT RATIO

This is similar to the gross profit ratio in that it expresses a known net profit as a percentage of known sales. For a ratio to be completely valid, comparisons should be made of figures which have a direct relationship with each other. When, therefore, we compare gross profit with sales this relationship exists as the gross profit is calculated after accounting for items which vary directly with sales, but net profit is struck after deducting items such as financial, administrative, and overhead expenses, which often do not vary in the same way. Nevertheless, net profit is important for many reasons and this ratio, when used in conjunction with the gross profit ratio, is also useful to bankers. If the gross profit ratio remains steady when the net profit ratio falls a banker should examine the detailed profit and loss account to find out what expenses have caused this result, and whether such expenses are extraordinary items, and should be non-recurring, or if a more fundamental change has taken place. An example of such a fundamental change would be the additional large borrowing for the purchase of an asset which is not generating sufficient income to cover the financial charges.

This ratio, however, is not often of much use when considering the accounts of the smaller private companies because the net profits can be kept at a low level when the proprietors decide to take out the net profit in the way of remuneration and, if necessary, plough back funds by way of directors' loans.

(c) EXPENDITURE TO SALES RATIO

When considering the net profit ratio it was mentioned that it was not a valid ratio on its own because certain debit items which appear in a profit and loss account are not directly related to sales. It is, however, possible to have a link between the gross profit ratio and the net profit ratio by calculating ratios for groups of debit items which appear in the profit and loss account. For example, the financial expenses can be segregated, and the administration expenses also, and ratios can be calculated for the total of these groups to the sales. Naturally, as these items are not specifically related to sales, a somewhat unreliable ratio is produced, but as sales provide the life blood of a business, so all expenses could be related in some way to sales.

These ratios become meaningful if comparisons are made year by year, and for management purposes they are useful in highlighting continuing or increasing costs. These ratios can also be taken further by dealing with the gross profit items too. Ratios can be calculated for wages to sales, and also for cost of materials to sales, and in these cases where there should be a direct relationship between the individual items and sales the ratios are most useful.

From the point of view of a banker the expenditure to sales ratios are useful as information, but in practice there will be no need to calculate them for successful businesses. When, however, a company appears to be getting into difficulties these ratios can be used to help to pinpoint areas of cost which need further examination.

CHAPTER 10

Balance Sheet/Revenue Ratios

Balance sheet/profit and loss account ratios – Rate of stock turnover – The creditor ratio – The debtor ratio – The stock ratio – The working capital ratio – The net return ratio – The validity of the balance sheet/profit and loss account ratios – The lending ratios – Investment ratios

Balance sheet/profit and loss account ratios

All the ratios in this group are based on the comparison of balance sheet figures with related figures in the revenue accounts.

(a) RATE OF STOCK TURNOVER

This is computed by evaluating the fraction:

$$\frac{\text{Cost of sales for the year}}{\text{Average stock}}$$

From *Example 19* $\quad X \; \frac{£161{,}000}{£13{,}500} = 12 \qquad Y \; \frac{£346{,}000}{£22{,}500} = 15.3$

That is to say, the amount tied up in stock is turned over on an average (*X*) 12 times in the year; a very satisfactory rate indeed. For (*Y*) it is 15.3 times. Stated another way, the money invested in stock is tied up on the shelves for

$$(X) \; \frac{365}{12} = 30 \text{ days} \qquad (Y) \; \frac{365}{15.3} = 24 \text{ days}$$

It should be especially noted that the *cost of sales* figure is used in this ratio, not the actual sales figure. The latter normally includes a profit addition. To the extent that this varies, it will vitiate the validity of this ratio for comparing the results of one year with another.

It is important to remember that the rate of turnover is an average figure for the whole stock. Where different lines are carried some will move much faster and some slower than the average. For instance, in a grocery business perishable provisions like bacon and eggs must obviously be cleared every week or two if heavy deterioration losses are to be avoided. On the other hand, bottled and canned goods can safely be held for much longer periods. Nevertheless, unless there is any marked change in the proportions of stock of different kinds handled in different years, inferences from changes in the rate of turnover from year to year will be of value. Other things being equal, the faster stock is turned over the better, for it is financially unsound to have capital tied up in stock (with consequent loss of return on capital) to a greater extent than necessary. It is equally important, however, to carry an adequate stock, both in quantity and variety, to satisfy all likely needs. The loss of profit on sales, and of goodwill, too, when a customer has to be told 'Sorry, we are out of stock', might quickly exceed the interest burden of the cost of the necessary additional stocks. The amount of stock which has to be carried must, of course, be determined largely by the ease and regularity with which replenishments can be obtained. Apart from supply considerations, a fall in the rate of turnover is a sign of overstocking or falling sales, or both; and an investigation into both purchasing and selling policy is indicated.

Using an arithmetic average for stock for this ratio is, of course, unsound as, for example, a low stock might have been held for 11 months of a year and a high stock for only one. However, if we consider this ratio for going concerns, normally during an accounting period excessively wide variations are not seen.

(b) THE CREDITOR RATIO

This ratio will be computed as follows:

$$\frac{\text{trade creditors}}{\text{factory purchases} + \text{trading purchases}}$$

From *Example 19 and Year A Balance Sheet, Appendix 1*

$$X \quad \frac{5{,}000}{10{,}000+43{,}000} = .094$$

$$Y \quad \frac{5{,}000}{100{,}000+185{,}000} = .0017$$

Length of credit taken

X 365×.094 = 34 days Y 365×.0017 = 6 days

It will be noted that the only creditor figure used is that directly related to purchases, taxation and dividend liabilities being ignored.

The *Y* term of credit taken is exceptionally low and suggests that the company could, with advantage, take longer credit, or in other words increase its current assets at negligible cost. On the other hand, it may indicate substantial purchases for cash on favourable terms which would be sound business.

It must always be remembered that a debtor has no prescriptive right to receive normal trade terms, or indeed any credit at all, and length of trade credit, whether on open account or acceptance, varies considerably. If general conditions deteriorate or a particular customer runs into difficulty, a curtailment of his credit is not unlikely.

When the creditor ratio is high, showing a term of credit longer than is customary in the trade, it means one of two things: either that the company is so strong that it can dictate its own terms to its suppliers, or that it is short of cash and cannot pay its accounts as they fall due. The latter is by far the more usual; but the former is by no means unknown. There should be no difficulty in practice in deciding which applies.

In interpreting the creditor ratio, the banker will naturally relate the balance sheet date to seasonal purchasing peaks; and also to the effect of inordinately large purchases just before the balance sheet date. Such exceptional purchases will often explain an abnormally high creditor ratio.

(c) THE DEBTOR RATIO

This ratio brings out the relationship between sales and outstanding amounts to be collected on sales at the balance sheet date. The fraction is:

$$\frac{\text{debtors and bills receivable}}{\text{sales}}$$

From *Example 19 and Year A balance sheet, Appendix 1*

$$(X)\quad \frac{24{,}500+7{,}500}{212{,}000} = .15 \qquad (Y)\quad \frac{24{,}500+7{,}500}{486{,}000} = .065$$

Accordingly, the length of credit allowed is:

$$(X)\quad 365\times.15 = 55 \text{ days} \qquad (Y)\quad 365\times.065 = 24 \text{ days}$$

The *Y* term looks short; a considerable proportion of cash sales is one possible explanation. Where this is a significant factor, the ratio involves bringing the debtor figure into relation with a sales figure to a substantial part of which (cash sales) it has no relation at all, and the quite logical basis of the ratio collapses.

The length of credit allowed to debtors varies widely from trade to trade, and is often longer in a retail business than in a manufacturing or wholesale business. But the retailer may have the advantage of cash sales to offset slow collections in connection with credit sales. As the creditor of one business is the debtor of the other, much the same considerations apply to both the debtor and creditor ratios. Exceptional sales just before the balance sheet date will, by inflating debtors, abnormally increase the debtor ratio and correspondingly increase the ostensible length of credit allowed.

(d) THE STOCK RATIOS

The purpose of the stock ratios appropriate to the various items which make up the stock – raw materials, work in progress, stock complete and ready for sale – is to establish the stock tie-up at the balance sheet date in relation to the amount of business done. How can this be measured? Clearly in a purely retail business the size of the business is determined by sales. But in a manufacturing or contracting business it is measured by the amount of production or work done. Now the value of production, as ascertained from the accounts, is sales (representing completed work invoiced), whether to outside customers or to own merchanting department, PLUS increase in work in progress (or MINUS decrease), PLUS increase in finished stock (or MINUS decrease.) In Example 19 all the finished stock has been 'sold' to the retail department and no stocks are retained in the factory account, except those of raw materials.

A word of caution is, perhaps, necessary about work in progress. In contractors' accounts it is customary to deduct progress payments from work in progress *in the balance sheet* and to extend a net figure for work in progress not paid for. But for the purpose of the stock ratios and to ascertain the true production figure, the gross work in progress figure should be taken, as it appears in the trading account itself.

From Example 19 the true production figures are:

(X) £99,000+£4,000 increase in work in progress = £103,000
(Y) £127,000–£5,000 decrease in work in progress = £122,000

RAW MATERIAL RATIO

(X) $\frac{5,000}{103,000} = .049$ (Y) $\frac{5,000}{122,000} = .041$

WORK IN PROGRESS RATIO

(X) $\frac{7,500}{103,000} = .073$ (Y) $\frac{7,500}{122,000} = 0.61$

Total factory tie-up .122 .102

Equivalent to:

(X) .122×365 = 45 days production (Y) .102×365 = 37 days production

The whole of the finished stock being in the merchanting department, the *finished* stock ratio will be based on sales, and the fraction will be:

$$\frac{\text{closing stock}}{\text{sales}}$$

The figures based on Example 19 will therefore be:

$$(X)\quad \frac{20{,}000}{212{,}000} = .094 \qquad (Y)\quad \frac{20{,}000}{486{,}000} = .041$$

Equivalent to:

$$365 \times .094 = 34 \text{ days} \qquad 365 \times .041 = 15 \text{ days}$$

With reference to all these stock ratios, it must be emphasized that the purpose is to establish the stock tie-up *at the balance sheet date.* It is for this reason that the final stock figure is employed and not the average stock as in the rate of stock turnover calculation.

(e) WORKING CAPITAL RATIO

This valuable ratio is designed to determine the amount of working capital required to sustain a given level of sales in a retail business or of production in a manufacturing business. The case of 'Manufacturers Limited', who conduct a hybrid business, partly manufacturing and partly merchanting, is more complicated and has been specially selected to demonstrate how the working capital ratio is extracted for both parts of the business. Only trade and expense creditors are taken into account, but current assets must be reduced by amount of non-trade creditors; in this case dividend and taxation £17,000.

Analysis of working capital
(from *Example 18, Year A*)

	Total (£'000)	Attributable to factory (£'000)	Attributable to warehouse (£'000)
Current assets			
Raw materials	5	5	—
Work in progress	7.5	7.5	—
Stock of finished goods	20	—	20
Debtors and bills	32	—	32
Liquid assets (£12.5)			
Less non trading creditors (£17)	(4.5)	say (2.2)	say (2.3)
	60	10.3	49.7
Less Creditors	5	say 2.5	say 2.5
	55	7.8	47.2

The factory working capital ratio deduced from Example 19 is therefore:

$$\frac{\text{working capital}}{\text{production}} = \frac{7.8}{53}\ (X) \qquad \frac{7.8}{120}\ (Y)$$

$$= 14.7\% \quad \text{or} \quad 6.5\%$$

That is to say, for every £100 of production at cost price £14.70 (or (Y) £6.50) of working capital is required.

The corresponding warehouses figures are:

$$\frac{\text{working capital}}{\text{sales}} = \frac{47.2}{212} \quad (X) \qquad \frac{47.2}{486} \quad (Y)$$

$$= 22.26\% \quad \text{or} \quad 9.71\%$$

indicating that for every £100 of sales £22.26 of working capital ((Y) £9.71) was employed at the balance sheet date.

The value of these working capital ratios is obvious, for they give an indication of the additional working capital which will be required for a contemplated expansion of turnover. Experience shows, however, that over and above the figure deduced for a given expansion, an adequate addition should be allowed to cover:

1. extra requirements during the transition period. Expanded production inevitably involves teething troubles and takes time to fructify;
2. the probability that the law of diminishing returns may operate: beyond a certain stage a progressively lower return may be expected from equal additional doses of capital;
3. an ample margin for the unexpected: the working capital ratio can only indicate a *minimum* order of magnitude.

It is the experience of most bankers that while usually business men fully understand and allow for capital requirements for buildings, plant and machinery, they tend to underestimate or even ignore the essential working capital; and in such cases the business is handicapped from the very start.

(f) NET RETURN RATIO

Like all profit ratios, this is usually expressed as a percentage. It shows the return for the year not on the issued capital but on the real capital or stake of the equity shareholders. But what figure of equity should be taken? The figure we want is the actual average effective equity capital employed in the business throughout the year. The balance sheet gives only the capital figures at the opening and at the close of the year. Which figure shall we take, the starting capital, the ending capital or an average figure? In so far as any accretion of capital is due to accruing profits, it might be reasonable to take the mean figure on the assumption that profits have accrued evenly throughout the year. But increases in the equity may also be due to further proprietors' capital invested in the business. In such cases the time of the year when such additions took place should be taken into account and the average effective equity capital calculated accordingly.

Working on Example 19, the net worth at the beginning of the year must be reconstructed in the light of the X and Y profit and loss accounts, the balance sheet for that date not being available. (Net worth is used in this example as there is no preference capital to be deducted to obtain the equity figure.)

(X)	£	(Y)	£
Final net worth . .	138,600		138,600
Add Decrease in carry forward, 13,400—10,000 .	3,400	*Deduct* Increase in carry forward, 15,100+10,000	25,100
Net worth at start of year .	£142,000		£113,500
(Assuming no fresh capital introduced)			
Average net worth . .	£140,300		£126,000
Net profit before taxation .	£56,600		£50,100
Net return ratio . .	40%		40%

These figures compare with 56.6% and 50.1% on the paid-up capital of the company.

As provisions for taxation may be affected by considerations other than the profits of the year in which they are made, the net return *before* taxation is the most reliable guide. Where this is unduly low it indicates over-capitalization or inefficient management, or both; or that, perhaps owing to competition, changing tastes or general depression, the business is no longer profitable. The net return is important because it roughly measures the ability of the business to attract and remunerate fresh capital in case of need.

(g) RETURN ON NET ASSETS

This ratio, also known as return on capital employed, is widely used as a measure of the efficiency of companies. It is calculated by dividing the profit before interest and tax by the net assets, which are the total assets minus the current liabilities.

Let us look at an abbreviated version of the year A figures for Manufacturers Limited.

	£	£
Fixed assets		153,600
Current assets	78,400	
Less current liabilities . . .	22,000	56,400
		£210,000
5% debentures		70,000
Net worth		140,000
		£210,000

The net assets are £210,000 (the total assets minus £22,000 current liabilities) which will be seen to be the total also of the funds provided by the proprietors and the debenture holders to run the company.

Looking at the other item in the ratio, the profit before interest and tax, it will be seen that if we start at the net profit figure for our calculation we shall have to add back the taxation and the interest paid on the debentures. Taxation varies from year to year according to fiscal regulations, and the figures for taxation must be eliminated from the ratio calculation to prevent distortion. As for the interest on the debentures, this must be added back to the net profit because we are in effect calculating the rate on all the funds provided by the proprietors and the long-term lenders.

The net return ratio, previously mentioned, gives the percentage of profit before taxation generated by the stake of the equity shareholders (i.e. ordinary share capital, profit and loss account balance and reserves). It therefore measures the gross yield on the equity stake and excludes any long-term borrowing from the calculation. It does not show whether the assets of a company (provided by all the shareholders and the long-term lenders) are being used efficiently; to decide this the amount of the long-term funds and the rate of interest on them must also be taken into account.

The return on net assets, however, does give a measure of efficiency in the use of the total funds at the disposal of the company. Whether or not a company chooses a method of financing which relies on proprietors' funds, or borrowed money, is for the company to decide, and the considerations are important, but they do not affect the efficiency of the company in dealing with the employment of its assets and the generation of profits from their use.

If we work now from Example 19, and take the net worth as computed for net return ratio we have the following figures:

	(X) £	(Y) £
Average net worth . . .	140,300	126,000
Add Debenture funds . . .	70,000	70,000
Equivalent to average net assets employed	210,300	196,000
Net profit before taxation . .	56,600	50,100
Add Back debenture interest .	3,500	3,500
	£60,100	£53,600
Return on net assets . . .	28.6%	27.3%

To obtain accurate comparisons it is, of course, necessary to take into account variations in the net worth throughout the year, together with variations in long-term borrowing. In other words an average figure for net assets must be calculated.

Summary

The difference between the inferences to be drawn from the balance sheet for year A when read in conjunction with the X revenue accounts and the Y, becomes clearly evident when the ratios deduced are tabulated below.

'Manufacturers Limited'

	(X)	(Y)
1. Factory gross profit	46.5%	5.5%
2. Trading gross profit	24%	29%
3. Rate of turnover of stock	30 days	24 days
4. Creditor ratio	34 days	6 days
5. Debtor ratio	55 days	24 days
6. Stock ratio (factory)	45 days	37 days
7. Stock ratio (warehouse)	34 days	15 days
8. Working capital ratio (factory)	14.7%	6.5%
9. Working capital ratio (warehouse)	22.26%	9.71%
10. Net return ratio	40%	40%
11. Return on net assets	28.6%	27.3%

All the accounting ratios of the last group (Nos. 3–11 above) have one characteristic and basic weakness. With the exception of Nos. 10 and 11 they seek to establish a relationship between one or more balance sheet figures showing the position *at a given moment of time* on the one hand, and revenue account figures for a whole year on the other, thus:

Ratio	Relating balance sheet figure(s) for	with	Revenue a/c figure
Rate of stock turnover	Stock (or average Stock)		Cost of sales
Creditor	Trade creditors and bills payable		Purchases (excluding transfers from works a/c)
Debtor	Debtors and bills receivable		Sales (or production)
Stock	Stock		Sales (or production)
Working capital	Working capital		Sales (or production)

All the profit and loss account figures are totals for the whole year and as such may be taken as fact. But there is no reason to suppose that the average weekly figure deduced from the totals would be correct for the closing weeks of the financial year, which alone have a natural and intimate connection with the position disclosed by the balance sheet 'Still'. It has already been suggested that the latter can be considered only in the light of the *immediate* preceding movements. If we were studying a golf swing with the help of a cinema projector, a 'still' at the moment of impact could usefully be studied in conjunction with the wind-up and the down-swing which went immediately before, or the follow-through which came immediately after, but would have no meaning at all in relation to sequences showing the player arriving on the tee, or moving off after his shot.

In relation to each of the balance sheet figures involved (for the working capital ratio perhaps six or seven will be used) the following questions must be asked:

1. how far is the figure itself accurate?
2. how far has it been affected (cf. the posed and unnatural photograph) by deliberate distortion?

and above all:

3. how far are the figures taken typical of those which have obtained for the same item(s) throughout the trading period?

The last question is vital to the validity of all these ratios. Unless the balance sheet figures are near enough to the effective average for the whole year we shall offend against the axiom that like must be compared with like. Clearly in practice it is almost impossible to establish either that the balance sheet figure taken is the correct one, or, in any case, that any ratio deduced will have any value in the forecasting of future developments.

The *creditor and debtor ratios* both suffered from two main defects:

1. the level of creditors or debtors at the balance sheet date is conditioned mainly by the buying and selling operations during the last few weeks of the year: if these were not at the average level for the year, the corresponding creditors and debtors figures will not be typical. Exceptionally high or exceptionally low purchases or sales just before the balance sheet date will substantially distort the ratios;
2. nowhere in the accounts will it be disclosed how much of purchases or sales were on credit and how much for cash. In the absence of this information any inference as to the length of credit taken or given is untrustworthy.

The debtors/sales ratio is the more important of the two and deserves some further comment. Where sales during the year amount to, say $4x$ and debtors to x, then the ratio is .25, indicating that the equivalent of 3 months' sales is tied up in book debts, though not probably or even necessarily the actual sales of the three months to the balance sheet date. Although the profit on these sales has been taken into account, it has not been received in cash. For we must remember that the sales ledger debits include all moneys owing and some of the debts may be of long standing. On the other hand, certain credit sales in the last three months of the account year may have been paid promptly, as little as a month after the sales.

A further important consideration is the proportion of cash to credit sales. It is obvious that if half the sales are for cash then a .25 ratio deduced from the accounts would mean that in fact the average debtor tie-up is six months (ratio .5), not three.

Consider the following figures supplied by a customer to his banker, analysing the debtors figure of £32,241 at 31st March.

Sales for	Amount owing £	% of total debtors
pre-October	1,945	6
October	1,934	6
November	2,587	8
December	3,861	12
January	5,491	17
February	7,073	22
March	9,350	29
	£32,241	100

For 29% of the debtors (March) no accounts had been issued at all by 31st March; and for a further 22% (February) the accounts had been sent out on 16th March, and very few had been paid by the 31st. In other words over half the debtors figure was entirely unaffected by the length of credit allowed. In the light of this break-down, is there any reality or logic in an attempt to relate the March debtors figure to the total sales for the year, £162,838; or any validity in the conclusion that customers were taking 14 weeks' credit? The banker must not be misled by traditional rule-of-thumb short cuts to knowledge. If the length of credit is really important it must be examined properly.

Nevertheless the ratio, taken in conjunction with the firm's credit terms, sheds some light on the efficiency of the accounts department and the quality of the debtors. Subject to the foregoing comments variations in the ratio from year to year can thus give a very useful suggestion of important changes both inside and outside the business.

Useful indications of the efficiency of businesses in control of their debtors and creditors can be obtained by comparing the length of credit given and received by other businesses in the same trade. Collation of these figures is often undertaken by trade organizations, but bankers are easily able to build up their own library of figures from the numerous balance sheets and profit and loss accounts they see.

Similar difficulties to those which apply to debtor and creditor ratios also apply to stock, both in connection with the rate of turnover and the stock ratio, with an added variable that the stock may not only be untypical in quantity, but also in the basis of valuation. That is to say, not only may the quantity of stock at the end of the year be lower (or higher) than the average, but by reason of recent market movements, may properly be valued at a figure lower (or higher) than the average cost for the year. Add to this the possibility that there may be deliberate undervaluation designed to throw profits forward to years when (it may be fondly hoped) taxation will be lower, and both the stock/sales and turnover ratios begin to qualify for the rough-and-ready class. In special cases, however, the rate of turnover of stock can be exceedingly useful.

It can often show when stock is grossly undervalued as the rate of turnover of stock is then too high to be readily accepted. Also it can give an indication when a large amount of unsaleable or obsolete stock is held as the rate of turnover of stock becomes exceptionally small. This is because the turnover of stock is related to all the stock held including the dead weight stock instead of to the proportion of stock which actually turns over.

The working capital ratio (working capital/sales (or production) rests on all the balance sheet items already discussed plus the liquid assets. It is subject to the characteristic defects of balance sheet/revenue comparison which have already been fully discussed in connection with the debtors/sales ratio. As a rough and ready indication of the tie-up per £100 of sales or production, when the adequacy of available funds for contemplated expansion is being considered it is useful, however, and cannot be rejected merely because inferences to be drawn from it are provisional only. Whether they are sound or not can be tested by enquiry. In practice, the banker finds it most valuable when it enables him to say, 'Your security and general position would justify the advance of £10,000 for which you ask. On the showing of your own accounts, this will not provide sufficient working capital for your proposed £50,000 contract.' The onus of demonstrating that £10,000 is enough then rests upon the customer and his accountant. If in fact it is, well and good; and the proof will have taught the banker more about the inner workings of his customer's business than he could have learnt in any other way. The outstanding warning given by experience is this: the most carefully drawn budget tends to be falsified in practice and the wise banker will insist on a wide margin of available resources, either provided by the facilities granted, or by the greater sum he is prepared in his own mind to concede, if and when it is needed.

The question of available resources leads to another related query: what is the ability of the business to attract fresh permanent share capital in case of need? On this question the *net return ratio* sheds some light. The main purpose of this ratio is to determine whether further doses of capital can profitably be assimilated by the business. It must always be remembered, however, that the current return on the net worth of the business will not necessarily be earned by additional capital. Sooner or later, perhaps much sooner than expected, the law of diminishing returns will operate.

Set out below are skeleton balance sheets and profit and loss accounts of a company making a trading profit of £3,000 and employing net assets of £10,000 which are provided by the proprietors in company A, and a combination of proprietors and mortgage funds in companies B and C. Let us now consider the effect of £5,000 increase in share capital, with a proportionate rise in trading profit and overheads (ignoring possible diminishing returns for the moment).

EXAMPLE 24

(1)

	Company A	Company B	Company C
	£	£	£
BALANCE SHEET CAPITAL AND FIXED LIABILITIES			
Net worth	10,000	8,000	5,000
Mortgage at 8%	—	2,000	5,000
Total proprietors' and loan capital	£10,000	£10,000	£10,000
PROFIT AND LOSS ACCOUNT			
Overheads	2,000	2,000	2,000
Mortgage interest	—	160	400
Net profit	1,000	840	600
Trading profit	£3,000	£3,000	£3,000
Net return ratio based on net worth	10%	10.5%	12%

(2)

	Company A	Company B	Company C
	£	£	£
INCREASE OF £5,000 IN SHARE CAPITAL			
Net worth	15,000	13,000	10,000
PROFIT AND LOSS ACCOUNT			
Overheads	3,000	3,000	3,000
Mortgage interest	—	160	400
Net profit	1,500	1,340	1,100
Trading profit	£4,500	£4,500	£4,500
Net return ratio	10%	10.3%	11%

It is clear from the example that:

(a) because the over-all return on the proprietors' funds employed, i.e. 10% on £10,000 in case A, is greater than the rate of interest paid on the loan capital, the rate of net return on the net worth will be higher where loan capital takes the place of part of the share capital as in B and C;

(b) when the trading profit increases pro rata the net return on new share capital will be lower than on existing net worth if there is any material amount of comparatively cheap loan finance. This is because the proportion of cheap finance diminishes as the proprietors' funds increase, and if it is not possible to increase the cheap finance in the same proportion a similar benefit will not accrue to the new capital subscribed. Nevertheless, an indication is obtained for the overall return on the total capital and this can be related to the dividend which is proposed on the enlarged capital, and a judgment made as to whether this will be acceptable to the market in the conditions applying at the time.

There are, however, many other factors which must be taken into account when the raising of fresh capital is contemplated. For example:

1. the additional capital may take considerable time before it brings in its full return;
2. the employment of additional capital may involve an increase in overheads, either higher in proportion than the increase in gross profit, or lower;
3. the profits for the year or years under consideration may have been raised or lowered by internal factors which no longer operate;
4. the fact that the profit for the years may have no relationship to the profits earned in its closing months or likely to be earned in the near future must be borne in mind;
5. changes in external conditions may make any forecast based on past figures completely wrong.

The foregoing survey of the more usual financial relationships suggests that the only completely logical and valid ratio is the gross profit ratio.

The rest of the ratios fall down as being based on comparisons between figures which are not strictly comparable at all. Nevertheless, they need not be discarded entirely by the banker who remembers at all times that:

1. a ratio by itself may be almost valueless;
2. changes in ratios for different years can be exceedingly suggestive;
3. such changes or inconsistencies between trends indicated by different ratios are invaluable if they promote intelligent and searching enquiry;
4. ratios generally contribute most to the lending banker's armoury as mnemonics impressing upon his mind the kind of relationship between different items in the accounts which it is important to watch;

and finally that

5. when several ratios, each in itself of indifferent evidential value, all point in the same direction their combined verdict may be irresistible. An example of how this works in practice will be seen when overtrading is discussed in a later chapter.

Lending ratios

There are no hard and fast lending ratios, and it is difficult, therefore, for a young banker to decide what to do. By studying balance sheets and profit and loss accounts, and by using ratios he will be able to reach a judgment on whether a balance sheet appears sound, and by comparing companies he will be able to gauge the relative strengths of them. This at least is a start.

Where overdrafts are granted for normal trading purposes a banker will be looking for working capital to increase as profits are made and retained in the business. This is a sign of a healthy business, and if the record of the company shows that it has been conducting its business in this way a banker should be able to have the confidence to back it. It is the working capital (i.e. the net current assets) to which the banker will be looking, and not to the fixed assets. The fixed assets are more of a permanent nature, and although they contribute to the well-being of the business, or should do if proper capital appraisals were made, it is the changing current assets and current liabilities which affect transactions which flow through the bank overdraft account.

If a company is profit-making the net current assets will increase, and a change in its trading results will be necessary for the net current assets to remain steady, and an even greater change will be necessary for losses to be made, and the net current assets diminish. If a banker has confidence in his customer he could advance one third of the net current assets on an unsecured basis, or, on occasions, go as high as half of the net current assets. This would be showing considerable confidence in the customer because the banker will be matching the customer's stake in the working capital. Any further proportion would establish the banker as the senior partner in the liquid position and this is not the function of a banker.

If a banker has security he can, of course, lend more with safety, but unless there are special considerations he should not be prepared to lend more than the amount of the proprietors' stake for the same reason that the banker's function is to be a banker, and not the senior partner in an enterprise run by a customer who obviously knows more about the business.

Additional investment ratios

To complete our review of ratios a brief description is given of a few additional ratios used by investment analysts. In the normal course a banker does not need to use these ratios when considering lending, but should have a knowledge of them to follow the financial press, and to give him a wide understanding. They can also be studied with advantage if a banker is thinking that the time has come for his lending to be lifted as he will be able to compare the ratios with those for other quoted companies, and make a judgment about whether the time is propitious to suggest going to the market for additional funds. These additional ratios particularly apply to companies with stock exchange quotations.

(a) RETURN ON THE EQUITY

This ratio is computed in the same way as the net return ratio except that after tax figures are used:

$$\frac{\text{earnings attributable to ordinary shareholders after tax} \times 100}{\text{amount of the shareholders' funds}}\%$$

This is an important ratio for investors because it takes into account all the factors which affect the company.

(b) EARNINGS PER SHARE

This is calculated from:

$$\frac{\text{earnings of ordinary shareholders after tax}}{\text{number of ordinary shares issued}}$$

The result is a figure which can be related to the nominal value of the ordinary shares, and provides an easy comparison with other companies. Naturally if earnings of 8p a share are related to a 25p share the comparative figure for a £1 share will be 32p.

(c) PRICE/EARNINGS RATIO

This is calculated from:

$$\frac{\text{market price of ordinary share}}{\text{earnings per share (as in (b) above)}}$$

If 8p is earned on an ordinary share and the price is 80p the price/earnings ratio will be 10, and if the market price is 120p the price/earnings ratio will be 15. It will, therefore, take the earnings attributable to the ordinary shareholders after tax either 10 or 15 years to be equal to the market price of the share, and the higher the price/earnings ratio the greater the regard of the investing public for the shares. This may well be because there is a greater expectation of future growth which puts up the market price, although, of course, there is a wide variety of factors which affect share prices.

(d) DIVIDEND YIELD

This is calculated from:

$$\frac{\text{dividend per share (pence)} \times 100}{\text{market price per share (pence)}} \%$$

Whereas the profit/earnings ratio deals with the after tax earnings of a share this ratio is concerned with the dividend which is paid and, of course, is of more immediate interest to shareholders.

(e) DIVIDEND COVER

It is important for investors to know not only the dividend yield but also whether the company's earnings safely cover the dividend, and if they can look forward with confidence to at least the same level of dividend in the future. The calculation is:

$$\frac{\text{earnings per share (after tax)}}{\text{dividend per share}}$$

(f) DEBT RATIO

This is calculated from:

$$\frac{\text{long-term debt}}{\text{equity capital}}$$

This ratio is not always calculated in the same way as sometimes short-term debt is also included. It also suffers from being described additionally as capital/equity ratio, or equity/debt ratio. When dealing with this ratio it is important to ascertain the basis of calculation. It is an important ratio as it shows the relationship between the funds which are provided for running the company. The greater the long-term debt as a proportion of the equity the higher gearing a company is said to have. The price of an ordinary share in a company which is highly geared is likely to fluctuate between wider extremes and more rapidly than a share in a low geared company. However, much will depend on the interest rate payable on the long-term debt. If the borrowing was arranged when interest rates were high there will be a continuing burden on the company and any advantage of gearing will be lost.

(g) INTEREST COVER (or TIMES INTEREST EARNED)

This is calculated from:

$$\frac{\text{earnings before interest and tax}}{\text{interest payable on loans}}$$

It shows the measure of safety available for the long-term loans and naturally if the cover is high the holders of the loans can feel secure as far as their income is concerned. The earnings before tax are taken because loan interest has to be paid regardless of whether a profit is made or not, and tax is payable on a profit only after loan interest has been met.

CHAPTER 11

Insolvency: Cash Circulation

When, as lending bankers, we examine accounts, what are we really looking for? Two main issues stand out: the nature of cash circulation and insolvency; the two are closely interlocked.

Insolvency

When lending, the banker is vitally concerned with the safety of his advance. He must assure himself that there is reasonable prospect of reductions and repayment if things go according to expectations and that if the unforeseen should happen and his customer should fail the assets, reinforced where necessary by third-party security, will realize enough to prevent loss to the bank. In other words, he looks at his borrower's accounts to satisfy himself that the customer is not insolvent.

There are two recognized kinds of insolvency:

1. 'going-concern' insolvency arises when the customer is unable to pay his debts as they become due;
2. 'gone-concern' (or commercial) insolvency arises when, on winding up and after realization of all his assets, the customer is unable to pay 100p in the £, i.e. when total liabilities exceed total realized assets.

The first arises, and indeed can only arise, while the business continues. Its essence is a shortage of *cash* of the right amount and at the time required and inability to raise cash by borrowing or otherwise: in other words an unliquid position. And the word 'liquidation' is aptly used to describe the winding up of a company, for that is exactly what happens. The assets are turned into cash. Clearly it is possible for an individual to be unable to pay his debts as they become due and still be able to pay 100p in the £ when his assets, including the fixed assets, are sold up. Equally it is possible for him to have ample liquid resources to meet current liabilities and yet, on winding up, to have insufficient to discharge his liabilities, including his long-term debts.

This is not the place to discuss bankruptcy law in great detail; but in practice, the majority of failures are precipitated by 'going concern' insolvency, which is normally the immediate cause of the most usual acts of bankruptcy, e.g.:

1. debtor filing a declaration that he is unable to pay his debts;
2. debtor filing his own petition;
3. giving notice that he has suspended payment;
4. failure to satisfy a bankruptcy notice within seven days;

and the probable underlying cause of most of the others, e.g.:

1. assignment of debtor's property for the benefit of his creditors;
2. fraudulent conveyance or preference;
3. avoiding creditors with the intent to delay or defeat them;
4. execution levied against debtor's goods.

Similarly, by far the most usual cause for the winding up of a company by the Court is that the company is unable to pay its debts, the tests of which are:

1. failure to pay or satisfy, within three weeks of service of demand, a creditor for over £200;
2. an unsatisfied execution issued by a judgment creditor;
3. proof to the satisfaction of the court that the company is unable to pay its debts (contingent and prospective liabilities of the company being taken into account).

It will be seen that none of the causes detailed above refers either in bankruptcy or company liquidation to inability *ultimately* to pay 100p in the £.

In considering a bankrupt's application for discharge, the Court may have regard to both kinds of insolvency and refuse or suspend discharge if the bankrupt has:

1. continued to trade after knowing himself to be insolvent: which means here inability to pay 100p in the £;
2. when unable to pay his debts as they become due has, within three months of the receiving order, given undue preference to any of his creditors.

Both kinds of insolvency are material to the validity of a floating charge under the Companies Act 1985. This provides that a floating charge created within twelve months of the commencement of the winding up shall be invalid (except as to the amount of cash paid to the company at the time of creation or subsequently) unless it is proved that immediately after the creation of the charge the company was solvent. The burden of proving that the company was solvent lies on the holder of the floating charge.

The company may be insolvent in either of two ways:

1. if the property 'left' is not enough to pay its debts. For this purpose all the assets and all the liabilities must be considered;

2. if the company is unable to pay its debts as they fall due (*London Counties Assets Co.* v. *Brighton Grand Concert Hall (1915)* 2 K.B. at p. 496). For this purpose it is immaterial that the assets exceed the liabilities. (*Hodson* v. *Blanchards* (*London*), *Ltd.* 131 *L.T. Newsp.* 9.)

If a banker, relying on a floating charge, is unable to prove solvency by *both* tests, it is little consolation that the debt remains although the floating charge is invalid; for his only remaining right of proof as an unsecured creditor may involve heavy loss.

The banker's special approach

It has already been stated that no prudent banker would become involved in an advance to a company if his only assurance of ultimate repayment was winding up and liquidation. He dare not do so in reliance on a newly taken floating charge as security for an already existing debt unless he is equally satisfied that on the current position the company can meet its debts as they become due. It is here urged that 'going-concern' solvency, and with an ample margin, should be the banker's paramount consideration. If there is a cushion of fixed assets in case of trouble, that is good: alone, it is not enough.

How then can the banker find the necessary assurance in the accounts of his customer? It might be assumed that if circulating assets exceed creditors and loans the customer is solvent. That is an over-simplification, although on a 'gone-concern' basis the statement may have some justification. But, on the 'going-concern' basis, the aggregate of creditors and loans is not the sole measure of cash requirements. Weekly wages may involve weekly requirements for cash which liquid assets and the inflow of collections cannot cover. It is notorious that when a business gets into serious difficulty it is often the inability to find wages which finally brings it to a stand-still and changes its status from that of a 'going concern' to that of a 'gone-concern'; and the ability of the debtors to provide ready cash is often misunderstood. It is too easy to think that the average monthly amount of debtors will be collected every month. The fact is, of course, that the amount received in any one month will normally be determined mainly by the amounts invoiced one, two or three months earlier (according to the length of credit customary in the trade) and has no relation at all to the total amount of debtors outstanding at any one time. Collections will tend to vary with credit sales, but with a time lag. Similar considerations apply to purchase and the payments which have to be made from time to time to trade creditors.

Particular problems occur with businesses which are having a poor trading experience, are approaching insolvency, or are perhaps only just solvent. In these cases it is often a struggle to obtain the right type of trading conditions, and longer credit has to be given (sometimes to financially weak businesses), and longer credit has been taken which can result in continued pressure from creditors.

It will be seen that there is no universal test of solvency for all businesses. Each business must be examined in relation to its particular circumstances. From the collection of liquid resources in the normal way current liabilities must be met, and current liabilities are not met from large book entries for debtors and stock, but only from the proportion which can be turned into cash.

The ebb and flow of cash is clearly the ultimate consideration. Its movements are illustrated graphically on the next page. It is quite clear that the life blood of this system is cash, which carries vitality into every stage of production up to finished stock. If there is any monetary anaemia the vitality of the whole organism quickly suffers.

It will not be overlooked that if raw materials, work in progress and stock are valued at *prime cost* all changes in the asset make-up from cash to stock will merely be changes in kind and not in value. It will be simply a case of asset for asset.

The next operation, the sale of stock, introduces an entirely new element. An asset, stock, valued at cost £C is exchanged for another asset, whether cash, debtor or bill receivable valued at £C+P, where P is the profit (or C−L, where L is the loss). When profit is made and *realized*, cash will steadily increase as it circulates to the extent of profits made. But this is not a closed circulatory system and there will be inevitable withdrawals as shown in the diagram. If the position becomes too full-blooded, excess cash may be drawn off within the system and invested (E: liquid investments).

If the withdrawals, which include payments of bank charges and loan repayments, exceed the normal cash increment from trading or special receipts, the strength of the organism will diminish. If such a condition is protracted the position may become so critical that only a liberal transfusion of fresh cash will restore normal health. It will be equally disastrous if the channels of circulation are clogged. Actual shortage of raw materials will stop production at its source; physical bottle-necks may retard work in progress, and the process may lag before finished stock emerges. Even when ample supplies of finished stock are coming forward, diminished sales and slower debtor collections may reduce the return of cash and create a position where the natural increase is insufficient to cover the withdrawals. This, in turn, brings about a fall in cash pressure at all the points where it normally boosts production and the whole cycle of circulation becomes sluggish.

Let us consider the illustration of the stopped cinematograph film and look at the diagram as a 'still'. The circulation of the current assets which may, at the balance sheet date, be either vigorous or sluggish, is notionally suspended. It will be clear that the values appearing at A, B, C, D, E and F in the balance sheet can tell us nothing about the *rate of flow* at the balance sheet date, nor indicate whether the return of cash to the pool (normally the bank) will provide an adequate margin over cash disburse-

EXAMPLE 25. The place of cash in a working business.

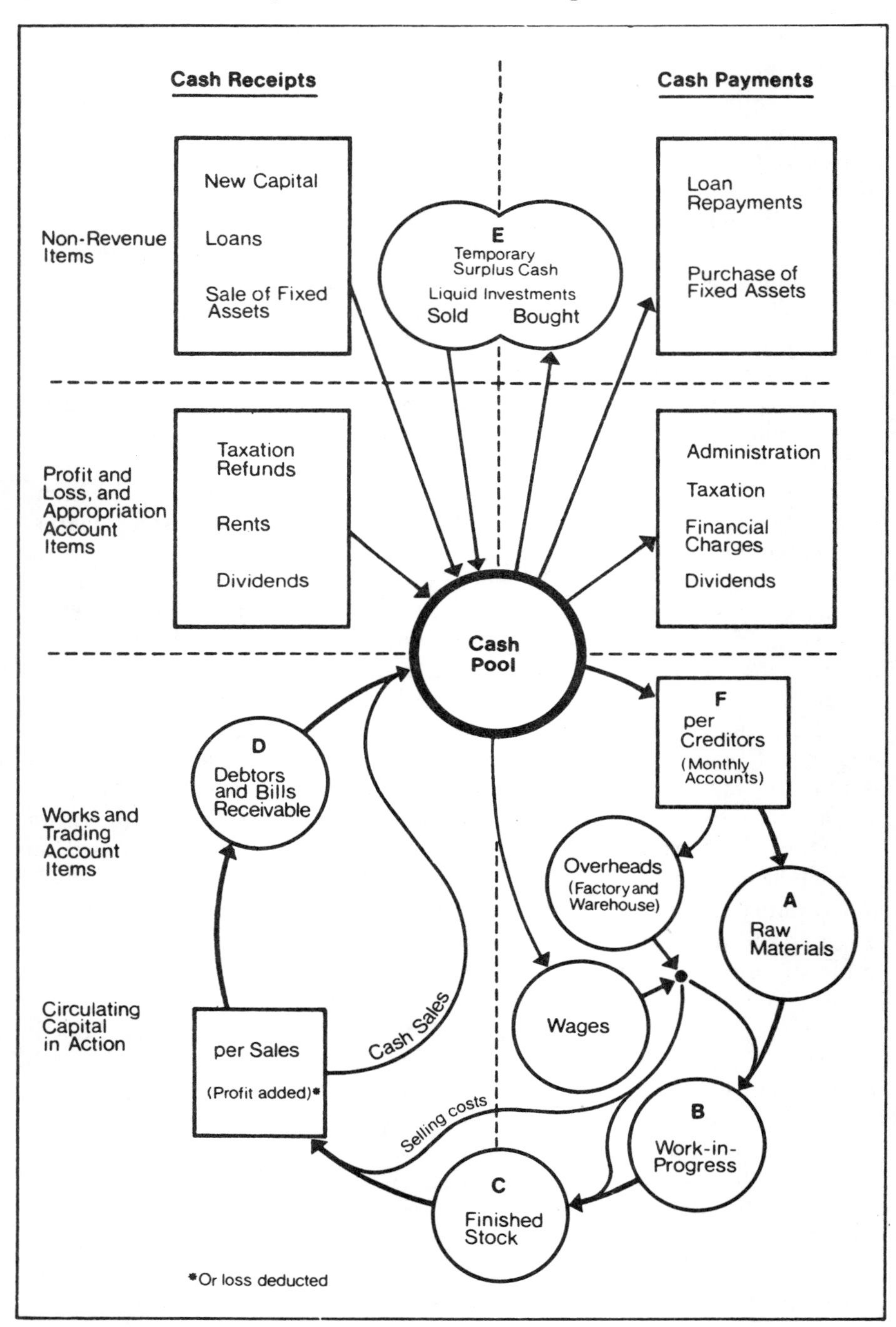

ments. The actual cash at bank and in hand, and other liquid resources (E), will, of course, be known, but at point A–D inclusive the balance sheet figures represent only potential cash.

The analogy of an electrical circuit is very apposite. Potential or voltage will do no work and yield no power unless there is an adequate amperage or rate of flow. Voltage multiplied by amperage=wattage or effective power; and just as a power of 1,000 watts will be given equally by 20 volts at 50 amps. or 250 volts at 4 amps., so in a business small circulating assets with a quick cash conversion rate will produce as much cash power as large circulating assets with a slow cash conversion rate. This perhaps throws some light on the old and eminently sound business adage, 'small profits and quick returns'.

If a banker looks at a balance sheet to ascertain whether on winding up his customer can pay 100p in the £, he will look in vain. And if the balance sheet is only a month old the current position will probably have altered materially. As far as the fixed assets are concerned, any relation between the book figures and realizable value is purely accidental, since normally the figures are based on historical cost, possibly written down to an estimate of value to the business as a going concern: their value as the empty shell of a defunct business is a matter of a fresh and direct appraisement.

The chief thing a lending banker wants to learn from his study of the accounts is whether the cash flow will be adequate to keep points A, B, C, and F properly supplied and to meet at least the demands of the overheads, including bank charges; and loan repayments: in short, to keep the business healthy and alive: and, if not, whether outside resources in the shape of available additional capital, further borrowing on the security of unencumbered assets, or the further sums he will himself be prepared to advance in case of need, will suffice to redress the position.

CHAPTER 12

Consolidated Accounts

Groups of companies – Requirements of the Companies Act – The purpose of consolidated balance sheets – The principles of consolidation – The purpose and nature of consolidated profit and loss accounts – Both designed for shareholders – Validity for creditors

Accounting developments have usually derived from alterations in the nature of the underlying business and from the changing purposes which business men wish their accounts to serve. As industry and commerce have grown both in range and complexity, and the number of enterprises operating as joint stock companies has continued to increase, there has been a strong tendency for amalgamations of interest to be effected by one company buying a controlling interest in another or others.

The earlier method was a direct purchase of the assets and goodwill, the vendor, if a company, being placed in due course into members' voluntary liquidation. What, then, are the reasons for this change in practice; what are the advantages of the groups of companies which are so widespread today?

1. a controlling interest in another company may be secured without:
   (a) incurring the expenses of amalgamation; or
   (b) having to find sufficient cash to acquire all the share capital or assets;
2. when shares are bought the expense of drawing conveyances and other documents of transfer is avoided. Share transfers in standard form will suffice;
3. the centralization of control of a group of undertakings is secured while maintaining their existing organizations, names and goodwill and—from the employee's point of view—without sacrificing loyalty to an established tradition.
4. there are often advantages in keeping a company on a going concern basis and in being able to group tax losses and profits within a group. When a company ceases trading its tax liabilities are crystallized.

When groups of companies grew up the managements of first-class holding companies started to present to their members consolidated balance sheets and sometimes consolidated profit and loss accounts. And in 1948 the legislature stepped in to impose the best practice (or an effective substitute) on all holding companies.

The relevant sections in the Companies Act 1985 are sections 229 to 233. The interpretation of the terms holding and subsidiary companies are contained in section 736. The main provisions are:

1. briefly a company becomes a subsidiary of a holding company if the holding company either owns more than 50% in nominal value of its equity share capital or controls the composition of its board of directors without the consent or concurrence of any other person;
2. every holding company (unless itself the wholly owned subsidiary of another British company, in which case the position of its subsidiaries is of interest only to its own holding company) is required to produce to its annual general meeting, along with its own accounts, group accounts;
3. such group accounts must, with certain exceptions, be in the form of consolidated balance sheet and consolidated profit and loss account which must comply as to form and content, with Schedule 4;
4. group accounts must give a true and fair view of the state of affairs and the profit and loss of the holding company and its subsidiaries as a whole, as far as concerns the members of the company, and must be so certified by the holding company's auditors;
5. where a consolidated balance sheet and a consolidated profit and loss account are produced (provided such profit and loss account discloses how much of the group profit is dealt with in the accounts of the holding company) the holding company need not lay its own profit and loss account before its members in general meeting. It must, however, state that it has taken advantage of this exemption.

In view of the emphasis which has been placed in Chapter 7 on the importance of reading the balance sheet, which is now available with last year's figures alongside for comparison, with the profit and loss accounts which link the two balance sheets, it is to be deprecated that under this last provision the shareholders and creditors of a holding company may be deprived of this valuable source of information about that company (though not about the group as a whole). Many holding companies, following the best accounting practice (which is still in many respects in advance of the minimum legal requirements) continue to publish both their own and a consolidated profit and loss account. Where this is not done and the holding company is his borrower the banker should be alive to the necessity in all suitable cases for calling for the holding company's own profit and loss account: or better still, for the complete profit and loss accounts.

The structure of consolidated accounts is an important branch of accountancy. The aim of this chapter is not, however, to discuss in detail the intricate mechanics of consolidation, but to arrive at an appreciation of the results and to grasp the realities which group accounts represent. For this purpose a summary of the main principles only will suffice.

Consolidated balance sheet

The purpose of a consolidated balance sheet is to show the holding company's members the position of the group as a whole, *vis-â-vis* the outside world. Accordingly:

1. inter-company debts and inter-company acceptances are cancelled out as are inter-company payments for interest, services, etc.[1]
2. stock which was bought by one company in the group from another in the group is reduced in value to its initial cost to the vendor company, whose profit on the sale is similarly reduced. It is of course quite proper for that profit to be shown in the individual accounts of the vendor company. But looked at *from the point of view of the group*, no profit will have been earned merely by the transfer of goods from one stock-room to another within the group; a sale must take place outside the group before it can be said to have earned a profit;
3. any profit realized on the transfer of a fixed asset within the group is similarly eliminated from the consolidated balance sheet, if the asset is still held within the group at the balance sheet date.

The method of consolidation as at the date of acquisition is, briefly:

1. to use the holding company's balance sheet as the framework for the consolidated balance sheet;
2. to bring in, in place of the asset 'investments in subsidiary companies' the actual assets and liabilities as at the date of acquisition the net amount of which will be the same as the total capital and reserves, i.e. the 'net worth' items from the balance sheets of the subsidiaries, the amounts of which represent the respective investments. It will be clear that a subsidiary's reserves and profit and loss balances *as at the date of acquisition* will not appear as such in the consolidated balance sheet. This follows from the fact that profits and surpluses already earned by subsidiaries are not profits or surpluses from the point of view of the group, but part of their capital and reserve total;
3. to make an adjustment, necessary to ensure that the consolidated balance sheet balances, where the net assets brought in do not exactly correspond in amount to the investment figure replaced. The adjustments are as follows:

   (a) where the net assets brought in exceed the investment figure, a balancing 'consolidation reserve' or 'capital reserve' is introduced in the consolidated balance sheet. This is similar to the reserve which

[1] There is one exception to this. If any inter-company acceptances have been discounted there will no longer be an item 'Bills receivable' in one balance sheet to set off against the item 'Bills payable' in another. The latter item is therefore retained in the consolidated balance sheet.

is created when a capital asset is revalued and its book value is written up. In fact that is exactly what has happened. The item is often accompanied by some such explanatory words as, 'being excess of the appropriate proportion of book values of net assets of subsidiaries at dates of acquisition of shares therein, over the cost, less amounts written off, of such shares';

(b) where the investment figure exceeds the amount of net assets brought in, there will be a shortfall in the assets of the consolidated balance sheet. To adjust this a goodwill item is created, either increasing existing goodwill balances or, better still, a balancing item is introduced. 'Excess cost of shares in subsidiary companies over the book value of the net assets acquired.'

4. where the holding company holds less than 100% of the share capital of a subsidiary, say 80%, it would obviously be incorrect just to bring in 100% of the subsidiary's assets and liabilities. There are two ways of dealing with this difficulty:

   (a) to bring into the consolidated balance sheet only 80% of the appropriate liabilities and assets;
   (b) to bring in the full liabilities and assets, and include on the liabilities side of the balance sheet a special liability item, 'minority shareholdings in subsidiary companies and reserves and undistributed profits attributable thereto'.

   The second method is preferable since it makes possible the retention in the consolidated balance sheet of the total assets controlled by the holding company and discloses both the existence and extent of an accountability to shareholders, outside the group.

Consolidated profit and loss account

While the purpose of the consolidated balance sheet is to show the shareholders of the holding company the position of the group *vis-à-vis* the outside world and the growth of the undertaking's net assets compared with the year before, the consolidated profit and loss account is designed to show the shareholders the total profits which have contributed to that growth, which are available from all its interests (including its own trading) to the holding company. It must, therefore, exclude the following things:

1. pre-acquisition profits of subsidiaries which, having been allowed for in the price of acquisition, will be treated as a capital item and not as a profit. For example, on 10th June company 'A' buys an 80% interest in the share capital of company 'B', which is all in the form of ordinary shares. The accounts of both companies are made up to 31st December

and company 'B' discloses a net profit of £16,000 for the year. Of this amount:

20%	=	£3,200	is attributable to minority interests.
$\frac{161}{365}$ths of 80%	=	£5,646	is attributable to pre-acquisition profits arising out of A's interest
$\frac{204}{365}$ths of 80%	=	£7,154	is attributable to post-acquisition profits arising out of A's interest

Only the £7,154 is true group profit to be brought into the consolidated profit and loss account of company A and its subsidiaries. The £3,200 will be included in the balance sheet with the appropriate part of the capital, reserves and profit and loss balance at 31st December under the item 'interests of the minority shareholders'. The £5,646 – pre-acquisition profits – is not brought in at all, since it is part of the capital and reserves acquired, the amount of which equals the net assets which *are* brought into the consolidated balance sheet.

The Companies Acts, from 1948 onwards, materially tightened up the position of holding companies and their subsidiaries and removed some anomalies. But it is still possible for a company D, 50% of whose equity capital is held by each of companies B and C, which are in turn subsidiaries of company A, to escape, even though, through its own subsidiaries, company A in fact controls all the equity of company D. There would accordingly be no obligation to include the accounts of company D in the group accounts of A even if all the group's real activities are conducted through D.[1]

There are still more than enough ways in which the intention of the legislature, which is to give to the holding company's shareholders adequate information about the group's affairs, can be defeated.

Associated companies

The relationship between a holding company and a subsidiary company is that the holding company must own more than 50% of the equity share capital of the subsidiary company. If only 50% or less is held, according to the Companies Acts there is no need to produce consolidated accounts. In effect, this means that all that is necessary is for the investing company to bring into its profit and loss account the dividends received and show the investment in its balance sheet at the lower of cost or market price.

This is not really satisfactory, especially when the companies have joint

[1] If, however, either company B or C controls the appointment of all or a majority of the directors of D, then D *will be* a subsidiary of A (Companies Act, 1985, Section 736).

ventures in which they hold 50% of the equity. Quoting the investment only on the purchase price in many cases does not give a true and fair view. The accountancy bodies, therefore, tackled this aspect in 1971 and produced a Statement of Standard Accounting Practice No. 1, which said that when a company conducts important parts of its business through other companies, whether it owns more or less than 50% of the equity share capital, the mere dividend received does not give shareholders adequate information.

It is interesting to see that the accountancy bodies emphasized the difference between a company's own accounts as a legal entity, and the consolidated accounts which show the results and the state of affairs of a group of companies as they concern the members of the parent company. This point should not be overlooked by a banker. Consolidated accounts are prepared for shareholders and not for creditors or bankers. The shareholder might be quite content to know that the company in which he owns shares has a variety of assets in various subsidiaries and associates which produce a certain total income, but a banker requires to know which company owns which assets, and how much profit is made by the individual companies.

What are the criteria for calling a company an associated company? The accountancy bodies said that when an investing company, or a group, is effectively a partner of a joint venture, or a consortium, then the company in which it has this stake is an associate company. Also if an investment is long term, or substantial, i.e. not less than 20% of the equity voting rights, then the company in which the investment is held is also an associated company. Finally, if a company or group is in a position to exercise significant influence over another company, and participate in commercial and financial policy decisions of that company, then that company becomes an associated company.

At this stage it must be considered how the accounts of the associated company are incorporated in the accounts of the investing company. In an investing company's own accounts the dividends received from the associated company are credited to the profit and loss account, and in the balance sheet the investment is quoted at the lower of the cost or market value of the investment. However, in the consolidated accounts the share of profits or losses is taken to the profit and loss account, and not dividends only, i.e. this is similar to the way in which the figures for a subsidiary company are incorporated in consolidated accounts. When it comes to the consolidated balance sheet, instead of bringing in all the assets and liabilities, as for a subsidiary company, the cost of the original investment, less amounts written off, is added to the share of post acquisition retained profits and reserves of the associated company, and this figure is shown. For example, if in a joint venture £50,000 was invested and this represented 50% of the equity capital of the joint venture and three years later the retained profits during the three years amounted to £20,000 the investing company would show in its consolidated balance sheet an asset under associated companies of £60,000 (£50,000 cost of investment, plus £10,000 share of retained profits).

There is no need for the specific assets of the associated companies to be quoted unless they are material for an understanding of the position. There must, however, be a note in the consolidated accounts showing the split of the accumulated reserves between the amounts retained by associated companies and the amounts retained by the group. It will be appreciated, therefore, that with this method of accounting for associated companies' profits shareholders who do not understand that the group is not a legal entity could obtain a very rosy picture of a group's affairs. A banker, on the other hand, should not be misled by the figures shown in consolidated accounts, but must look at the individual accounts of the companies to which he is lending and make appropriate enquiries. It is only in this way that a proper understanding is obtained.

The banker's approach

The lending banker, as a creditor, has an approach quite different from that of the shareholders, and our present purpose is to enquire how far consolidated accounts help him as a creditor of a holding company.

The balance sheet of his borrower may show as a substantial, perhaps as its main, asset investments in and advances to subsidiary and associated companies. His problem is to determine the real value of these assets and especially the true current position of the company. How far can the consolidated accounts furnish the answer?

There are three aspects of consolidated accounts with which the lending banker is especially concerned:

1. the limitations which affect all accounts are present to at least the same extent in all consolidated accounts with the added possibility that a consistent basis of valuation may not have operated throughout the group;
2. consolidated accounts are designed primarily for the information of *shareholders* of the holding company;
3. they relate to a notional integration of companies which, in fact, remain separate legal entities; the creditors of any one company can look for the payment of their debts to *the assets of that company alone*. The group as such has no legal existence.

The last two aspects merit further examination.

Group accounts designed for shareholders

The Companies Act, 1985, underlines the lessons of accounting history that group accounts are intended and designed for the information of shareholders only, when it provides that the group accounts laid before a company in general meeting shall give a true and fair view of the affairs of the group 'so far as concerns the members of the (holding) company'. This aspect is strongly emphasized by the sections permitting the directors of a holding company to omit the laying of group accounts with its own if they are of the opinion that, in the case of any subsidiary, group accounts would be of no value to the members of the holding company: or to present group accounts in a form other than that of consolidated balance sheet and profit and loss account, if they are of the opinion that the necessary information may be better appreciated by their members if presented in some other form. In each case the sole criterion is the interests of the holding company's shareholders. Neither the legislature nor the accountancy profession is here concerned with creditors and others having dealings with the holding company.

Example of consolidated accounts

A study of an example will help the reader to appreciate the points already covered, and will bring out the main principles of consolidation in practice. This will assist with understanding consolidated accounts, and it will be seen how such accounts are only of limited assistance to the bankers and creditors of a holding company.

Example 26 comprises the following items:

A. the balance sheet of a holding company in simple form;
B. consolidated balance sheet of the group on the same date;
C. a consolidated balance sheet of the subsidiary companies only, derived mainly by deducting the figures in A from the figures in B. A footnote explains the more complicated method of computing the 'net worth' figure: the actual figures for the share capital of the subsidiary companies cannot, of course, be extracted from A and B;
D. shows the computation of all the figures in the consolidated balance sheet affected by the existence of either minority interests or pre-acquisition profits and reserves. This computation in conjunction with the relative balance sheets will help the reader to a real understanding of the points involved;
E. the simplified balance sheets of the three subsidiaries.

Appraising the consolidated balance sheet

While the apparent 'net worth' in A is high, over three-quarters of the total assets consist of amounts invested in or lent to subsidiary companies. The strength of the company, in so far as it can be disclosed by this balance sheet, therefore stands or falls by the value of these assets.

The current position – of prime importance to the banker – is not very strong and certainly not very liquid, unless the advances to subsidiaries are both good and liquid.

What light does the consolidated balance sheet (B) throw on the position?

1. It is seen for the first time from the 'interest of outside shareholders' items, that at least one of the subsidiaries is not wholly owned by Tricolour (Holdings) Limited;

2. there is a substantial excess cost or goodwill 'asset' which may or may not be justified by the true value of the assets;
3. nevertheless net worth is substantial and the balance sheet is on the face of it sound;
4. both bank overdrafts and bank credit balances appear. In consolidating the accounts the not unusual practice of setting off the overdrafts of certain companies in the group against the credit balances of others and showing a net figure only has not been followed. No such right of set off will exist in fact even where all the companies bank with the same bank. To quote a net figure would therefore seem contrary to the requirement that the consolidated accounts must present a true and fair view of the affairs of the group. Similar considerations arise where any outside creditor of one company in the group is at the same time the debtor of another. Unless there is some right of set off specially created by agreement or by process of law (e.g. a garnishee order) the accounts should reflect the underlying realities and show the figures as the independent liabilities and assets they are;
5. the current position is both strong (ratio 1.92) and reasonably liquid. Debtors and cash combined exceed current liabilities. The fact that creditors exceed debtors (drs./crs. ratio .75) may require explanation. Nevertheless the general impression conveyed by the consolidated balance sheet is one of satisfactory balance and reasonable strength. Can this impression be trusted? Does the consolidated balance sheet represent (albeit imperfectly as a balance sheet must) any underlying reality which has meaning for and can give assurance to a lending banker or other creditor of the holding company?

The answer is required to two questions: the value of the holding company's investments and the soundness of its loans to one or more of the subsidiary companies.

With regard to the first, the consolidated balance sheet does disclose that the price paid for the shares of subsidiary companies exceeded the book values of the net assets acquired to the extent of £64,219 and unless there is a substantial goodwill value or an undisclosed reserve concealed by the undervaluation of the assets of subsidiaries, *prima facie* too much has been paid. But in fact the consolidated balance sheet can help little as to the value of the holding company's investment.

What of the loans and advances? It must be remembered that inter-company indebtedness has been eliminated and all the current liabilities remaining are due to people outside the group. But this elimination is based solely on the fiction that the group is an entity and that there is no greater difference between the component parts of the group than between the separate departments of one business. This is a fallacy and no outside party who is owed money by one of the constituent companies can look for satisfaction of his debt *beyond the assets of that company*; certainly not to

EXAMPLE 26

A

Tricolour (Holdings) Limited

BALANCE SHEET 30TH SEPTEMBER

	£	£
FIXED ASSETS		
Tangible assets		
Sundry fixed assets at cost *less* amounts written off		58,000
Investments		
Investments in subsidiary companies at cost		297,355
CURRENT ASSETS		
Stocks		
Raw materials and consumables	3,592	
Work in progress	14,429	
Trade debtors	18,954	
Loans to subsidiary companies	57,854	
Cash at bank and in hand	7,922	
	102,751	
CREDITORS: AMOUNTS FALLING DUE WITHIN ONE YEAR		
Trade creditors	33,886	
Net current assets		68,865
Total assets *less* current liabilities		424,220
CREDITORS: AMOUNTS FALLING DUE AFTER ONE YEAR		
5% 10 year notes		35,000
		£389,220
CAPITAL AND RESERVES		
Called up share capital		300,000
General reserve		70,000
Profit and loss account		19,220
		£389,220

EXAMPLE 26 (continued)

B

Tricolour (Holdings) Limited and its subsidiary companies

CONSOLIDATED BALANCE SHEET AS AT 30TH SEPTEMBER

	£	£
FIXED ASSETS		
Intangible assets		
Excess cost of shares in subsidiary companies over net assets at date of acquisition		64,219
Tangible assets		
Sundry fixed assets at cost *less* amounts written off		265,691
CURRENT ASSETS		
Stocks		
Raw materials and consumables	72,170	
Work in progress	97,905	
Debtors	108,385	
Cash at bank and in hand	82,304	
	360,764	
CREDITORS: AMOUNTS FALLING DUE WITHIN ONE YEAR		
Bank loans	42,781	
Trade creditors	145,195	
	187,976	
Net current assets		172,788
Total assets *less* current liabilities		502,698
CREDITORS: AMOUNTS FALLING DUE AFTER MORE THAN ONE YEAR		
5% 10 year notes	35,000	
6% debenture stock	20,000	55,000
		447,698
Interest of outside shareholders in subsidiary companies		37,551
		£410,147
CAPITAL AND RESERVES		
Called up share capital		300,000
General reserve		86,000
Profit and loss account		24,147
		£410,147

EXAMPLE 26 (continued)

C

Consolidated balance sheet of the subsidiaries of Tricolour (Holdings) Limited

30TH SEPTEMBER

	£	£
FIXED ASSETS		
Tangible assets		
Sundry fixed assets at cost *less* amounts written off		207,691
CURRENT ASSETS		
Stocks		
Raw materials and consumables	68,578	
Work in progress	83,476	
Debtors	89,431	
Cash at bank and in hand	74,382	
	315,867	
CREDITORS: AMOUNTS FALLING DUE WITHIN ONE YEAR		
Bank loans	42,781	
Trade creditors	111,309	
Amount due to holding company	57,854	
	211,944	
Net current assets		103,923
Total assets *less* current liabilities		311,614
CREDITORS: AMOUNTS FALLING DUE AFTER ONE YEAR		
6% debenture stock		20,000
		£291,614
Capital and reserves and profit and loss account		*£291,614

* Ascertained as follows:

Investment in subsidiaries (from holding company's balance sheet)	297,355
Excess of consolidated balance sheet figures over holding company's figures for:	
Reserves	16,000
Profit and loss account	4,927
Interest of outside shareholders from consolidated balance sheet	37,551
	355,833
Less excess cost figure from the consolidated balance sheet	64,219
	£291,614

EXAMPLE 26 (continued)

D

Computation on consolidation of figures for reserves, profit and loss account, outside shareholders' interest and excess cost

(The holding company has an 80% interest in Redwing Limited: the other subsidiary companies are fully owned)

Details		As at date of acquisition	Post acquisition	Acquired by holding company	Reserves	Profit and loss account	Outside shareholders (20% interest in Redwing Ltd.)
CAPITAL		£	£	£	£	£	£
Redwing Ltd.		100,000	—	80,000			20,000
Whitelock Ltd.		50,000	—	50,000			
Bluestone Ltd.		75,000	—	75,000			
RESERVES							
Redwing Ltd.		40,000		32,000			8,000
			20,000		16,000		4,000
PROFIT AND LOSS							
Redwing Ltd.		15,823		12,658			3,165
	Profits		11,929			9,543	2,386
Bluestone Ltd.		5,832		5,832			
	Profits		1,512			1,512	
				255,490		11,055	
Deduct							
Whitelock Ltd.		22,354		22,354			
	Losses		6,128			6,128	
				233,136		4,927	
Add							
Tricolour (Holdings) Ltd.					70,000	19,220	
			Cost of acquisition of shares in subsidiaries	297,355			
Figures carried to consolidated balance sheet B				Excess cost £64,219	£86,000	£24,147	£37,551

EXAMPLE 26 (continued)

E

Redwing Limited

BALANCE SHEET 30TH SEPTEMBER

	£	£
FIXED ASSETS		
Tangible assets		
Sundry fixed assets		54,985
CURRENT ASSETS		
Stocks		
Raw materials and consumables	7,972	
Work in progress	6,211	
Debtors		
Trade debtors	47,492	
Loan to fellow subsidiary	12,543	
Cash at bank and in hand	74,382	
	148,600	
CREDITORS: AMOUNTS FALLING DUE WITHIN ONE YEAR		
Trade creditors	15,833	
Net current assets		132,767
Total assets *less* current liabilities		£187,752
CAPITAL AND RESERVES		
Called up share capital		100,000
Reserves		60,000
Profit and loss account		27,752
		£187,752

continued overleaf

EXAMPLE 26 (continued)

E *continued*

Whitelock Limited

BALANCE SHEET 30TH SEPTEMBER

	£	£
FIXED ASSETS		
Tangible assets		
Sundry fixed assets		93,790
CURRENT ASSETS		
Stocks		
Raw materials and consumables	6,277	
Work in progress	21,883	
Debtors	13,442	
	41,602	
CREDITORS: AMOUNTS FALLING DUE WITHIN ONE YEAR		
Bank loan	18,492	
Trade creditors	37,528	
Loan from parent company	37,854	
	93,874	
Net current liabilities		(52,272)
Total assets *less* current liabilities		41,518
CREDITORS: AMOUNTS FALLING DUE AFTER ONE YEAR		
6% debenture stock		20,000
		£21,518
CAPITAL AND RESERVES		
Called up share capital		50,000
Profit and loss deficit		(28,482)
		£21,518

EXAMPLE 26 (continued)

E *continued*

Bluestone Limited

BALANCE SHEET 30TH SEPTEMBER

	£	£
FIXED ASSETS		
Tangible assets		
Sundry fixed assets		58,916
CURRENT ASSETS		
Stocks		
Raw materials and consumables	54,329	
Work in progress	55,382	
Debtors – Trade	28,497	
	138,208	
CREDITORS: AMOUNTS FALLING DUE WITHIN ONE YEAR		
Bank loan	24,289	
Trade creditors	57,948	
Loan from parent company and fellow subsidiary	32,543	
	114,780	
Net current assets		23,428
Total assets *less* current liabilities		£82,344
CAPITAL AND RESERVES		
Called up share capital		75,000
Profit and loss account		7,344
		£82,344

the assets of any other company in the group. The consolidated balance sheet has therefore failed to answer the legitimate questions of the creditor simply because it is based not on reality but on a notional approach valid only for the members of the holding company and not even fully valid for them. It is accordingly necessary to fall back on the individual balance sheets of the subsidiary companies themselves which, it should be noted, a member of the holding company is not entitled to receive and which a creditor of the holding company will never have access to (except on the files of the companies' registry), unless he is in a position to insist on their production.

From the three subsidiary balance sheets themselves it will be seen that real capital of £254,063, made up as follows (but with no direct indication of the extent of pre-acquisition reserves and profits):

	£	£
REDWING LIMITED		187,752
WHITELOCK LIMITED		
Capital	50,000	
Less Profit and loss account deficit .	28,482	
		21,518
BLUESTONE LIMITED		82,344
		291,614
Less Outside interests		37,551
		£254,063

was acquired on the investment of £297,355 by the holding company. In the full accounts a statement must be included (usually in the notes attached) giving the proportion of the nominal value of each class of share in a subsidiary held by a holding company.

What of the value of the £57,854 advanced to subsidiary companies? Of this, £37,854 is due from Whitelock Limited, whose balance sheet discloses an extremely weak current position with total current liabilities (including the holding company's loan) plus bank overdraft at £93,874, more than double the current assets £41,602. This loan has, therefore, all the appearance of a lock-up and may not be recoverable in full.

The balance of the advances is to Bluestone Limited £20,000 (£32,543, *less* £12,543 borrowed from Redwing Limited). Here the current assets exceed the current liabilities (current ratio: 2) but are predominantly unliquid and again the loan must be regarded as a lock-up.

This position could not have been deduced from the consolidated balance sheet at all, which is indeed not only an unsatisfactory source of information to the lending banker, but is sometimes (as in this case) positively misleading.

As far as day-to-day control is concerned, the holding company is certainly in a position to secure the utilization of the resources of Redwing Limited to repay its own loans to the other two subsidiaries or to discharge the latter's or its own heavy current liabilities. Whether the directors of Redwing

Limited can properly utilize that company's funds in this way is quite another question. They are in a fiduciary position charged with the duty of conducting the company's affairs and controlling its resources in the interests of the company as a whole. They are not entitled as a matter either of law or ethics to exercise their powers for the benefit of any other company, nor for the exclusive benefit of 80% of the shareholders (i.e. the holding company) to the detriment of the 20% minority.

Protection was first given to aggrieved minorities by the Companies Act, 1948. To what extent it has succeeded in curbing such misuse of directors' powers is difficult to ascertain. Shareholders are notoriously apathetic and the new powers have been only lightly invoked. There can be no statistics to show how far their mere existence has acted as a deterrent. The Companies Act 1985 continued the protection in section 459. The section provides *inter alia* that any shareholder who complains that the company's affairs are being conducted in a manner oppressive to some part of the members (including himself) may petition the Court which may make such order as it thinks fit whether for regulating the company's affairs in future, or otherwise. And even where a subsidiary company is wholly owned and section 459 is inapplicable, the misuse of its funds for the benefit of the holding company may, if loss is caused by it amount to a misfeasance or breach of trust which, under section 631, will render any director(s) concerned liable to make restitution on the liquidation of the subsidiary company.

Whatever doubts there may be as to whether the directors of a holding company can make available the resources of the group to meet its own liabilities, it is impossible for a creditor to achieve the same result in his own right and by his own actions. Under pressure from a creditor of the holding company, Tricolour (Holdings) Limited, its directors might, but certainly cannot be made to, make available the resources of Redwing Limited to satisfy his debt.

A receiver appointed by the creditor under his debenture could borrow such resources, but could do so only by incurring a liability to repay which he would have to discharge, and the creditors would not be advantaged. If no debenture is held and liquidation of the holding company is forced the shares in the subsidiaries would be sold but the direct use of the subsidiaries' resources would be almost impossible; the liquidator would have the utmost difficulty in forcing the liquidation of the subsidiaries and the distribution of their assets to himself as shareholder. This of course also applies to associated companies.

All this adds up to the conclusion that any banker who lends or is asked to lend to a holding company must beware of being misled by strength in the group which is out of his reach. Before reading a consolidated balance sheet he should say to himself 'This balance sheet is what would be produced if the whole groups were one legal entity. It is only correct, it only has meaning on that assumption: *the assumption is never valid.*' With this

EXAMPLE 27

Tricolour (Holdings) Limited and its subsidiaries

CONSOLIDATED PROFIT AND LOSS ACCOUNT, YEAR TO 30TH SEPTEMBER

	£	£		£	£
Interest on loan capital (gross)		2,950	Surplus from trading		76,666
DIRECTORS' EMOLUMENTS			INCOME FROM INVESTMENTS		
Fees	2,000		Trade	10	
Other	11,833		Other	189	
		13,833			199
AUDITORS' REMUNERATION					
Parent company	42				
Subsidiary companies	170	212			
Corporation tax due		22,805			
ATTRIBUTABLE TO OUTSIDE SHAREHOLDERS					
Proportion of profit for the year	5,918				
Surplus for the year (Note (i))	31,147				
		£76,865			£76,865

	£	£		£	£
Transfers to specific reserves		20,000	Surplus for the year		31,147
SUBSIDIARY COMPANIES			ITEMS RELATING TO PREVIOUS YEAR		
Appropriations	4,836		Taxation adjustments	943	
Carried forward	4,927		Provisions no longer required	2,438	
		9,763			3,381
PARENT COMPANY					
Balance forward (Note (ii))		19,220	Balance from previous year		14,455
		£48,983			£48,983

Notes: (i) This is the year's surplus attributable to the Group.
(ii) Carry forward, corresponding to profit and loss balance in holding company's balance sheet: with subsidiaries, carry forward (previous item) corresponds to consolidated balance sheet profit and loss account.

caveat in mind the banker can then look to the consolidated balance sheet for indications of progress in the group as a whole which indirectly and on long-term will enure for the benefit of the holding company.

Consolidated profit and loss accounts

How far do the foregoing reservations apply to group profit and loss accounts? Example 27 is a typical consolidated profit and loss account which shows what profits, attributable to the interests of the holding company, have been made during the year, how they have been dealt with and the extent to which they are held by the holding company and by the subsidiaries, respectively. They therefore do exactly what they purport to do: all the unappropriated profits disclosed, after the portion attributable to outside shareholders has been allowed for, is available and ultimately distributable to the members of the holding company. This is of course subject to normal financial prudence and in this respect a consolidated profit and loss account is no different from that of an individual company. The consolidated profit and loss account may therefore be accepted as valid.

Consolidated accounts including an associated company

Examples 26 and 27 included subsidiary companies only in order not to confuse the position by including associated companies. We should now look

EXAMPLE 28

Consolidated profit and loss account

	£	£
Profit (including subsidiaries)		X
Share of profit *less* losses of associated companies		X
Profit before taxation		X
Corporation tax (including subsidiaries)	X	
Associated companies	X	X
Profit after taxation		X*

	£
*PROFIT AFTER TAXATION	
By investing company	X
By subsidiaries	X
In associated companies	X
	X

Note: Of the profit attributable to members of the investing company the amount of the dividends is dealt with in the accounts of the investing company.

briefly at an example which includes associated companies. Firstly we will deal with the consolidated profit and loss account, and it has already been explained that the share of profits or losses must be incorporated in consolidated accounts and not dividends only. However, a note of the dividends received should be shown as in Example 28 which follows the guidance given in the Statement of Standard Accounting Practice No. 1.

Where the consolidated balance sheet is concerned the incorporation of associated companies is relatively simple as an asset under investments is shown for associated companies being the cost of the investment plus the share of retained profits since the investment was made. The split of reserves between the amounts retained by the group and those retained by associated companies will appear as a note to the accounts.

CHAPTER 13

Appraisal of Capital Expenditure

Pay-back method – Rate of return – Cash flows – Discounted cash flow – Net present value – Annual value – Sensitivity analysis – The final decision

When a person starts a business he is rightly expected to examine carefully his projected income and expenditure before embarking on the exercise. The same considerations of careful evaluation should naturally be made after the business has started when additional capital expenditure is contemplated. Nevertheless, insufficient attention is given to this aspect by many businesses and little or no planning is evident, particularly in the smaller businesses.

A banker often comes across this problem because many of the propositions put to him are for providing finance for buying capital assets. It is necessary, therefore, for bankers to have a knowledge of the methods which can be used to appraise capital investment projects to appreciate whether or not a customer is using sophisticated methods or, possibly, none at all in his evaluation of such projects.

Most businesses find it necessary to invest capital from time to time and, ideally, provision should be made annually for the eventual replacement of assets, or for buying additional assets. In times of inflation replacement costs are much greater than original costs and, apart from the depreciation provision, there should also be a provision to make up the shortfall.

If a company is expanding, additional plant and machinery is often needed, and this also requires expenditure which must come from income, borrowing, or raising of fresh capital. Many companies, however, do not plan properly and are often faced with the need to replace a piece of equipment, or to buy a new piece of equipment, without the necessary resources. An *ad hoc* basis of dealing with capital expenditure is hardly sufficient.

However, even if foresight has been used and the necessary resources have been conserved it is still necessary to calculate the total expenditure and the total income which will be received from use of the new equipment, and to evaluate whether it is right from the investment point of view for the company to spend money in this particular way. It may also be that several items of capital expenditure are possibilities, and then it is necessary to evaluate and compare all possibilities to see which expenditure should have priority.

Complete accuracy of an appraisal is impossible. Nevertheless this is not a reason to discard a proper appraisal as otherwise any investment decision is decided on instinct, flair, or luck. These particular attributes are often assumed by an individual to be possessed by him, but a business enterprise in which much capital is invested and on which many people depend for their employment should not be endangered by chance or by expenditure on capital equipment which cannot generate an adequate return.

There is also added benefit in making a proper appraisal, especially if the appraisal is made by people who will be involved in dealing with the equipment after it has been installed. Naturally a full appraisal cannot be made at the lowest level, but as many people as possible should be brought into the appraisal process. They will then understand what is expected from the investment, and this knowledge should be of benefit to the whole enterprise. Quite often in such circumstances the manager of a particular department will see that the investment proposed will be uneconomic, and he will be able to see that an alternative is possible within his particular department. The knowledge of his existing activities, work force and premises may enable him to make an alternative suggestion whereas the board of directors will not have such detailed knowledge. It is far better, from everyone's point of view, to have as many of the work force as possible involved in the appraisal.

A wrong decision on a large capital investment can be a burden on a company for many years, and instances have occurred where an excessively large capital investment which has not turned out satisfactorily has had the effect of driving a company into liquidation.

Some of the methods used are as follows:

Pay-back method

This is a simple method which is easily understood, and in consequence is often used by companies who attempt to appraise the worth of capital expenditure. It consists merely of estimating the number of years it will take before gross income from the investment will cover the capital cost. By gross income, in this instance, is meant the income from the investment after expenses, but before tax and depreciation.

EXAMPLE 29

	£	£
Cost of investment		100,000
Gross income – year 1	5,000	
year 2	15,000	
year 3	20,000	
year 4	30,000	
year 5	30,000	
Total income after 5 years		£100,000

It will be seen from Example 29 that the investment generates its full cost in five years and gives a measure upon which to assess the effectiveness of the investment. If, however, we look at another investment for a similar sum and consider that, in this instance, the gross income will be received on a pattern which is the reverse of that shown in Example 29 we would have the following table:

EXAMPLE 30

	£	£
Cost of investment		100,000
Gross income – year 1	30,000	
year 2	30,000	
year 3	20,000	
year 4	15,000	
year 5	5,000	
Total income after 5 years		£100,000

In Example 30 the cost of the investment is also covered in a five year period but, obviously, we have insufficient information to judge which of the two investments is the better. We do not know what the income is likely to be subsequently, nor whether the piece of equipment will have some value or not at the end of its life. A further drawback to the system is that the figures are considered in gross terms whereas, to be accurate, net figures after tax should be considered.

Investments in companies are made out of retained earnings which have been taxed, or from borrowing which has to be repaid out of net-of-tax income, or from funds provided by shareholders whose dividends will be paid out of taxed income. All tax implications should be taken into account, not only from the income point of view, but also after considering the tax implications of expenditure. From time to time capital allowances have been granted on expenditure for capital equipment, and this effectively reduces the cost. A further fault of a pay-back method is that timing differences are not taken into account.

In Example 29 £5,000 was recovered in the first year whereas in Example 30 £30,000 was recovered in the first year. Obviously recovering one's money quickly is worth more than recovering the same amount over a longer period of time.

There are many drawbacks in the pay-back method, but it is still useful for considering certain types of project where the income generated is regular, or with a consistent trend. A decision maker can then take a reasonably accurate view, especially when other aspects and assumptions are also quoted to him, before the investment decision is made. Nevertheless, the method is inexact and is not of great use when comparing the suitability of various investment projects. It does, however, indicate whether the amount of the investment will be recovered quickly, and often the effect of a quick return of cash is important for the viability of a business.

Rate of return method

This method has various names but the most usual are 'rate of return', 'return on investment', or 'the accounting method', and the object is to specify the income generated as a percentage of the capital expenditure. The income used is generally the gross income before tax, but after expenses and depreciation. This income can be expressed as a percentage of capital, and can be used on the basis of the first year's income, the expected peak income, or an average income over several years.

As an illustration similar figures are used as in the two examples in the pay-back method:

EXAMPLE 31

Investment 1

	£	Cumulative income £	Average cumulative income £	Average rate of return %
Cost of investment . .	100,000			
Gross income – year 1 . .	5,000	5,000	5,000	5
year 2 . .	15,000	20,000	10,000	10
year 3 . .	20,000	40,000	13,333	13.3
year 4 . .	30,000	70,000	17,500	17.5
year 5 . .	30,000	100,000	20,000	20
Total income after 5 years .	£100,000			

EXAMPLE 32

Investment 2

	£	Cumulative income £	Average cumulative income £	Average rate of return %
Cost of investment . .	100,000			
Gross income – year 1 . .	30,000	30,000	30,000	30
year 2 . .	30,000	60,000	30,000	30
year 3 . .	20,000	80,000	26,666	26.6
year 4 . .	15,000	95,000	23,750	27.7
year 5 . .	5,000	100,000	20,000	20
Total income after 5 years .	£100,000			

Over five years both investments produced an average of 20% on the original cost of £100,000, but it will also be seen from the cumulative rate of return that, dependent on the number of years taken to compute an average, so the rate of return will vary greatly between the two investments.

In the first year only £5,000 is produced from the investment in Example 31 compared with £30,000 from the investment in Example 32. If the first two years are taken together, and the gross income for the two years is averaged, the average rate of return for the first investment improves to 10%. This rate of return continues on an increasing trend, whereas for the second investment the rate of return is on a decreasing trend. In the fifth year they are the same but, no doubt, in the sixth and subsequent years they will be different again.

It is difficult to compare the two investments by this method and, in fact, it is impossible to compare any investments merely by taking a percentage figure and ignoring all other aspects.

In the rate of return method it is usual to make a deduction for depreciation, but depreciation is a book entry and it is only appropriate to use a depreciation figure if the amount involved is accurate. As will be seen, the final value of the investment has not been taken into account in the calculations.

There are many ways in which the figures used for this method can be improved. Net of tax figures can be used and also, instead of using the initial capital, the average capital employed after depreciation can be used. However, whatever refinements are built into the system the basic faults remain.

Both the pay-back method and the rate of return method are inexact, mainly because timing differences are not taken into account. In the pay-back method there is a bias towards investments which bring profits quickly, whereas the rate of return method favours projects where the average rate of return is greater. However, there is no need to reject these methods as completely worthless although they are certainly inexact and of little use when considering complicated projects.

Cash flows

In the illustrations considered so far simple figures have been used but, in practice, it is not so easy to obtain a composite view without a table showing the cash flows in and out of the company on an annual or monthly basis. For example, the expenditure on capital equipment can be spread over a number of years and, of course, income can vary from year to year also.

Previously it was mentioned that the correct way of assessing a capital investment was to consider the after tax position, not gross figures. To consider the after tax position it is necessary to know when tax is paid, and what allowances are granted on capital expenditure.

Although there are some exceptions, generally tax on profits is payable nine months after the end of a company's year, except for companies in existence before 5th April, 1965, when the tax is paid on 1st January in the year following the fiscal year in which the company's year end falls, i.e. if a company makes up its books for the year ending June 1977 its year end will fall in the fiscal year 1977 to 1978, and tax will be payable on 1st January, 1979.

As far as capital allowances are concerned the amounts will be regulated by the annual Finance Acts.* Let us assume that a company may claim allowances for 100% of capital investments. This amount would be allowed as a deduction from profits; taxation on the full amount would be retained by the company at the taxation rate in force. For example, with capital allowances at 100% and with say, a 40% corporation tax rate a company spending £100,000 on capital equipment would have a £40,000 reduction in the tax it would have to pay.

Depreciation is not allowed as a deduction from profit for tax purposes, and by claiming capital allowances a company will, in effect, have written off its depreciation in the first year. Naturally it has no further amount which it can write off in subsequent years. If depreciation was allowed for tax purposes, and capital allowances did not exist, a company would spread the retention of tax over the years in which the capital item is written off. The tax advantage to a company claiming capital allowances is therefore because of the timing difference, and as large amounts are involved it is very important in calculating the return on capital.

Let us now look at the cash flows of a profitable company which can use all its capital allowances (an unprofitable company will not be paying any tax and will not get the benefit of capital allowances). We will assume that the corporation tax rate is 52%, and the company is one incorporated before 5th April, 1965.

The company has an old machine which, although still of use, is an out-of-date model and would have no value if scrapped. The company can buy a modern replacement for £100,000 and to install the machine would entail initial expenses of £6,000. The new machine would be able to operate in such a way that there would be a saving of £9,000 in stock. There would also be a saving on wages and other expenses of £20,000 in the first year, and the company's accountant estimated that inflation would mean that such savings would increase by 10% per annum. At the end of five years the company would expect to sell the machine for £20,000, and replace it with another model. The cash flows on an annual basis would then appear as shown in Example 33.

For the sake of simplicity all the figures are put into the table as at the year end, and the tax payable on 1st January has been looked upon as if

*As from 6th April, 1986, capital allowances have been withdrawn but as they could be re-introduced in the future (or replaced by some similar allowance) this illustration is included to show that all items which could have a financial bearing on the investment decision should be included in the calculations.

it was paid on the previous day. In practice it would be more accurate to work with monthly figures.

It will be seen that up to the start date £106,000 has been spent on the investment and £9,000 saved on working capital. The capital allowances on the total expenditure would be saved in tax on 1st January in year two and so this has been entered in the total at the end of year one. The savings on wages have been put in the appropriate years, and the tax in respect of these savings follows in the same way as for the capital allowances. There is no scrap value of the out-of-date equipment, but even if there had been it would not have been included as it is usual to consider any scrap value, or sale proceeds of replaced equipment, as belonging to the evaluation of the previous capital expenditure, otherwise such items could be double counted in both the evaluations of the old and the new equipment.

EXAMPLE 33

	1	2	3	4	5	6
Year	Investment	Working capital	Savings on wages etc.	Capital allowances	Tax on increased income	Net cash flows
	£	£	£	£	£	£
0	(100,000)	—	—	—	—	—
	(6,000)	—	—	—	—	—
		9,000	—	—	—	(97,000)
1	—	—	20,000	49,920	—	69,920
2	—	—	22,000	—	(10,400)	11,600
3	—	—	24,200	—	(11,440)	12,760
4	—	—	26,620	—	(12,584)	14,036
5	20,000	—	29,282	—	(13,832)	35,450
6	—	—	—	(10,400)	(15,226)	(25,626)
	(86,000)	9,000	122,102	39,520	(63,482)	21,140

If we look to the rate of return method which was mentioned previously, we can consider the rate of return on the average capital employed after taking depreciation into account. For this purpose the first three columns of the cash flow chart can be used. The cost of the initial investment in the machine was £106,000 and sale proceeds of £20,000 are received after five years. If depreciation is spread over five years we get the following figures:

Average capital employed

	£	
Cost of machine	106,000	
Less Sale proceeds	20,000	
	£86,000	over 5 years

Average depreciation
£17,200 per annum

Capital employed each year – year 1	106,000	
year 2	88,800	
year 3	71,600	
year 4	54,400	
year 5	37,200	
	358,000	
Less Reduction in working capital	9,000	
	£349,000	over 5 years

Average capital £69,800

We must now look at the income generated over the period and the total of column 3 comes to £122,102 but, of course, the depreciation has to be written off this income as depreciation has to be provided from total receipts in the normal way. We therefore get the following:

	£	
Gross income (as per column 3)	122,102	
Less Total depreciation	86,000	
Gross income after depreciation	36,102	over 5 years

Average income £7,220

The average income of £7,220 on the average capital of £69,800 is 10.3% per annum, which is calculated after depreciation, but before tax.

This, therefore, is a refinement on the rate of return method previously set out, but it still has the disadvantages of dealing with before tax figures, and not taking into account the timing of the expenditure and the receipts.

If we use the cash flow table (Example 33) for the pay-back method it will be seen that the initial outlay is £97,000, and this is recovered in five years from gross receipts (column 3). No consideration, however, is taken of the value of the machine at the end of the period. The pay-back method could also be refined by taking the average capital employed, as already deduced for the rate of return method at £69,800, and this would be recovered in just over three years.

Discounted cash flow (DCF)

Timing differences are very important when considering the receipt and expenditure of money and the whole basis of interest rates is built on time for the use of money.

In looking at the cash flows chart (Example 33) we see that in year three the net cash flows received were £12,760, but what is that figure worth as at the start date three years earlier? This will depend on the interest rates during the three years, and an estimate would have to be made of the rate to be applied and the sum of £12,760 would have to be discounted at that rate.

All the net cash flows, as shown in column 6, can be discounted back to the start date, and by trying various discount rates it is possible to find out which rate brings the total of all the cash flows to nil at the start date. If, for example, 10% was the rate that did this it would prove that the net income generated by the capital investment was 10% over the period. The point now is to find out how to calculate easily the discount rate which will do this.

If a pound is invested at 5%, at the end of a year it will be worth $£1 \times \frac{105}{100} = £1.05$. If the investment is left at the same interest rate for a further year the original pound will be worth $\left(£1 \times \frac{105}{100}\right) \times \frac{105}{100} = £1.1025$. Similarly for a third year the figure at the end of the second year would have to be multiplied by the fraction $\frac{105}{100}$. A formula can, therefore, be worked out. If we call the principal sum 'P' and the interest rate fraction 'IR', at the end of one year the sum invested will have risen to $P \times IR$, at the end of the second year it will have risen to $P \times (IR)^2$. For the third year the principal sum will have risen to $P \times (IR)^3$, and so on. All that is necessary to find the discount rate is to alter the formulas to $\frac{1}{P \times IR}$, $\frac{1}{P \times (IR)^2}$, $\frac{1}{P \times (IR)^3}$, and so on.

Using the interest rate of 5% the discount rate for one year will be $\frac{1}{1.05}$ or 0.952, and for two years $\frac{1}{1.1025}$ or 0.907. It is quite easy to construct discount tables, but these can also be bought quite easily.

The formula can also be written as $\frac{1}{(P+I)^n}$ where 'I' is the rate of return (as opposed to the interest rate fraction as shown above) and 'n' is the number of years.

Example 34 shows the discount factors for rates between 5% and 12% for ten years.

EXAMPLE 34

Year	5%	6%	7%	8%	9%	10%	11%	12%
1	0.952	0.943	0.935	0.926	0.917	0.909	0.901	0.893
2	0.907	0.890	0.873	0.857	0.842	0.826	0.812	0.797
3	0.864	0.840	0.816	0.794	0.772	0.751	0.731	0.712
4	0.823	0.792	0.762	0.735	0.708	0.683	0.658	0.636
5	0.784	0.747	0.713	0.681	0.650	0.621	0.594	0.567
6	0.746	0.705	0.666	0.630	0.596	0.565	0.535	0.507
7	0.710	0.665	0.623	0.584	0.547	0.513	0.482	0.452
8	0.677	0.627	0.582	0.540	0.502	0.467	0.434	0.404
9	0.645	0.592	0.544	0.500	0.460	0.424	0.391	0.361
10	0.614	0.558	0.508	0.463	0.422	0.386	0.352	0.322

Using column 6 in the cash flows chart (Example 33) we now have to discount back to the start date the annual cash flows and, by trying various interest rates, find out which one will bring the present value of the net cash flows to nil. A few efforts, which are quite simple to work, will quickly find the desired discount rate. I have used discount rates of 11% and 12% and the resultant figures are shown in Example 35.

On the capital investment at the end of each year the return is therefore just under 12% net of tax. To get a more detailed figure interpolation can be used, i.e. the difference between the 11% figure of £1,328 and the 12% figure of (£197) is £1,525. The difference covers the one percentage point difference in the rates, and the 12% figure can be reduced by $\frac{197}{1,525}$ which is 0.13%. The discount rate to bring present values of the cash flows to nil is therefore 11.87%. This method of interpolation is not absolutely correct, but the difference is too slight to be material for the purposes of capital appraisal programmes.

It must be borne in mind, however, that the discount percentage produced is based on various assumptions, the most important being that the figures in the chart of cash flows will be correct, and that the timing of income and expenditure will also be correct.

EXAMPLE 35

Discounted cash flow

Year	Net cash flows	Discount factor at 11%	Present value	Discount factor at 12%	Present value
	£		£		£
0	(97,000)	1.0	(97,000)	1.0	(97,000)
1	69,920	0.901	62,998	0.893	62,438
2	11,600	0.812	9,419	0.797	9,245
3	12,760	0.731	9,328	0.712	9,085
4	14,036	0.658	9,236	0.636	8,927
5	35,450	0.594	21,057	0.567	20,100
6	(25,626)	0.535	(13,710)	0.507	(12,992)
	£21,140		£1,328		(£197)

It is sometimes contended that appraisal of projects by the use of a discounted cash flow percentage figure to bring the net cash flows to nil is not the best method of comparison. For example, if two projects are evaluated and the first one shows a return of 12% whereas the second one shows a return of 10% it is not always correct to assume that the project showing the higher return is the better one.

This is illustrated simply by considering which is the better investment of:

1. lending £100 at 10% for one year; or
2. lending £200 at 9% for two years.

It would not be right to consider that the 10% investment will turn out to be the better one as other aspects have also to be taken into account. The amount available for investment must be considered, together with the time for which it will be available. The risk associated with both loans must be taken into account, and also the rates of interest must be compared with the rates of interest current in the market place to decide whether or not the rates are correct in respect of the risks. A further important point to be considered is whether there are better opportunities for other investments.

Net present value (NPV)

The net present value is calculated in the same way as the discounted cash flow by discounting the future cash flows to a start point and deducting the original cost at the start point. However, instead of finding the discount rate which will bring the resultant figure to nil the result will show the net present value at the rate of discount applied.

For example, let us take two projects and imagine that the annual cash flows have been worked out in the same way as in the previous cash flow chart. We will also assume that a company requires a rate of return of 6% net after tax. The annual net cash flows will, therefore, have to be discounted at the 6% rate and a comparison of the two projects is shown in Example 36.

EXAMPLE 36

	Project 1			Project 2		
Year	Net cash flows	Discount factor at 6%	Present value	Net cash flows	Discount factor at 6%	Present value
	£		£	£		£
0	(11,560)	1.0	(11,560)	(39,360)	1.0	(39,360)
1	2,000	0.943	1,886	8,000	0.943	7,544
2	2,000	0.890	1,780	18,000	0.890	16,020
3	3,000	0.840	2,520	20,000	0.840	16,800
4	4,000	0.792	3,168			
5	5,000	0.747	3,735			£1,004
			£1,529			

Project 1 shows a present value of £1,529, and project 2 shows a present value of £1,004. The theory is that with the present value of project 1 being greater than that of project 2 it would be more advantageous to invest in project 1. All that has been done is to compare the result of two projects using the same discount rate instead of finding out the discount rates which will reduce the cash flows to nil. Nevertheless, there is an important difference which will be apparent if we use widely dissimilar figures and calculate both the NPV and the DCF of two cash flows as per Examples 37 and 38.

EXAMPLE 37

Calculation of NPV at 6%

	Project A			Project B		
Year	Net cash flows	Discount factor	Present value	Net cash flows	Discount factor	Present value
	£		£	£		£
0	(6,957)	1.0	(6,957)	(72,470)	1.0	(72,470)
1	1,000	0.943	943	70,000	0.943	66,010
2	1,000	0.890	890	8,000	0.890	7,120
3	1,000	0.840	840	2,000	0.840	1,680
4	2,000	0.792	1,584			£2,340
5	5,000	0.747	3,735			
			£1,035			

EXAMPLE 38

Calculation of the DCF rate of return

	Project A			Project B		
Year	Net cash flows	Discount factor at 10%	Present value	Net cash flows	Discount factor at 9%	Present value
	£		£	£		£
0	(6,957)	1.0	(6,957)	(72,470)	1.0	(72,470)
1	1,000	0.909	909	70,000	0.917	64,190
2	1,000	0.826	826	8,000	0.842	6,736
3	1,000	0.751	751	2,000	0.772	1,544
4	2,000	0.683	1,366			
5	5,000	0.621	3,105			nil
			nil			

In Example 37 the net present values of the cash flows are greater for project B than for project A, but Example 38 shows that the return from the cash flows is 10% for project A and this is better than the 9% obtained on project B. There is, therefore, a conflict between the two methods, but this has been brought about by comparing investments for vastly different amounts, for cash flows which are obtained over different periods of time, and which have differing patterns. Conflicting results from the two methods can also occur if multiple discount rates are used.

These differences are mentioned merely to give a composite view of the DCF and NPV methods. It is not necessary to stress them and discard the methods because of these minor differences. The overall gain in using these methods of evaluation is considerable, and they are far superior to other methods.

On the occasions when projects are compared which require the investment of substantially different amounts an indication of the better project can be given by comparing the ratios of the net present values to the capital sums invested.

Annual value

Some capital projects can be compared with each other by using the annual value (or charge) which will be necessary to amortize fully the cost during a stated period of years. Equal amounts, to include both interest and capital, are calculated which will, after the required number of years, be sufficient to pay for the capital sum and satisfy all interest. The annual value is then compared with the annual income.

This method also recognizes the two aspects, (1) replacement of the original cost, i.e. full depreciation, and (2) interest on the capital employed, but it differs from the DCF and NPV approaches by use of the sinking fund concept. This concept is that an annual sum can be put aside which will increase by interest additions to provide an exact sum at the end of a given number of years.

For example, if £20,000 is provided as depreciation at the end of each year, and this sum is invested at 10% per annum, the total at the end of three years will be £66,200.

Between the end of the first year, when £20,000 is put aside at 10% per annum, and the end of the second year when a further £20,000 is added, interest of £2,000 is generated which also is added to the capital sum. In the interval between the end of the second year to the end of the third year interest of £4,200 is generated and, of course, there is no interest earned on the third instalment as it is added at the end of the third year.

At end of	Brought forward	Sinking fund	Interest at 10% p.a.	Cumulative total
	£	£	£	£
Year 1	—	20,000	2,000	22,000
Year 2	22,000	20,000	4,200	46,200
Year 3	46,200	20,000	—	66,200

It follows that if a capital project costs £66,200 it will require £20,000 per annum in depreciation over three years at an interest rate of 10% to cover the capital cost. It is not necessary for the instalments of £20,000 to be put into any specific investments as they can be retained and used in the business. The instalments required for different periods of time and interest rates can be calculated, but tables are published (showing the amount by which a £ accumulates at different rates of interest) which make the calculations simple.

This has dealt with the recovery of the capital cost, but the other aspect which has to be taken into consideration is the interest on the capital sum provided. The sums of £20,000 per annum are generating interest to provide sufficient for replacement of the capital sum at the end of the period, but meanwhile £66,200 has been invested in the project, and at an interest rate of 10% the annual interest charge is £6,620. The total annual value to amortize fully the project in three years is £20,000 plus £6,620, making £26,620. This sum can be compared with the annual income. It will be seen that this method differs from the DCF and NPV methods by ignoring the timing of allowances and payments of tax and also by using a calculation for depreciation; DCF and NPV use capital allowances when applicable instead of depreciation.

However, the annual value calculations can be adjusted to account for tax, but this makes the method cumbersome, especially if there are several other variations in assumptions. The discounted cash flow techniques are simple in comparison and more widely used. Annual value is useful if dealing with projects with a long life and regular income, and as a quick rough guide to the annual income required. A quick approximation can be calculated by assessing depreciation to be on a straight line basis and, therefore, the capital sum being recovered equally during the life of the project. Interest on the capital sum will be high at the start of the project and low towards the end, and can be averaged. For example the straight line depreciation of £66,200 over three years is £22,066 and interest on half of £66,200 at 10% is £3,310. The annual value is, therefore, £25,376 approximately.

Sensitivity analysis

In calculating the discount rates, net present values, and other rates of return of projects, various assumptions have to be made, and the more complicated the project the more assumptions will be necessary. Estimations concerning timing of expenditure, receipt of grants, delay in reaching full production, interest rates and other assumptions must be judged, and these may subsequently turn out to be incorrect. To understand whether, perhaps, a timing delay in delivery, or a change in interest rates, will affect the viability of the project several calculations should be made with changed assumptions. Conclusions can then be drawn to indicate which factors are vital to the viability of the project, and which ones have little effect. This sensitivity analysis is important if the final decision is to be made with all aspects considered, and the area of uncertainty as small as possible.

The final decision

What is the correct rate of discount or interest to use in assessing projects against each other? A 6% rate of discount and 10% interest have been used in the examples studied, but are these the right rates, or how should the correct rates be established? A company might well look at the return on its existing capital by reference to its profit and loss account and balance sheet, and decide that any future projects must bring a return of at least the rate already earned by the company.

However, this reasoning is incorrect, as the rate of return which is required from a project must reflect the risk involved in the project. The return required on an investment in a gold mine in a politically unstable country must be much greater than that of running a confectioner's shop in the middle of a busy High Street.

It is, of course, possible to decide on a rate of interest or discount which fully compensates for the risk in the project or, alternatively, to decide on the minimum acceptable rate and then look at the risk as a separate exercise. The minimum acceptable rate is often taken as the rate of return on U.K. government borrowing. If the rate on three-month Treasury Bills is taken this can be regarded as risk free, and projects which are not risk free, or are for longer periods than three months, cannot be justified if an additional appropriate sum cannot be earned.

Also, as mentioned when discussing discounted cash flow, a decision maker cannot just work on a single set of comparative figures, and the same qualifications apply to all methods of assessment.

A decision maker must view both the results obtained and the assumptions used. All factors must be taken into account including the amount involved, the timing of cash flows, the rate of discount or interest in relation to risk, and possible other opportunities, before a reasoned judgment is made on the facts presented. There is no doubt, however, that by carefully calculating the DCF return, or the NPV, and with appropriate sensitivity analyses, that a decision maker will have a better idea of the returns expected and will, therefore, have to use less guesswork in making his final decision.

CHAPTER 14

Taxation

Corporation tax – Taxable profits – Advance corporation tax – Capital allowances – Stock relief – Deferred taxation – Cash flow – Value added tax – Income tax – Tax in balance sheets – Preferential tax liabilities

The taxation of companies is a specialized subject and no attempt will be made in this chapter to deal in detail with all aspects involved. A specialist text book should be studied for a complete understanding, but we will deal here with the overall effect of taxation on the company accounts and see how it affects the work of a lending banker.

Tax naturally plays a large part in the affairs of companies, and adequate planning of a company's finances cannot be made without looking at the after tax position of a company's activities. We have seen how this is related to particular projects in the chapter on the appraisal of capital expenditure, and we can now, therefore, leave this aspect and look at taxation generally in relation to a company's results. We shall look at the results produced by companies as shown in their profit and loss accounts and balance sheets, and consider the effect of taxation on these results.

At first sight it might seem to be a very simple matter in that a company makes profits and then pays tax on these profits, and that is the end of the matter. However, taxation is far more complicated than that. Profits can, of course, be calculated in different ways, and the figures produced by companies are not always the ones accepted by the revenue authorities. Also, of course, there are specific requirements about some items which can be deducted from profits before tax is calculated, and some items which are not allowed to be deducted for tax purposes. The computation of profits for tax is, therefore, different from the accountancy computation.

Corporation tax

The tax on the profits of companies is called corporation tax. The rate of tax is fixed by Parliament in the Finance Act each year, and the rate is fixed for the preceding year. This means that companies have to estimate the amount of corporation tax due, and adjustments have to be made subsequently. Corporation tax is charged both on a company's profits and on its capital gains, but the rate on capital gains is less than that on trading profits. There is also a lower taxation rate for companies which have small profits.

Date for payment of tax

Some companies get longer periods of credit for payment of their tax than others. Companies formed before 6th April 1965 normally pay tax on 1st January following the fiscal year in which the year end of the company falls. For example, if a company's year end falls on 30th September 1985, its accounts will fall in the fiscal year 1st April 1985 to 31st March 1986, and it will be due to pay its tax on 1st January 1987. When the company produces its accounts for the following year up to 30th September 1986 it will again be assessed for tax, and the tax will be due on 1st January 1988. It follows that when the company produces its accounts for the year up to 30th September 1985 it will be showing two amounts due for corporation tax, one due on 1st January 1986 and the other on 1st January 1987. This company has fifteen months credit on each payment of tax.

The situation, however, is different for companies formed after 6th April 1965 which have to pay tax nine months after the end of their financial years, or one month after the date of assessment.

There is, however, no need for a banker to enquire when a company was formed. He will be able to find out from the balance sheet what length of credit is allowed to the company by the revenue authorities because the dates when corporation tax is due are generally stated on balance sheets.

Explanation of terms used

ADVANCE CORPORATION TAX

When a company makes a qualifying distribution, such as a dividend, it is required to pay corporation tax. This payment is known as advance corporation tax (ACT), and the amount of the ACT depends on the amount of the standard rate of income tax. In effect, the amount paid in dividend is regarded as a net amount and a calculation is made to gross this amount up to a sum which if income tax was deducted from it at the standard rate would leave the same sum as a net dividend. The amount by which the dividend is theoretically grossed up becomes the ACT, and the amount of the tax is imputed to shareholders by issuing a tax credit. If the tax is at 30% in the £, and the dividend is £7,

$$\text{the ACT is } \frac{\text{the dividend (£7)} \times 3}{7} = \text{£3}$$

The general principle is that a company has to make quarterly returns for ACT purposes at which time it will pay the revenue authorities. Also it may set off the advance corporation tax against its total liability for corporation tax.

QUALIFYING DISTRIBUTIONS

This is a dividend, or any other distribution such as a capital dividend, or a distribution of the company's assets, but it does not include a distribution such as a stock dividend, or a bonus issue of shares. When a qualifying distribution is made the payment of advance corporation tax is involved.

FRANKED PAYMENT/FRANKED INVESTMENT INCOME

A qualifying distribution, plus the ACT, is called a franked payment. In the hands of a recipient it is known as franked investment income, i.e. it is the distribution, plus the amount of the advance corporation tax imputed to the distribution.

NON-QUALIFYING DISTRIBUTION

This covers such matters as bonus issues of shares, or securities on which no payment of ACT is required. A non-qualifying distribution can, therefore, not be a franked payment, nor franked investment income. It is received, or paid, without the addition of any tax credit.

MAINSTREAM CORPORATION TAX

This is the total liability for corporation tax less the ACT already paid. The amount of ACT which can be set off against corporation tax is limited in effect to the amount of the standard rate of income tax which could be imputed to shareholders if all the company's profits for the year were distributed. For example, if the corporation tax rate is 52% and the standard income tax rate 35% the mainstream corporation tax liability cannot be reduced below 17% of taxable profits.

CAPITAL ALLOWANCES

These are the allowances which by the Capital Allowances Act and the Taxes Acts are deductible from trading profits for computing income for tax. The most important was the allowance given for expenditure on machinery and plant. This was previously at a rate of 100% first year allowance which meant, in effect, that the entire depreciation of newly-bought plant and machinery could be written off in the first year. If subsequently the machinery was sold there would be a liability for tax on the amount received on the sale, known as a balancing charge. As from 6th April, 1986 capital allowances have been withdrawn.

STOCK RELIEF

This is relief which was allowed in the Finance Act 1975 to compensate companies to some extent for the inflationary aspect concerned with the replacement of stock. It has since been withdrawn.

THE CALCULATION OF TAXABLE PROFITS

As previously mentioned the normal accounting profits have to be adjusted in the tax computation as follows:

Deduct
1. franked investment income;
2. any stock relief claimed (if applicable);
3. capital allowances (if applicable);

Add back
4. any disbursements for non-business purposes;
5. legal and professional charges arising from capital transactions;
6. expenses for business entertaining (other than in connection with overseas customers or the company's own staff) which are not allowable;
7. depreciation charges which may have been replaced by capital allowances;

Adjust
8. for capital profits and losses;
9. for any interest received or paid net (i.e. after deduction of income tax) so as to show the gross amount in each case;
10. by adding back any balancing charges and deducting any balancing allowances (i.e. when capital allowances on equipment have been claimed in previous years and the equipment is later sold an adjustment may be necessary, either by way of a charge or an allowance, and will depend on the amount realized on the sale).

There are also provisions for excess advance corporation tax to be set off in different accounting periods, and also for set off for losses. Where groups of companies are concerned losses and allowances can be transferred around the group (provided the parent owns at least 75% of subsidiaries).

Deferred taxation

There is a further aspect which we must consider which arises out of accountancy provisions. We will, first of all, consider this in relation to plant and machinery.

From an accountancy point of view plant and machinery should be depreciated fully over the expected life of the asset; that is a full 100% will appear in the accounts over a period of years for depreciation until the asset is disposed of as scrap. To help companies re-equip the Government introduced capital allowances whereby, in effect, depreciation could be accelerated for taxation purposes. The capital allowances were, for some years, 100% of the cost of the equipment, and this meant that for tax purposes the entire value of the asset could be written off in the first year. As the normal accountancy method is to write off an annual amount of depreciation this, of course, differed from the 100% capital allowance written off in the first year.

For example, if the cost of an item of equipment was £100 and it was to be depreciated at £20 per year for five years, instead of the company's profit being reduced by £20 each year for tax purposes, a reduction of £100 would be made in the first year with nothing in the following four years. Obviously it would not be right to produce accounts showing the full £100 deduction in the first year only as this would seriously upset comparison of the figures year by year. In these circumstances a deferred taxation account was set up to spread the taxation on the capital allowance received in the first year over the number of years of expected life of the equipment. In this case the life of the equipment was five years and we will consider the corporation tax rate as 50%. Therefore tax not paid on the 100% first year allowance on £100 would be £50. This sum (less the proportion applicable to the tax on normal depreciation for the first year, i.e. £10) would be credited to a deferred taxation account which would then be reduced by £10 in each of the following four years.

If we now consider that in the second year the equipment was sold for its written down value of £80 this amount would have to be taken into account for tax purposes, and the tax on it, i.e. £40, would have to be paid. It will be seen, therefore, that the amount put aside on the deferred taxation account was really a reserve for the contingent liability of the equipment's being sold. If, however, in the second year as well as selling the equipment for its written down value of £80 a further piece of equipment costing £100 was bought the £40 would not have to be paid in tax: it would be offset against the 100% capital allowance on the new equipment. It will be seen that if the cost of buying equipment in any one year at least equals the amount realized from sales that the amount put on a deferred taxation account was not paid to the revenue authorities. All that a deferred taxation account does, in these circumstances, is smooth out the capital allowances over the expected life of the asset, and no tax is actually paid.

There seems no point in adding to deferred taxation accounts if there is little possibility that the additional amounts will be paid in tax. This was acknowledged by the accountancy bodies in the issue of SSAP15 whereby all balance sheets after 1st January 1979 have to show deferred taxation only if it is reasonably certain that the amount shown thereon will be paid in tax. The deferred taxation account is, therefore, one related to timing differences where tax would, in the normal way be due, but, by legislation, the payment can be delayed until a future time.

However, SSAP15 also requires companies to include a note to the accounts showing the full contingent liability for deferred tax with details of the principal categories involved.

It will be appreciated that if a company purchased more plant and machinery annually, sufficient for the capital allowances at least to cover the deferred taxation running off the account, it would not have to meet the tax bill which would otherwise be due. Capital allowances were reduced to 75% as from 6th April, 1984, 50% as from 6th April, 1985 and withdrawn as from 6th April, 1986. Writing down allowances only are now permitted for tax computations. Deferred taxation accounts will now, in consequence, be running down.

Tax in the profit and loss account

How is a lending banker able to judge the amount of the profit generation which has been ploughed back into the company? This is an important aspect as far as a lending banker is concerned as it not only tells him what amount is available for repayment of borrowing, but also how much of internally generated funds are available to support the purchase of new

EXAMPLE 39

Calculation of cash flow

Z Company Limited

PROFIT AND LOSS ACCOUNT FOR THE YEAR TO 30TH JUNE, YEAR A

	£
Profit before tax (and after all expenses and deductions, including depreciation of £3,000)	10,000
Less Tax	4,300
Profit after tax	5,700

BALANCE SHEET AS AT 30TH JUNE, YEAR A

	£	£
Fixed assets		20,000
Current assets	15,000	
Less Current liabilities (including proposed dividend, £1,400, and ACT thereon, £600)	13,000	
		2,000
		22,000
Less Corporation tax		
due 1st January, year B	2,700	
due 1st January, year C	3,400	
		6,100
Net assets		£15,900
Shareholders' funds		12,900
Long-term liabilities		3,000
		£15,900

CASH FLOW (i.e. profits made and retained in the company's business)		
Profit before tax		10,000
Add Depreciation		3,000
		13,000
Less Corporation tax	3,400	
Proposed dividend	1,400	
ACT thereon	600	
		5,400
Cash flow		£7,600

assets, or the increase of working capital. Firstly, the profit is calculated after making a book entry for depreciation. This is a book entry only, and no cash has left the business, therefore the amount of the depreciation has to be added back to the net profit. Subsequently the amount payable in tax has to be deducted but there is no point in deducting the amount shown in the profit and loss account as this figure could be a combination of both corporation and deferred tax. The amount which must be deducted is the corporation tax liability in the balance sheet applicable for the same accounting year. From the resultant figure must then be deducted the amount of the dividend paid out and also the associated advance corporation tax (see Example 39).

Value added tax

This tax is one on supplies: both goods and services. It is a tax on the ultimate consumer; the intermediaries between the initial producer and the final consumer act merely as agents for the collection of the tax. The tax is imposed on imports of goods into the United Kingdom and the supply of goods and services by businesses in the United Kingdom. There is no value added tax on exports.

Value added tax is now levied at two different rates:

1. zero rate applies to items such as food and other items supplied in providing catering, water, newspapers, journals, periodicals and books. It also applies to fuel and power, children's clothing, and certain drugs and medicines, and to exports;
2. standard rate applies to other goods and services;

The goods quoted in these two categories are not a complete list. For this it is necessary to obtain the appropriate publication from the customs and excise authorities. Also, of course, variations can be made in the goods which come in the different categories. Most traders are required to register for the purpose of collecting and paying this tax, and they then have to keep records of the inputs and outputs of tax.

Inputs arise when a trader buys goods and services on which value added tax has to be paid in due course. Outputs arise when the registered trader sells goods and services. He therefore has both inputs and outputs and every quarter must make a return to the customs and excise authorities showing both. A balancing amount is then paid to, or received from, the customs and excise.

Certain goods and services are exempt from VAT, including such items as sales or leases of land, insurance, postal services, betting, finance, health and some education. Although it might seem that being zero rated and exempt are similar it is better for a business to be zero rated than exempt as, whereas in both cases there is no VAT on the supply, there is also no credit allowed for the tax on the inputs of the business if it is exempt. It can, therefore, not claim back these inputs, whereas the zero rated business can. For example, an assurance company is exempt and collects no tax on premiums on a life policy, but the life assurance company is not able to obtain repayment of inputs on those services for which it pays and uses in its life assurance business.

Small traders are defined from time to time in relation to the amount of annual sales. If they qualify they need not register. But a small trader can register voluntarily; and this could be to his advantage. In any case he will have to pay VAT on his own purchases of goods and services. If he registers he can set off the input VAT payable against the VAT he will then have to charge on what he sells. But only he can decide whether the time and effort involved in collecting and recording VAT on his sales will be worth his while.

Where group companies are concerned no payments need be made between members of the group for supplies between themselves.

Therefore a business is merely a collecting agency. The tax is paid by the final consumer. The business itself is only ultimately responsible for VAT on purchases which it keeps itself for its own business, such as fixed assets. There is, of course, a considerable amount of unpaid work as a tax collector which a company has to perform, but the tax affects a company's affairs in other ways too.

The company can either be a net payer of VAT or a net receiver, and in some ways it is better to be a net payer as then the business has the use of the VAT collected until it is paid. The businesses which have this advantage are generally those with cash sales. The VAT is collected immediately, whereas with sales on credit the VAT is not received until some time later. From a banker's point of view, although the VAT in these circumstances may serve to reduce the overdraft on an account, it must also be kept in mind that in the case of weak customers the VAT can turn out to be a preferential liability if the company should go into liquidation, or a receiver is appointed. With weak companies a banker will want to know about the amount of VAT kept in hand for the revenue authorities. He can, of course, obtain a rough idea on this by looking at the amount of the quarterly payment. He will not be able to find out the amount from the balance sheets because VAT will be included in either the debtors or the creditors, and not quoted separately. When monthly or quarterly current assets and current liabilities figures are required by a banker he should check to see that the VAT payments (if payments are normal for the company) are included at the due times and that the cheques in payment also go through the banking account at the correct time. Delay in payment is a sign of weakness.

Incidentally, in the profit and loss account the turnover figure which is quoted should not include the value added tax. However, with the debtor figures including the amount of VAT the ratio of debtors to turnover is distorted. Normally the distortion is not great.

Exporters are at a disadvantage because, although they have to pay VAT on goods supplied to them, they cannot charge VAT on their exports. This means that the companies are out of pocket to the extent of the VAT until they can reclaim it, which they are entitled to do because exports are zero rated.

Income tax

Companies are required to deduct income tax at the basic rate when paying loan interest, mortgage interest, debenture interest or royalties. Income can also be received from which the basic rate of tax has been deducted. This occurs on such items as loan interest received, or income received from British Government Securities from which income tax is deducted at source. Such income, known as franked investment income received, can be set off against the deductions which a company has made when paying loan interest etc., and the balance, if any, can be set off against the corporation tax on the profits for the year.

Presentation in balance sheets

Taxation, in all its forms, impinges on many aspects of business life, and it is interesting to see where in balance sheets, items for taxation occur. Normally items for corporation tax are seen in balance sheets, but other items are often amalgamated with debtors and creditors. Example 40 will illustrate.

If we now examine the balance sheet for items where tax is mentioned we see the following:

1. *Deferred taxation*. This is an account for spreading timing differences and the full contingent liability will be shown in the note to the accounts.
2. *Corporation tax due 1st January, year B*. This is the corporation tax assessed on the profits for the year before that of the balance sheet at which we are looking and is due to be paid within twelve months.
3. *Corporation tax due 1st January, year C*. This is the corporation tax due on the profits of the business for year A. It will be seen, therefore, that eighteen months elapses from the end of the financial year of the business until tax is due to be paid. This indicates that the company was formed before 1st April 1965, as otherwise tax would be due nine months after the end of the company's year.

4. *Pay As You Earn.* This is the amount of tax deducted from wages and salaries due to be paid to the revenue authorities. The collector of taxes requires this tax to be paid on the due dates and does not take kindly

EXAMPLE 40

Taxation items in a balance sheet

BALANCE SHEET AS AT 30TH JUNE YEAR A

		£'000	£'000	£'000
	FIXED ASSETS			
	Freeholds			80
	Plant and machinery			40
	Fixtures, fittings, tools and equipment			9
	Investments			7
				136
	CURRENT ASSETS			
	Stocks		8	
	Trade debtors		15	
	Other debtors			
8.	V.A.T.	3		
9.	Advance corporation tax recoverable (on interim dividend)	1		
10.	Advance corporation tax recoverable (on final dividend)	3		
11.	Income tax recoverable	1		
	Cash	6	14	
			37	
	CREDITORS: AMOUNTS FALLING DUE WITHIN ONE YEAR			
	Trade creditors		12	
	Other creditors including taxation and social security			
12.	Social security	1		
4.	P.A.Y.E.	1		
5.	V.A.T.	2		
	Proposed final dividend	7		
2.	Corporation tax due 1st January year B	8		
6.	Advance corporation tax on dividend	3		
7.	Income tax	1	23	
			35	
	Net current assets			2
	Total assets *less* current liabilities			138
	CREDITORS: AMOUNTS FALLING DUE AFTER MORE THAN ONE YEAR			
	Loans		8	
3.	Corporation tax due 1st January year C		10	
1.	Deferred taxation		10	28
				110
	CAPITAL AND RESERVES			
	Called up share capital			100
	Reserves			8
	Profit and loss account			2
				110

to giving longer credit. However when companies get into financial difficulties, they often delay payment of this tax and when liquidation, or receivership, occurs a substantial amount of PAYE is often found to be owing.

5. *Value added tax.* This is the tax due on the sales of the company and has to be paid quarterly. Both PAYE and VAT are normally included in creditors and are not specified separately.

6. *ACT on dividends.* It will be seen that it is proposed to pay a final dividend and advance corporation tax on the dividend must also be paid to the collector of taxes.

7. *Income tax.* This is the tax which has been deducted from interest payments made and is, therefore, due to the collector of taxes.

8. *VAT.* This is the value aded tax on the asset side of the balance sheet and is, therefore, due to be recovered from the customs and excise on purchases made for which the company is not the final consumer.

9. *Advance corporation tax recoverable on interim dividend.* This is the amount of tax paid to the collector of taxes when the interim dividend was distributed to shareholders and it can be offset against the full liability for corporation tax when it is due to be paid, i.e. on the 1st January, Year C.

10. *Advance corporation tax recoverable on final dividend.* This is the same amount as shown among the current liabilities for the advance corporation tax on the dividend. When the dividend is paid the advance corporation tax has also to be paid, but this amount of tax is not lost entirely to the business because it can be set off against the full liability for corporation tax. The amount, therefore, generally appears both as a liability and as an offsetting asset. If, however, a company does not anticipate being liable for mainstream corporation tax for some time the amount of ACT recoverable is not then shown as an asset but is written off. This situation occurs because of anticipated losses, and it is also common with companies which have large overseas income and little liability for corporation tax.

11. *Income tax recoverable.* This is the amount of tax which has been deducted from the interest payments received on investments. The amount is normally netted with the income tax due to be paid and only one figure would appear in the balance sheet.

12. *Social security liability.* Deductions from wages and salaries for social security benefits are now of substantial amounts and, added to an employer's contributions, can combine to give a company a material liability especially if it has a large number of employees.

It will be seen that items for taxation appear in many sections of the balance sheet, and it is as well for bankers to appreciate this and to know when payments are due, what payments can be offset, and when a company gets into difficulties, what items are preferential liabilities. Preferential liabilities have already been mentioned in chapter 6, but as far as taxation occurs these are repeated as follows:

1. outstanding taxes for the period of twelve months before the appointment of a receiver, or the date of a company going into liquidation;
2. PAYE for the same period of one year;
3. VAT for the same period of one year;

Both items for corporation tax shown in the balance sheet will be preferential liabilities, but against this will be offset the net amount of advance corporation tax which is due to be recovered. All the PAYE and VAT would normally become preferential as it would be unusual for either of the authorities to allow these items to outstand for a period of one year. The net amount of income tax if a debit will also be a preferential liability.

CHAPTER 15

Various Balance Sheets

Two farming balance sheets – Professional partnership – An association – A hotel company – Extractive company – Property investment company – Retail drapery company – Chain store company

The varied balance sheets considered in this chapter have been selected to fulfil three main purposes:

1. to show that all balance sheets have the same basic structure and are susceptible to the same kind of analysis;
2. to familiarize the reader with balance sheets of non-industrial undertakings;
3. to provide the opportunity of making comments on any special features of interest. In the course of these comments it is hoped that some understanding of the kinds of inference which can be safely made will grow.

For reasons which are dealt with fully in Chapter 17, no attempt whatever will be made to indicate how much bank accommodation would be justified by these different balance sheets.

For the convenience of the reader the specimen balance sheets have been collected together in a separate section at the back of the book. Please see Appendix 2, pages 302–16.

BALANCE SHEET A SOLE TRADER : TENANT FARMER

BALANCE SHEET RATIOS

	%	%		%
Real capital		26.9	Fixed assets	55.4
Current liabilities			Current assets	44.6
Bank	34.1			
Sundry creditors	39.0			
		73.1		
		100.0		100.0
Current ratio		.61	Liquid ratio	nil

Real capital provides approximately 50% of the fixed assets. 50% of the fixed assets and all the current assets are provided by creditors; on the face of it, a very vulnerable position.

Net profit—10¼% on turnover: 12% on total assets employed at the end
(before tax) of the year: 44% on 'net worth.'

This balance sheet is not subject to the Companies Act and the farmer may prefer to have the same format as has been used in the past.

If we look first at the capital account we see that a good profit has been made but drawings are very low. This is quite usual with a farmer's balance sheet and one is left wondering how a farmer is able to live on such small drawings. However, he has his house to live in and various expenses are taken out of the farming account which otherwise the farmer would have to pay out of his drawings. However, the balance sheet is not one which is normally accepted by the inspector of taxes and the farmer, or his accountant, will have to argue the question of drawings with the tax authorities.

There seems to be quite a large bank overdraft and, in fact, this is greater than the amount of the capital account, but if we look at the other side of the balance sheet we see that the freehold house and freehold cottages are in very low figures, and a revaluation of these properties would, of course, increase the farmer's capital account. Presumably the properties are worth substantially more and are probably security for the bank overdraft.

The creditors at over £84,000 are well in excess of the debtors of only £12,000. However, farmers run their businesses extensively on long credit, and the merchants support them pending receipt of harvest proceeds.

When we look at the date of the balance sheet we see that it is 25th March, and it seems unusual, therefore, to have such a large amount in creditors when the harvest proceeds from the previous year should have been collected. There appears to have been a large amount of money spent during the year on plant and machinery, motor tractors and motor lorries, and one wonders whether this farm is in the process of being modernized and brought up-to-date with new equipment. Enquiries will have to be made about this because if the new equipment will enable bigger profits to be made this is, of course, vital to the whole consideration of the farmer's affairs.

Looking at the current assets the only amount of note is that for the valuation and, where farmers are concerned, the valuation although specified among the current assets quite often contains an element of fixed assets. This is because the value of cattle is included and cattle, such as cows which are kept for the milk they produce, are therefore part of the farmer's fixed assets. The same applies to all other cattle which are kept not for sale but some other purpose such as breeding, or for the sale of wool. In the present instance, however, the amount for cattle and sheep is relatively small, but that for crops and cultivations is large.

We have already commented on the unusual aspect of having a large amount of creditors at the 25th March and, of course, it would be unusual also to have a large amount of crops and cultivations at the same date. A further enquiry on these points is necessary, but before making enquiry of the farmer it would be better to look at the profit and loss account to see if this throws light on the subject.

PROFIT AND LOSS ACCOUNT

	£
Sales of:	
cattle and sheep	4,152
wheat, oats and barley	23,136
sugar-beet	5,982
market garden produce	47,928
hay and straw	393
Total sales	81,591
Grants	3,840
Contract work	2,528
Tenant right	351
	£88,310

It will now be seen that the main activity is market gardening and this, of course, is the answer to the problems we have posed. The turnover should be rapid and provide quite substantial cash. Nevertheless, the balance sheet and the profit and loss account do not give us the full information which we require and certain suppositions have had to be made. Undoubtedly further enquiries are necessary and the bank manager will have to talk to the customer about the figures revealed, but in order to get a full idea of the customer's business he will also have to visit the farm.

He will be interested in the acreage farmed broken down to show the extent of use for arable, pasture, horticulture, rough grazing and woodland and to see how the effective acreage compares with the capital employed. If the number of cattle (ascertained by dividing a fair average price into the valuation figure) indicates an overloading of the pasture, further enquiry may reveal any of the following:

1. that there was actual over-stocking at the balance sheet date;
2. that pedigree herds are carried and the fair average price applied was, in fact, too low;
3. that at peak periods additional pasture is rented.

Well drawn accounts shed valuable light on the type of farming carried on. But in no industry is it less safe to rely on accounts alone. If factories should be seen, farms and farmers should be visited and known intimately. The difference between 'farming to quit' and keeping the land in good heart will often not show in the face of the accounts. It is obviously vital for a banker to know whether satisfactory profits are the result of good husbandry or of 'bleeding' the land.

There is, however, one aspect of the accounts which is very important and that is that the farmer in his capital account, regardless of whether the house and cottages are under-valued, has still not provided for all the funds to cover the fixed assets. To have a successful business the proprietor (together with a long-term lender if necessary) must provide the funds for the fixed assets, and also a proportion of the current assets, but in the present case the creditors and the bank are providing what must be regarded as permanent capital. There may, of course, be reasons for this and possibly among the creditors' figure there is an amount which can be regarded as a long-term loan or, on the other hand, possibly the bank overdraft, or part of it, has been provided on a temporary basis pending the injection of more capital. Whatever the reason, the fact will remain that if the proprietor does not provide sufficient money to cover all the fixed assets, or have access to long-term funds for this purpose, he will be in financial difficulty which will mean constant trouble with the bank and his creditors until he has rectified the position.

BALANCE SHEET B — FARMING COMPANY

BALANCE SHEET RATIOS

	%		%
Fixed assets	20.9	Capital	6.5
Current assets	79.1	Loan	45.6
		Effective real capital	52.1
		Bank overdraft	31.8
		Other current liabilities	16.1
	100.0		100.0

Current ratio 1.65
(taking overdraft as a wholly current liability)
Liquid ratio nil
The effective real capital (including the loan)
is invested 40.1% in fixed assets
59.9% in current assets

100.0%

Net profit – 10.9% on turnover
12.3% on total assets employed at end of year

The capital structure of this tenant company (no land is owned) is suggestive. The main capital has been put up by way of loan, rather than subscribed share capital, to keep the position flexible though not for the more usual reason of saving capital duty, for this has already been paid on the authorized capital of £18,000. The bank will probably have taken a letter of postponement to place the loan at the back of the queue, along with the issued share capital. Losses have been made in the past, but the profit rate is now reasonably good in relation to both turnover and total assets employed. Compared with balance sheet A, fixed assets are low, and it is fair inference (which the trading account will confirm) that the main activity is dairy-farming and stock raising, with just sufficient arable farming to provide fodder, give the pasture a rest and, incidentally, earn the subsidies.

It is usual for all farm accounts (whether of companies or sole traders) to have the valuation of stock made by a professional valuer. Tenant right corresponds to work in progress in an industrial balance sheet, and is based on expenditure incurred in ploughing, manuring, seeding and agreed building work for which, had the tenant relinquished possession on the balance sheet date, he would have been entitled to compensation as part of the new tenant's ingoing: a proportion of rent and other overheads can reasonably be added. For an owner-farmer the corresponding term could be 'cultivations': but as the basis of valuation is the same in either case, the terms are usually regarded as interchangeable. As in industrial accounts an increase (reduction) in cultivations or tenant right is added to (deducted from) sales to ascertain the true turnover.

BALANCE SHEET C — PROFESSIONAL PARTNERSHIP

BALANCE SHEET RATIOS

	%		%
Capital	61.0	Fixed assets	16.8
Current liabilities	39.0	Current assets	83.2
	100.0		100.0

Current ratio 2.1

This balance sheet is not subject to the requirements of the Companies Act. Capital, comprising capital and drawings accounts, covers the fixed assets and over 50% of the current assets. Net profit is 42.4% of total out-turn: and 49.1% on capital employed at end of year.

It will be noted that unlike most commercial and industrial balance sheets, this one lists the liabilities in order of payability, with current liabilities first and proprietors' claims last and the assets in order of liquidity, from cash to goodwill. The large provision for income tax is a reminder that this tax is always payable by a partnership and not by the partners personally, even though the amount assessed is based on their individual returns.

The tie-up in debtors, accrued fees (work in progress) and expenses not yet charged up is high in this type of practice: in this case equivalent to

75.6% of the year's turnover. Cash and investments at £60,000 look ample until it is seen that practically the whole of this amount is due in income tax, the staff bonus scheme or to the estate of a deceased partner, and all these liabilities might well have to be paid without delay.

	£
Income tax	16,816
Staff bonus	11,226
Estate of deceased partner . .	24,573
	£52,615

Sundry creditors have nearly doubled and may contain a sufficient overdue element to absorb the balance of the cash and investment at an early date. It is also noteworthy that the current assets have become much less liquid in character. Accounts immediately receivable are little over half those at the end of the previous year, while the amounts tied up in fees and expenses not yet chargeable, are nearly £20,000 higher. In fact a close examination reveals a position of near stringency: and part of the reason.

G. Smith's capital and drawings account balances amounting to £31,400 have been lost to the business and £7,000 in cash has already been paid out. The last remnant of a similar cash drain to another deceased partner is indicated in the previous year's figures (Estate of G. Williams, dec., £978). The drawings accounts of the three surviving partners have been augmented during the year by no less than £19,000, and they have each injected £6,000 in capital. The paying out of a deceased partner, like the payment of taxation, requires cash and thus falls on the business where it hurts most.

The payments to Thomas of £1,920 represent part of the purchase price of another practice. As it is clearly the intention to charge the cost up to partners' drawings accounts and not to leave this item in the balance sheet capitalized as 'goodwill', there seems little point in keeping this item in the balance sheet at all.

Turning to the profit and loss account (which for the reader's convenience is barred off into three sections to correspond with the trading, profit and loss and appropriation accounts of a trading company) the high profit rate 42.4% is noteworthy though not at all excessive where personal expert service is being sold and its cost is not directly charged against profits. The lower divisible profit on a higher out-turn (10% up) prompts enquiry.

However the overall position is strong, the earnings are high, and the ploughing back of profits is large. Additionally, there is a freehold property which could be used as security and altogether the partnership should have no difficulty in getting a bank to agree to reasonable facilities for normal trading plus, if necessary, some term loan moneys.

BALANCE SHEET D — CLUB, OR SIMILAR INSTITUTION

This is a typical balance sheet for a professional association, club or similar body. It is, of course, not subject to the requirements of the Companies Act. The freehold premises are no doubt held by trustees on behalf of the association. The only item which calls for comment is the accumulated fund which corresponds to members' capital and with the reserves constitutes the association's 'net worth'.

In nearly all cases this fund has been built up out of past surpluses in income and expenditure account which takes the place of the more usual profit and loss accounts presented by business undertakings. Another possible source is legacies and similar benefactions.

As on the termination of the association any surplus is presumably divisible between the members for the time being, a substantial accumulated fund is at once the reason and justification for an entrance fee for new members. If this particular association has 4,000 members, each new member joining acquires an interest (taking the assets at book value) worth about £10. This fact is often overlooked when the committee of the club decides to reduce or waive the entrance fee for a period, to attract new members.

An unincorporated association's balance sheet is, in essence, similar in character to that of a company and requires from a lending banker the same assessment; but such an association presents special legal and technical difficulties in relation both to borrowing and the giving of security.

The liquid position is, of course, always important to a banker, but in the present case the current assets at £16,000 are well in excess of the current liabilities. The fact that there was a deficit being an excess of expenditure over income for the year is of no consequence if the liquid position is substantial and in this case as well as the current assets there are, of course, the investments of over £50,000.

A club or an institute does not try to make a profit, but is more interested, after the initial period of building up a substantial base, in keeping expenditure and income more or less in line.

BALANCE SHEET E — HOTEL COMPANY

BALANCE SHEET RATIOS

	%		%
Goodwill	16.9	Capital	41.5
Fixed assets	58.6	Loans	33.6
Current assets	24.5	Current liabilities	24.9
	100.0		100.0
Liquid ratio	0.4	Current ratio	1.0
On year end assets	4.1	Net profit (before tax) on turnover	1.7

The balance sheet is of a public limited company and, as is normal, few details have been set out in the balance sheet. The details will appear in the notes to the accounts. In this example, the notes are not included but bankers must beware that notes are an integral part of the accounts and must be studied thoroughly.

This type of presentation is a popular one as it shows the main figures only, and is more digestible for people not well versed in financial affairs. It will be seen that shareholders have contributed £1,035,000 but loans of £850,000 have been arranged and there is also bank borrowing of £200,000.

It will be seen that the amount contributed by shareholders and the amount contributed by loans and from borrowing are more or less equal. With this sort of proportion for the provision of funds we should immediately look at the fixed assets to see how much the shareholders have provided and how much has been provided from loans. We cannot overlook the goodwill item as this is £430,000 and has to be deducted from the shareholders' funds. There is, therefore, only an amount of £605,000 left and with fixed assets at £1,480,000 the bulk of the fixed assets are, therefore, provided by the loans. This is not too healthy a sign and much will depend on the interest rate payable on the loans, and whether the loans become repayable shortly. For full details it would be necessary to refer to the notes to the accounts, but from the brief details provided it will be seen that the bulk of the loans, apart from bank borrowing, will not be due to mature until at least five years. If the interest rate is high indicating that the company had to raise funds under adverse conditions this will weigh heavily on the company in both poor years and good. If, however, the loans were obtained at low interest rates then the shareholders will have the benefit of this gearing during good years.

If we now turn to the current position we see that liabilities slightly exceed assets. No unsecured lending is, therefore, justified and from the accounts so far it will be appreciated that all the lenders would wish to have security and this, in fact, is what has happened. Generally with hotels when it comes to a sale each hotel would have to be sold not only with the premises, but with all the fixtures, fittings, carpeting and equipment. The only security of any worth would, therefore, be a debenture as then the hotels could be sold complete.

With the lending being so spread it will probably be the case that some of the lenders will have a debenture, and other lenders will have charges over the fixed assets. If trouble arises in these circumstances the lenders will have to agree together both on the sales of the hotels and the split of the proceeds, in order to be able to negotiate with potential buyers.

The profit and loss account shows that turnover was up during the year, and in consequence, trading profit increased from £19,000 to £30,000. The net profit on turnover at 1.7% was, however, extremely small. The interest on loans was a relatively large amount of £95,000 in both years, and a considerable increase in trading profit will have to be achieved before shareholders can get a good return on their investment. Altogether it will be seen that the borrowing of the company will be causing it some problems for some years as the profits generated are insufficient to make a sizeable impact on the overall liabilities.

BALANCE SHEET F — EXTRACTIVE INDUSTRY

BALANCE SHEET RATIOS

	%		%
Capital	57.0	Fixed assets	36.8
Current liabilities	43.0	Current assets	63.2
	100.0		100.0

Current ratio 1.5 — Liquid ratio negligible

Capital represented by:	
Net fixed assets*	35.5%
Working capital	64.5%
	100.0%

* But see below regarding the position of stocks of stone.

This balance sheet presents some interesting features. Share premium account is shown separately in accordance with the requirements of the Companies Act, 1985 as also is the revaluation reserve which is a capital reserve and cannot be distributed as a dividend.

Only one-third of the current assets is provided by proprietors' capital (after deducting fixed assets) and the bank overdraft has the appearance of a lock-up. The fact that the bank is prepared to lend £52,000 on the security of certain of the company's properties, suggests that the balance sheet valuation of £80,000 is conservative. Ridding values, the cost of removing the overburden and uncovering the stone ready for blasting is the quarryman's equivalent of the manufacturer's work in progress. Road development, also included in current assets, is of a similar nature. The existence of a substantial work in progress item in addition to riddings suggests that the company also runs a substantial stone masonry department. It is interesting to observe that in a mining company's accounts, development expenditure is usually treated as a fixed asset and has to be incurred mainly before production begins: in a quarry company riddings and roads proceeding step by step with the extraction of stone are current assets.

In accordance with the Companies Act 1985 development costs can only be carried forward in special circumstances and, in such cases, the notes to the accounts must state the reasons for capitalizing the costs and the period over which they are being written off.

A noteworthy feature of this balance sheet is the substantial amount written off the properties. A company established expressly to exploit a wasting asset like stone or other mineral deposits is under no legal obligation to make good such wasting assets out of profits.[1] Provided the members appreciate that their dividends contain a return of capital ingredient (albeit wholly taxed as income like normal life annuities) no one is deceived or injured if, when the deposits have been worked out, there are few assets left.

In the present instance the quarrying of stone could be subsidiary to the company's main activity of manufacturing or processing stone. In that case, the stone lying on the company's quarry properties might properly be regarded as stock in hand and fall to be revalued year by year, in the same way as industrial stocks of raw materials; such stocks of stone would then be included in the circulating assets.[2] The principle may, in fact, have been followed in the present case in the course of writing down the value of properties, even though, because of the difficulty of segregating the stock ingredient, they are still grouped with the fixed assets.

In lending to extractive industry the banker will always have in mind the fact that he is dealing with wasting assets, however they may be treated in the accounts.

BALANCE SHEET G

This is in a simple form, but the notes, of course, must cover all the aspects which, according to the Companies Acts, must be disclosed.

Dominating the figures in this balance sheet is that for the property at £50,000. The other assets are relatively small. The capital employed covers all the fixed assets, plus the net current assets, because there is no borrowing at all. The profit and loss account discloses that the gross return on the rent receivable is reasonably good but expenses are heavy for collecting this rent, and the after-tax profit gives shareholders a poor return.

BALANCE SHEET G — PROPERTY INVESTMENT COMPANY

BALANCE SHEET RATIOS

	%		%
Capital	88.2	Fixed assets	85.1
Current liabilities	11.8	Current assets	14.9
	100.0		100.0

Current ratio 1.3 — Liquid ratio 1.3

Where property investment companies are concerned there is generally a more or less fixed income, especially if there are old leases. This is because the rents are fixed with possible periodic reviews, but there can be no dramatic change from one year to the next. To see whether the company is using its assets properly it will be necessary to know the current value

[1] Lee *v.* Neuchatel Asphalte Company, 1889.
[2] Bond *v.* The Barrow Haematite Steel Co., 1902.

of the freehold property. If, through inflation and changes of values, the property is really worth £100,000 the shareholders would have a poor investment as the assets would not be generating their full potential. However, the full potential will take a long time to be realized because of the difficulty in raising rents. Also, of course, the retained income is small and even if, as in the present case, there is no borrowing against the property it would be very difficult to gear the company satisfactorily. This is because if any further property was bought on borrowed money to increase income there would be little to contribute from the income of the present property to repay any borrowing incurred.

The previous year's figures are also included as an illustration of what is required by the Companies Act 1985. Whenever figures are quoted it is a requirement of the Act that comparative figures are also shown. The profit and loss account in this illustration is only in summary form. A format as specified by the Act can be seen in Appendix 1.

BALANCE SHEET H — DRAPERY RETAILERS

BALANCE SHEET RATIOS

	%		%
Capital and reserves	34.5	Fixed assets	73.0
Loans	22.4	Current assets	27.0
Current liabilities	43.1		
	100.0		100.0

Current ratio 0.63 Liquid ratio 0.11

This balance sheet is given in greater detail as the notes referring to items in the balance sheet are added on an additional sheet. This balance sheet, therefore conforms fully to the requirements of the Companies Acts. The balance sheet ratios which are shown above bring out some salient points. For example, the fixed assets are not covered by the capital provided, and are not covered either by the capital and loans combined. Therefore all the current assets and part of the fixed assets are provided from current liabilities. It will be necessary, therefore, to refer to the current liabilities and see what the individual items show.

If we look firstly at the creditors we see they are at £130,000 and if we compare this with the turnover of £2.5 million we see that the creditors account for less than one month's turnover and, therefore, are at a relatively small amount. Hire purchase creditors are not very large for the figures seen in this business. The bank overdraft of £160,000 is also less than one month's turnover. The drapery trade is seasonal in some respects but there are several seasonal products each year and also it is normal to have one or two special sales each year. It looks, therefore, as if the bank overdraft should swing satisfactorily. The other amounts in current liabilities are those for tax and proposed dividends and are relatively small.

The £320,000 due to associated companies is a large sum and, indeed, provides the key to the whole balance sheet. If this money is a long-term loan to Drapery Shops Limited then it is, of course, really being used for fixed assets. As the amount is included in current liabilities it is unlikely that this is the case and enquiries will have to be made about the associated companies. It is particularly necessary because the only other evidence in the accounts about such associates is a trade loan of £1,000. There are two reasons for a company to be classified as an associated company:

1. if the investing company is effectively a partner in a joint venture, and
2. if the investing company has an interest in the associated company which is long-term and substantial, i.e. not less than 20% of the equity voting rights.

In both cases it is essential that the investing company participates in financial policy, and has a significant influence over the associated company. It seems odd, therefore, that a trade loan of £1,000 would give such an interest in an associated company which is in business on such a scale that the associated company could allow Drapery Shops Limited credit of as much as £320,000. There is something unusual about this, but an enquiry of the directors of Drapery Shops Limited will probably throw some light on the situation. In any event it certainly looks as if the liability cannot be classed as long-term, but is correctly designated among the current liabilities. It is obvious now that Drapery Shops Limited is not properly financed. It is trying to finance its fixed assets out of its current liabilities, and will have the greatest difficulty in dealing with its current liabilities out of its current assets, regardless of the fact that its turnover is £2.5 million per annum. The directors, no doubt, are trying to increase the turnover because most of the trade is for cash, debtors being only a relatively small figure in the balance sheet. With the increased cash coming in the directors are, therefore, struggling to pay their liabilities. At the same time they will be wishing to increase their turnover even more and here we have a typical overtrading situation. More capital or long-term money is required. Whether this can be obtained will depend on the directors' personal finances, or whether they can get other people to contribute.

As for the loan side we shall have to look at the security available to any lender. If further borrowing was contemplated a lender would, no doubt, require security. If we look at the notes to the accounts we see that the freeholds are valued at £900,000, but there are loans of £350,000 and a bank overdraft of £160,000 which are secured against these deeds. It may be possible to raise some more money, but much will depend on the forced sale value of the freeholds. It will be seen from Note 7 that during the year a further loan of £40,000 was taken out, and this is repayable in two years' time. This, of course, will cause some trouble for the company by that time, especially so if we look at Note 10 which shows capital commitments are as much as £57,000 at the end of the year.

The company is ploughing back the bulk of its profits and it could well afford to take out another loan. However, in the last year 12% had to be paid for a loan, and the amount that was raised was insufficient for the company's real requirements. Possibly the relatively high interest rate curbed the directors' willingness to borrow sufficient funds. Altogether the company has the elements of overtrading in it, and is not properly financed, so that it has continuing difficulty in meeting its current commitments as they become due.

BALANCE SHEET I — HIRE PURCHASE AND INSTALMENT CREDIT FINANCE

BALANCE SHEET RATIOS

	%		%
Capital and reserves	40.9	Goodwill	3.9
Loans	19.3	Fixed assets	87.0
Current liabilities (inc. bills payable)	39.9	Current assets	9.1
	100.0		100.0

Current ratio 0.27 Liquid ratio 0.15

Here, at first sight, we have a very odd situation in that fixed assets are so large and they are not paid for by the capital, or the capital plus the long-term liabilities. In fact, most of the current liabilities must be included before the fixed assets can be covered. The current ratio is very small, as also is the liquid ratio, and altogether the situation of the company looks a distinctly unhappy one. However, it is necessary to know something about hire purchase finance companies before coming to any proper conclusions about the balance sheet.

These companies generally have regular income coming from well spread contracts and they are, therefore, able to arrange for loan repayments to be matched against income coming in. If we look at the fixed assets we see that only £200,000 is in properties and the rest is either in plant and equipment on lease, or in rental equipment. These items are probably placed among the fixed assets as it is the income which is generated by putting the equipment out upon lease or rental which provides the income of the company. Nevertheless, much of the finance necessary to provide such equipment will appear among current liabilities. For example, acceptance credits can be arranged in such a way that they are repayable on a monthly basis and gradually run down or, alternatively, can be reinstated when more equipment is put out on rental. The same can apply to bills payable and to the loans which appear among the current liabilities.

It will also be seen that among other liabilities are bills payable and loans, and these will be the liabilities which do not require to be settled within twelve months of the balance sheet date. With this knowledge the balance sheet, of course, takes on a different aspect. Of course, it will be necessary to know if the liabilities are properly matched against income, and this can only be found out by proper enquiry of the company. If we assume that they are properly matched and that the profits generally remain at around £180,000/£200,000 we can see that the real current liabilities which must be matched against the current assets can be whittled down to:

	£
Taxation	40,000
Creditors	300,000
Bank overdraft	100,000
Dividends	1,000
Total	£441,000

This figure is, therefore, less than that of current assets. Naturally if the company is not properly run the deposits will quickly disappear, and renewal of acceptance credit lines and other loans will not be easy to obtain. Much, therefore, depends on the proper financial management of the company.

Another point we might note is that plant and equipment on lease remains in the ownership of the hire purchase company and all the capital allowances can be claimed by the company. We therefore see that the tax figure is very low in relation to the profit which, of course, is because of the capital allowances. An entry in respect of the timing difference would appear in the deferred taxation account.

		£
outside lenders	Deposits	200,000
	Loans	220,000
	Acceptance credits . . .	100,000
	Bills	800,000
	Bank overdraft	100,000
	Other loans	1,000,000
	Other bills payable . . .	300,000
		£2,720,000

How is the business financed? The proprietors have only provided £1,509,000 (£1,709,000 less £200,000 goodwill) and the company relies heavily on outside lenders, i.e. the £2,702,000 shown in the list above.

Outside lenders are providing more towards running the company than the proprietors, but this is not unusual for this type of company. If the proprietors are old established and of proved financial acumen lenders will put up much more than the proprietors. The sound running of the company in these circumstances is particularly important as otherwise loan funds will quickly be withdrawn or will not be renewed.

It is also to be noted that the figure for goodwill is the same in both years. This must be examined further as the Companies Act 1985 states that goodwill must be written off over a period chosen by the directors and must not exceed the useful economic life of the goodwill. Possibly an explanation could be that some writing off has taken place but more goodwill has been purchased in the year.

BALANCE SHEET J — CHAIN STORE COMPANY

BALANCE SHEET RATIOS

	Current year %	Previous year %		Current year %	Previous year %
Shareholders' funds	73.2	72.9	Fixed assets	85.7	86.5
Debentures	8.1	8.7	Current assets	14.3	13.5
Deferred tax	4.0	3.5			
Current liabilities	14.7	14.9			
	100.0	100.0		100.0	100.0

	Current year	Previous year		Current year	Previous year
Current ratio	0.97	0.91	Liquid ratio	0.42	0.41
Debtors/creditors	0.37	0.36	Net profit ratio	11.7	12.8
Debtors/sales	5.7 days	7.3 days	Stocks/sales	20.9 days	24.8 days
Working capital sales	nil	nil	Return on net assets	19%	16%
Dividend yield	6.5%	6%	Dividend cover	3.3 times	3 times
Debt ratio	1 to 91	1 to 83.5	Interest cover	30.2 times	23.9 times

This balance sheet is in the usual abbreviated form which is normally used nowadays. It would also be necessary to have notes attached to give the information required by the Companies Act, and to elaborate on some of the figures quoted. The notes are not attached in this instance as they are not required for analysing this particular balance sheet. As many ratios as can be calculated from the figures provided have been quoted in addition to the usual balance sheet ratios. With this information all the figures come immediately to light and we can get a good idea of the company's business.

Firstly we can see that the shareholders have provided the main part of the funds, but even so the shareholders' funds plus the debenture stock do not add up to sufficient to cover the fixed assets. There is only a small shortfall, however. Current liabilities in both years are in excess of current assets, but the amount involved is very small. In the current year it is only £10,000, and with a turnover of £3,500,000 per annum the turnover on one day will be approximately equal to the shortfall in the working capital. With this amount of cash coming in the company has nothing to worry about with its liquid position and, of course, profits are being made and if ploughed back into the working capital will soon redress the deficit. The liquid ratio is small, but this is of no consequence because, if we look at the detailed figures in the balance sheet, we see that the immediate payments are only for creditors and the dividend. This amounts to £215,000 whereas the debtors and cash total £155,000 and the cash coming in will enable the company to meet its liabilities quite easily. This is further emphasized by looking at the stock/sales ratio. In the current year stock is turned over every 20.9 days which is a remarkably quick turnover of stock. As it is not unusual to find that it takes companies 60 days on averge to collect their debtors it will be seen that in this particular company the stock is much more liquid than an average company's debtors.

The debtors/sales ratio is very small because most of the sales of this company are for cash. The return on net assets shows an increase from 16% in the previous year to 19% in the current year and, in fact, with all the ratios it will be seen that a better position is shown in the current year than in the previous year. The dividend yield, of course, will be important to shareholders and will affect the stock market price of the shares. It will be seen that the dividend is covered more than three times and the interest cover on the debentures is also adequate. The ratio of debt to shareholders' funds is very small indeed.

Looking now at the profit and loss account we see that in both years a good plough-back of profits is made and altogether the figures show the results of what must be a thriving company.

* * *

The specimen accounts examined here have disclosed the widest variations in the balance of the key ingredients in the balance sheet:

Proprietors' capital	varying from	88.2%	to	26.9%	of total funds
Current liabilities	,, ,,	73.1%	to	11.8%	,, ,, ,,
Fixed assets	,, ,,	90.5%	to	16.8%	,, ,, ,,
Current assets	,, ,,	83.2%	to	9.5%	,, ,, ,,
Current ratio	,, ,,	2.1%	to	0.3%	,, ,, ,,
Liquid ratio	,, ,,	1.3%	to	nil	

The same basic ingredients have been combined in differing proportions to produce dishes of infinite variety. A study of these differences and a search for the underlying reasons will bring home the lesson that no accounts can be read intelligently without a working knowledge of the nature of the particular business.

Lack of space has excluded the accounts of many types of undertaking – shipping, insurance, aircraft operation, contracting, building finance (building societies), catering, newspapers and a host of others, which all have features of special interest. The earnest student will take the opportunity of studying them all, item by item, as they come his way and will find it rewarding to build up his own dossier of varied balance sheets as an essential part of his technical library.

CHAPTER 16

Over-trading

Nature – General causes: inflation: taxation – Internal causes: mistakes of financial policy – Results – Signs in accounts – The cure

Judgment in lending is the real test of a banker's skill. The need of many would-be borrowers for increased cash resources is clear enough, but in a number of cases the advance would obviously entail so great an element of lock-up, that the banker would prefer not to become involved. A not insignificant number of the industrial and commercial concerns of this country – especially the smaller ones – are short of working capital and up-to-date equipment and still have a struggle to expand or even maintain their turnover: in fact are on the verge of over-trading.

The nature of over-trading is simply stated. It is a matter of trying to maintain a scale of operations with insufficient resources. An analogy suggested by our examination of cash circulation in Chapter 11, is that of an anaemic man striving to do work too heavy for him and in danger of final and fatal exhaustion. In accountancy circles over-trading is often graphically described as 'over-blowing the balloon'. It is an apt metaphor. Over-trading involves impressive size; an increasingly thin margin of safety; a sense of strain; and the danger of sudden collapse. Another analogy, equally helpful, is suggested by the proverb 'If too many irons are put in the fire, none will come out hot.' If the process is carried to the limit the fire may be put out altogether.

To appreciate the danger to a banker of over-trading by a borrowing customer and the importance of the banker's not becoming too far involved, he must have an understanding of:

(a) its causes;
(b) its effects;
(c) the warning signs which can be recognized in his customer's accounts, and in the bank account;
(d) the steps which can be taken to improve the position.

The causes of over-trading fall into two classes: general causes which affect all kinds of businesses and internal causes arising from the course of an individual business and from the temperament and financial policy of the proprietors themselves.

General causes

INFLATION AND TAXATION

One of the root causes of over-trading is inflation and the consequent general rise in prices and wages. To maintain a constant physical level of business, a manufacturer is now faced with a continually increasing tie-up of capital in fixed assets and in every one of the circulating assets. The problem of replacing or renewing fixed assets which deteriorate and become out of date is a continuing one. In addition the weight of increasing circulating assets in terms of money presses on manufacturer and merchant alike.

The accountancy profession has been well aware that, what has been called a modest rate of inflation, a rate of 3%–5% per annum, distorts accounts over a period of time. A rapid increase in the inflation rate brings more immediate problems. We have experienced inflation in the United Kingdom for a long time but this intensified during World War II and continued subsequently until the 1970s when rapid inflation was experienced. Costs then increased at unprecedented rates and it was not always possible to pass on the price increases. Some markets would not stand the increases and companies had to face a contraction in sales, or a drop in their margins. Statutory price controls were introduced for many products, and again this prevented companies from passing on increases in costs which they had suffered. The result has been to deplete the liquid resources of companies.

The 1980s have seen a reversal of the inflationary trend but it still remains a powerful troublesome force and only strong government pressure seems able to prevent a recurrence of the difficulties experienced when the inflation rate was well into double figures in the 1970s.

Historical accounting methods have not been adequate to make adjustments for inflation and the Government has not been prepared (except temporarily in the case of stock) to accept any adjustments for inflation when making calculations for taxation.

We have previously dealt with depreciation methods and have shown that depreciation as written off in accounts is insufficient to provide for replacement machinery. Extra sums have to be provided at the time of replacement merely to keep the business in the same position as it was previously.

Historical accounts have in fact been misleading because, in many cases, larger book profits have been shown whereas, after taking into account inflation and the extra funds required to run the businesses the real profits have decreased. Also as the historical profits have been taxable the combined result of the additional cash requirements for the businesses and the additional tax has been to deprive businesses of much needed liquidity.

Let us look at a simple set of accounts (Example 41) for a ten year period and imagine that an average inflation rate of 6% per annum persists over the period. This is not a high rate compared with what has been seen in the United Kingdom in the 1970s, and will therefore not overstate the case. An inflation rate of 6% per annum builds up to approximately 80% over a ten year period (6% for the first year, then 6% on the increased amount for the second year, and so on).

An opening balance sheet is shown, then a profit and loss account for the ten year period, and then a closing balance sheet.

It will be seen that the proprietors had a net worth of £417,000 at the outset and subsequently the company retained profits after payment of tax (assumed at 52%) and after payment of dividends of 11% (net of tax in shareholders' hands). The retained profits of £225,000 when added to the initial net worth of £417,000 gave a final net worth of £642,000. The company at the end of the period is in a very liquid state with cash of £316,000. One could easily be forgiven for thinking that the company had done well.

EXAMPLE 41

BALANCE SHEET 31ST MARCH

	£'000	£'000
FIXED ASSETS		
Freehold factory at cost		50
Plant and machinery at cost	200	
Less depreciation	20	180
Total fixed assets		230
CURRENT ASSETS		
Stocks	195	
Debtors	150	
Cash	34	
	379	
CREDITORS: AMOUNTS FALLING DUE WITHIN ONE YEAR		
Trade creditors	143	
Dividend	27.5	
Taxation	21.5	
	192	
Net current assets		187
		£417
CAPITAL AND RESERVES		
Called up share capital		250
Reserves		160
Profit and loss account		7
		£417

PROFIT AND LOSS ACCOUNTS SUMMARIZED, 10 YEARS TO 31ST MARCH

	£	£
Sales		11,318
Cost of manufacture	9,846	
Opening stock	195	
	10,041	
Less Closing stock	386	
Cost of sales		9,655
Gross profit		1,663
Less Overheads	441	
Depreciation	180	
		621
Disposable profit		1,042
Less Corporation tax at 52%	542	
Dividends	275	
		817
Retained profit		£225

Assumptions: 1. constant physical stock turned over four times a year;
2. steady increase in average prices;
3. trading profit 13% on sales.

The fact is, however, that although the net worth has increased by 54% the inflation rate has been much greater and liquidity too has not kept pace. The plant and machinery has now been fully depreciated and will need to be replaced; if we assume that new machinery costs 80% more than it did ten years previously the new machinery will cost £360,000 instead of £200,000. This purchase of machinery will absorb all the cash and also entail borrowing of £44,000 and the net current assets will be depleted by £360,000 to £232,000. The resultant figure is below the equivalent for net current assets at the beginning of the period. They were then £187,000 and if increased by 80% the equivalent would be £336,000.

Additionally we see that taxation has taken the large sum of £542,000. A corporation tax rate of 52% is a high one, but this does not tell the whole story. This is because taxation has been calculated on profits deduced from historical accounting methods, whereas the real profits are, in fact, much less. No allowance has been made for the imaginary profits on stock appreciation. More money is required, under inflationary conditions, to replace stock and merely to retain the same position, but the additional income being received from stock sales is taxed as profit before taking into account this fact. A similar position arises with replacement of machinery in that the additional £200,000 required for replacement has been taxed as profit whereas it is, really, a tax on the capital assets of the business. (Since

BALANCE SHEET AT END OF 10 YEARS

	£	£
FIXED ASSETS		
Freehold factory at cost		50
Plant and machinery at cost	200	
Less depreciation	200	nil
Total fixed assets		50
CURRENT ASSETS		
Stocks	386	
Debtors	252	
Cash	316	
	954	
CREDITORS: AMOUNTS FALLING DUE WITHIN ONE YEAR		
Trade creditors	266	
Dividend	28	
Tax	68	
	362	
Net current assets		592
		£642
CAPITAL AND RESERVES		
Called up share capital		250
Reserves		350
Profit and loss account		42
		£642

6th April 1974 for some years a measure of relief on stock appreciation was allowed, but has not been included in the example in order not to confuse the issue.)

The company has, therefore, been badly affected by two forces:

1. inflation: the retained profits have not been sufficient to cope with the effects of inflation and the effects have not been revealed by the accountancy methods used;
2. taxation: this has depleted the company of much needed liquid resources as the taxation rate has been high and has been calculated on profits from which insufficient allowance has been made for the replacement of capital. The result is, therefore, to put strain on liquidity.

Internal causes

1. DEPLETION OF WORKING CAPITAL

We have already examined the comparatively limited number of ways in which working capital can be depleted. All of these will ultimately, if not immediately, involve a disbursement of actual cash. The most common errors in financial policy which can bring about cash shortage and a condition of over-trading are:

1. denuding a business of essential cash and endeavouring to maintain the turnover without it;
2. attempting to expand the volume of business beyond what is justified by the resources available. The two policies often operate together.

A manufacturing company had been running successfully for many years with a turnover of £300,000, gross profit of £90,000 and net profit of £42,000 per year. The paid-up capital and reserves amounted to £60,000. The current assets had been steadily maintained at twice the amount of the current liabilities, with a very liquid position, cash in hand (some £66,000) more than covering current liabilities of £60,000. There was a change of control.

The new directors were not content to continue in the old-fashioned factory, held on a long lease at £3,000 per annum, as it restricted the prospects of expansion. They therefore decided to buy a larger factory for £165,000, borrowing £108,000 on the security of the freehold and using most of their available cash to complete the purchase. The change appeared to involve an increase in overheads of under £3,000 a year. In fact, it was found impossible to continue the business with the reduced working capital remaining, and the projected expansion of turnover was out of the question.

Within 12 months they were borrowing £42,000 from the bank under a comprehensive debenture. At the end of the second year they were £39,000 in excess, mostly on wages account, and at one time the total bank debt was as high as £120,000. The bankers then said 'No more'. Meanwhile creditors had become critically high at nearly six months' purchases. The circulation of current assets had been so clogged that the tie-up in stocks and work in progress was equivalent to nearly three months' production (as against an average of four weeks under the previous 'unenterprising' management). Bank charges alone exceeded twice the original rent: the management were distracted and at their wits' end; and instead of the former net profit of £42,000 a loss of £6,000 was made in the third year. Mainly by an ill-judged depletion of liquid resources a sound business had been brought within three years to the verge of collapse; and this in spite of the fact that by blood and sweat production had been maintained.

Sadder, wiser, and sobered by this staggering reversal of fortune, the directors decided to retrace their steps and re-liquefy their position by selling the factory to an investment trust, reserving a long lease to themselves at £9,000 a year. The penalty for their unfortunate finance will lie heavily on the company for many years. The business will be saddled with three times its former rent; a bank overdraft of £60,000; and an annual burden for bank interest and for reductions (which will have to be found out of net profits *after* taxation). On this basis the distributable profits will be less than half those available under the old regime. For obvious reasons certain facts and figures have been changed. But in all essentials this is a true story of over-trading brought about entirely by a voluntary over-investment in fixed assets. The same sort of effect will follow the voluntary depletion of cash resources by:

1. the premature repayment of long-term loans;
2. excessive drawings or dividend distributions;
3. the investment of cash in other businesses by way of loans or share purchase.

The most difficult case of all is where the fall in working capital is the result of losses. The constant replenishment of the cash pool from the most usual source – realized profits – no longer occurs. The position may well be reached where remaining resources are insufficient to finance an increased turnover; and without increased turnover sufficient gross profit cannot be earned to cover irreducible overheads and show a profit. Faced with this situation, the lending banker's problem is not to decide whether to step in; only when. A practical example is discussed in some detail in Chapter 18.

2. OVER-EXPANSION

During the Second World War the industry of this country was under official pressure to achieve maximum output of goods and manufactures needed for the war effort. It did not matter whether adequate capital was available or not. Very liberal assistance was given by the banks under the arrangements made with the appropriate government departments, who themselves assisted with factories and machinery, raw materials to be processed, and liberal progress payments. It was the heyday of the little man when, metaphorically speaking, the village blacksmith was encouraged to produce tanks. Every little back street had its workshop where essential work proceeded night and day under conditions which in normal times would reduce a factory inspector to apoplexy. But those times were not normal and after the war it was necessary to return to sound financing principles.

However it is easy to have over-emphasis on production as the supreme objective and an airy disregard of the elementary rules of sound finance and there is a natural tendency of the practical man to think in terms of the tangible things he knows and understands. When he allocates his available capital he remembers the workshop, the machinery, the jigs and the tools, and tends to ignore more remote considerations like working capital to finance stocks, work in progress and debtors. It is all very well to want to make money as quickly as possible and plan the most ambitious scale of production which can be financed. But there is a hard time before any *entrepreneur* who omits essential working capital from his calculations and fails to allow a wide margin for the unexpected which seems to happen so frequently.

Any banker with wide lending experience will have examined many budgets and financial forecasts in connection with advances. How often are they falsified by the event! Some of the most troublesome accounts are those where a concern has undertaken contracts beyond its power to finance. It has always been sound policy to make haste slowly: but never more essential than when the expansion of even the most successful business is heavily retarded by excessive taxation. Moreover, the greatest danger of over-expansion is just at the point where the business is most successful and the manufacturer or merchant, eager to make hay while the sun shines, extends his operations over as wide a field as possible. The seeds of over-trading are so often sown in the good years.

He gets caught worst who deliberately ignores warnings and goes on over-blowing the balloon until it bursts. All this is largely a matter of business sense and acumen; of knowing when to stop; and having enough strength of character to act accordingly.

The following typical case (disguised like the previous one, but the true story in essentials) will illustrate the dangers of over-enthusiasm.

A small one-man company was engaged in retailing certain bread-and-butter supplies and equipment to industry. On sales of £90,000 he was making a gross profit of £25,500 (29%) and a net profit of £10,000. The following year there was a shortage of supplies which reduced his sales to £63,000 but with gross profit £22,200 (35%), some savings in overheads still made possible a net profit of £9,000. A satisfactory little business; although at this stage an optimistic temperament, bewitched by the increased rate of gross profit, had led to considerable over-stocking, and creditors exceeded debtors by 112%. Stock at the end of the year was equivalent to six months' average sales, at £31,500. The accounts at the close of the following year showed sales back to £90,000, gross profit £27,000 (down to 30%), net profit £4,800 (overheads having risen by £7,500), and stock up to £40,500.

At this stage he took the balloon firmly between his lips and blew hard. He approached his bankers for as much finance as they were prepared to provide to build up stocks which would not be pressed for sale. Facilities up to £75,000 were sanctioned, partly against third party security and partly against a debenture. A warning was given that over-trading was dangerous and the scale of trading should be adjusted so that the account worked easily within the limit; and reduction at the end of twelve months would be expected.

The reduction did not materialize and the accounts for the next year showed why. Sales were up to £165,000 with gross profit £43,500 (now only 26%). Creditors were double at £42,000 and stock at £81,000. Apprehension about the heavy stock had promoted an expansion of the selling organisation during the year at a cost of £30,000 and a net loss of £8,700 was made. Nearly double the work and worry for worse than no reward!

The bank account had lost its resilience and instead of showing a healthy swing settled down heavily round the permitted limit, with occasional excesses as the following figures show:

Bank account
(limit after year 1, £75,000)

	Highest overdraft	Lowest overdraft
Year 1	£28,000	(in credit)
Year 2	£76,000	£38,000
Year 3	£84,000	£68,000

Vulnerable and difficult though his position had become, the merchant remained oblivious of his danger and went to his bankers for further help. He was prepared to explain away the smallness of his net profit and pointed with pride at the greatly increased turnover. He claimed that with continued support from the bank there was scope for even further expansion. Business was good, the outlook promising and the only difficulty was to meet the monthly accounts as they fell due – hardly surprising when the creditors' figure represented over six months' purchases. Further help was refused. Shortly afterwards this decision was more than justified when creditors started pressing, many suppliers refused further deliveries except against cash and a long fight back to a position of liquidity and safety began. This was only possible when a complete change of attitude took place: it would not have been possible at all had the crisis (which was never far way) been precipitated by any marked deterioration in general trading conditions. By no means all who so tempt fate are as fortunate.

It might well be wondered why the bank was so generous in providing the facilities without which such a disastrous over-trading position would not have arisen. Certainly it would have been better to refuse, but there are occasions when because of other connections of the customer, or the guarantor, a banker has to lend more than his reason tells him he should. In such circumstances all he can do is to point out the pitfalls and insist that sufficient security of a liquid nature is deposited to enable him to restore the lending to reasonable proportions if he so wishes.

Unfortunately, a man who thinks that all will come right if he increases turnover, regardless of the small resources upon which to do it, will rarely learn that overtrading is unsound. When his business collapses he will blame some unexpected event for his troubles and will not see that he has so over-extended himself that there was bound to be some unfavourable event which would topple him. If he gets a further opportunity he will generally over-trade again; he is unlikely to be deterred from pressing for a larger overdraft because a bank manager preaches good sense to him. Occasionally such a person will change his attitude, but this is very rare.

It may be as well to insert a reference here about what can be a dangerous form of over-trading which is sometimes practised. It is employed mainly by the merchanting community to enable them to carry a much higher turnover than their financial resources justify by making use of 'married' documentary credits. These are generally referred to as back-to-back credits. This is not the place for a detailed explanation but, briefly, they arrange for their banker to open a documentary credit in favour of the merchants from whom they are buying goods and at the same time arrange for their own buyers to open covering credits in as near as possible identical terms, so that their banker can take up the documents under the first credit and recoup himself with trifling delay by presenting them and collecting cost plus profit under the covering credit. There are numerous snags in this type of business and it is only necessary here to say that the security provided by the covering credit is by no means as complete as is sometimes supposed. When goods are in short supply and there is little risk of the ultimate buyer wishing to repudiate his bargain, things pass off quite smoothly. As soon, however, as a break in the seller's market occurs, there is no limit to the pretexts under which the buyer can refuse to accept the goods which are then left in the banker's hands or in those of his agent, often in a foreign country. There may then be no alternative but to re-ship them to a more suitable market at considerable expense or to sell them on the spot for what they will fetch.

Over-trading by means of confirmed credits is no sounder than over-trading in any other form, and the banker will be on his guard against supporting a customer with small capital too far in this direction. This is especially the case as the documents which may possibly be left in the banker's hands may themselves fall short of the desired standard and represent something less than a complete title to the goods. Even when the documentary business proceeds smoothly, technical difficulties are so frequent that often the banker finds himself in the position of having to give indemnities to secure payment, for which the counter-indemnity of the customer may be by no means adequate cover. Losses arising from such indemnities are likely to occur more frequently when trading conditions deteriorate.

The results of over-trading

Some of the effects of over-trading may be inferred from the two cases which have been described. They all follow, directly or indirectly, from a shortage, not primarily of assets, but of *cash* and may be briefly summarized as follows.

1. DIFFICULTY IN FINDING WAGES

This is the most immediate and dangerous result. If wages cannot be paid the balloon will be pricked at once and complete collapse will follow. The trader's dilemma is sometimes immediately passed on to his banker who is, quite unfairly, given the choice of finding the wages against his better judgment or putting his customer out of business. The banker's problem, as difficult as it is unpleasant, is to decide exactly when to say, 'No more!' In the case of a company the preferential position in liquidation of advances for wages may enable the banker to go a little further than would be safe if the customer were a sole trader or firm.

2. DIFFICULTY IN PAYING TAXES

PAYE payments, representing tax deducted under code from all wages and salaries, are payable monthly. Value added tax is payable quarterly, corporation tax once a year and advance corporation tax quarterly. Quite properly the Inland Revenue does not look kindly on trading with public money which is what in fact occurs when tax payments fall into arrears. And so pressure from the tax collector is often the proximate cause of bringing a company down.

3. INCREASED COST OF PURCHASES OWING TO:

(a) inability to accept special opportunities. In many a business opportunities arise from time to time to acquire stocks at bargain prices for cash. If cash is not available to snap up such bargain lots, substantial additional profits will be missed;

(b) hand-to-mouth buying. Bulk buying is cheaper than buying in small quantities. When cash is short and suppliers are becoming difficult the 'over-trader' may be forced to buy piecemeal at unfavourable prices;

(c) selecting sources of supply because long credit is obtainable, not on the prime criteria of quality, price and value;

(d) loss of discounts. One of the earliest effects of over-trading is inability to pay accounts early so as to earn the discounts allowed for prompt payment.

The extent to which cash discounts benefit a buyer is often not realized. Assume that purchases are £120,000 per annum and the monthly accounts are £10,000. Six weeks credit is received. The balance sheet will thus show creditors £15,000. Supposedly 2½% *actual* is allowed on prompt payment within 14 days. £10,000 is borrowed at 12% per annum: annual cost £1,200. Discount received during the year 2½% on total purchases £120,000=£3,000: Profit £1,800: surely a very good justification for the balance sheet reading:

	£
Loan	10,000
Creditors (2 weeks' credit) .	5,000

4. REDUCTION IN EFFECTIVE SALES FIGURE BY:

(a) pressing stock for sale. Where the particular form of over-trading involves the holding of excessive stocks these may have to be thrown on the market at drastically reduced prices;

(b) discounts allowed. Where the need for cash is pressing it may be necessary to tempt debtors into prompter payment by offering liberal discounts. This has the effect of reducing the sales figure.

5. EXPEDIENTS TO RAISE MONEY

After all normal securities have already been pledged, the harassed trader will be forced to try other expedients to raise cash. They may be many and various but they usually have this in common; they are all expensive. The following list is by no means exhaustive:

(a) charges over plant and machinery, often by sale to a finance company and buying back on onerous hire-purchase terms;
(b) sales of book debts, or factoring;
(c) unsecured loans at high rates justified by the real element of risk involved.

Such expedients usually weigh heavily upon the profit and loss account, even if the trading profit can be maintained.

It should be noted that because a company arranges sales and lease back, or factoring, it does not automatically follow that it is over-trading. These transactions can be perfectly sound financially for some companies; much depends on the circumstances. A company which is over-trading, however, is pressed for time and has insufficient strength to be able to bargain with the result that it has to pay dearly for the cash it requires.

6. GENERAL DIFFICULTIES WITH CREDITORS

When the trader has persuaded all those of his creditors who are willing to draw bills upon him (for a consideration) and thus extend his credit, he can do no more than resist, as far as he is able, the increasing pressure which will inevitably follow. A period of trying to stop too many holes with too little material will follow, fraught with worry and anxiety. Fear of writs and worse will be his constant companion.

Moreover, a considerable interruption in normal supplies will be inevitable, with unfortunate effects on production, sales and goodwill.

7. PRESSURE ON DEBTORS

In times of depression this will be unavoidable and may well cause resentment in the minds of good and long-standing customers who, perhaps are also affected and have their own difficulties. Irreparable damage to goodwill may result, which will affect not only current sales but future business when better times return. If the trader can induce his debtors to accept bills, some early cash may be secured by discounting; but, as has been stressed before, this is merely borrowing from the future to meet pressing liabilities in the present and may aggravate, while it temporarily postpones, the ensuing crisis.

8. OBSOLETE PLANT AND MACHINERY

Shortage of cash will inevitably prevent necessary replacements of machinery; and may even imperil proper maintenance. Inefficient working, with unavoidable interruptions for breakdowns and repairs, cannot fail to leave its mark both on the volume of production and the rate of gross profit earned.

Over-trading is, in effect, caused by a business being over-extended. An individual can generally appreciate when dealing with his personal finances that difficulties quickly follow when he has taken on commitments which are too large for his income, and the same applies in business. The effect is that the receipts are not sufficient to meet expenditure, extended credit has to be taken, top prices have then to be paid for supplies, profit drops and the snowball effect of this cycle continues and, in fact, becomes worse if at the same time the company is still trying to extend itself even more.

Most bankers must have been saddened by instances of sound businesses being brought to the verge of collapse and sometimes finally wrecked by over-trading. And it is saddest when the proprietors are worthy, hard-working men whose only fault is that their enthusiasm is greater than their financial acumen. So often the pathetic thing is that the immediate objective, increased turnover or better premises, plant and machinery, is achieved; but because working capital has been unduly depleted, the ultimate prize, increased *net* profits, eludes the grasp. The risks, the worries and the all too frequent penalties may be incurred for nothing.

It is, of course, all a question of degree. Merely to maintain production it is often imperative that plant and machinery be renewed. Obsolete and outworn plant will usually reduce profits for at least two reasons: maintenance charges will be unduly heavy; and breakdowns will involve loss of production. To expend money on essential replacements, and to borrow from the bank or elsewhere for the purpose, will be perfectly sound business provided cash resources are maintained at an adequate level. It is when the nice balance between fixed and working capital is unduly disturbed that trouble almost inevitably follows.

In protecting his bank from losses in difficult times in which over-trading will always be one of the greatest dangers, the wise credit man will look once at the accounts and twice at the man behind them. In his temperament or character the very first warning of this danger can often be discerned.

Nevertheless, a close watch on the accounts and any interim figures obtained is of vital importance.

Signs of over-trading in accounts

1. One of the earliest signs of over-trading in a company's figures is a tendency for the debtors/creditors ratio to fall progressively. This will happen when creditors increase more rapidly or fall more slowly than debtors. It may be caused by increasing difficulty in paying creditors as

they become due; by creditors remaining static or increasing with growing stocks while debtors fall in step with decreasing sales; and by an undue fall in debtors as a result of increased and generally undesirable pressure;

2. without corresponding increase in turnover (i.e. sales or production):
   (a) increases in bank borrowing or loans;
   (b) increases in creditors, usually accompanied by
   (c) undue increases in stock of all kinds – i.e. materials, work in progress and finished goods;
3. the appearance of bills payable where this is not customary and is not accounted for by changes in the nature of the business. This may indicate extensions of time by trade creditors (at a price) or borrowing on accommodation paper;
4. an unexplained reduction in bills receivable, suggesting discounting. This will be revealed by a footnote to the balance sheet referring to the contingent liability in respect of bills discounted, but can only be inferred from periodical interim figures by an undue fall in this item;
5. a fall in the working capital ratio

$$\text{i..e.} \quad \frac{\text{working capital}}{\text{production}} \quad \text{or} \quad \frac{\text{working capital}}{\text{sales}} \quad ,$$

   indicating increased business without a corresponding increase in working capital;
6. (a) In the early stages the rate of gross profit may be maintained with a steady fall in net profit owing to increasing expenses;
   (b) in the later stages there is a fall in the gross profit rate as well;
7. above all, a progressive fall in liquid resources, and in the ability of the undertaking to raise fresh money by borrowing, as one pledgeable asset after another goes into pawn. A fall in liquid resources can easily be seen by examining the statement of sources and application of funds which has already been discussed.

The bank account

The lending banker is in the fortunate position of having a source of information not usually available to other creditors, namely the bank account itself. The alert branch manager will keep an eye open for the following signs of over-trading:

1. an increasing tendency for excesses to occur, especially round the normal time for payment of the monthly accounts. There will be requests for permission to overdraw in anticipation of money which is certain to come

in next week or next month: in short, to borrow from future receivables to meet current payments. This is similar to an abnormal discounting of bills receivable, and equally a portent of growing difficulties;

2. a less vigorous swing between the highest and lowest balances over a week, a month or other suitable period. The balance will swing narrowly either side of zero; or either side of any overdraft limit which has been arranged;
3. continual pleas for assistance with wages, which at times provide for the banker a regular weekly problem;
4. a marked tendency for monthly accounts to be paid progressively later in the month. Often it will be found that cheques are drawn and dated at the usual time, but that their issue is deferred until cover is available in the account;
5. cheques to suppliers in even amounts suggest payments on account to keep creditors quiet. A similar but less easily detected sign is frequent and irregular payment, probably on a cash with order basis to suppliers who, in easier times, were paid once a month only. Each means that the customer is paying what he can, when he can: not when he should. An increasing number of smaller cheques is often seen, indicating that purchases are being made wherever credit and supplies can be found. When things become really difficult there may even be increasing drawings of actual cash from the bank, if that is the only kind of payment certain suppliers will accept.

The cure

In general the cure for a state of over-trading is simple enough to prescribe: either a smaller coat, or more cloth! But when the trader has already cut out half the coat on too large a scale and has insufficient cloth to complete the garment, there will be unpleasant gaps open to the chill winds.

It is easy enough to say to a trader who has bought too much stock on credit, 'You must concentrate on reducing your stocks and curtail buying.' But the cure is easier to prescribe than to follow. Stocks must take their time to turn into cash via debtors: the pace cannot be forced except at heavy loss, which will help no one. Curtailing buying is just as difficult. There is nothing a supplier dislikes more than stale and dormant accounts followed by the cessation of orders. To pursue such a policy is to invite heavier pressure for payment and a refusal to supply except for cash the odd lines which *must* still be bought.

Where over-trading has been induced or increased by an over-investment in fixed assets, it may be feasible to re-liquefy the position by finding someone else to invest the capital and by renting the fixed assets instead. This will be possible with land and buildings which are adaptable to many types of business and well situated for labour supplies and transport. It may not be so easy where the buildings are specialized, and the continuance of rent payments rests on the success of a business which is already in difficulties. That a concern takes the initiative in selling its own factory is a clear admission that all is not well. The same considerations apply to plant and machinery which can be sold to a hire-purchase company and re-purchased on hire-purchase terms. This is indeed giving hostages to fortune; for failure to maintain the payments will entail the loss of the plant which is the core of the business, and that may well mean the end of everything.

Whether the condition of over-trading is due to lack of wisdom or external misfortune, the only real cure is more cash. If that is not available there is no choice but to sell the business as a 'going concern', for what it will fetch, or to hang on grimly and fight and hope. It is here that the quality of the man behind the business will be really tested. Courage and resourcefulness transcend figures and balance sheets. There are cases where the banker, knowing his man, will withdraw his support at the earliest signs of serious over-trading: there are cases too where, knowing his man, the banker will be justified in backing him in spite of the figures. It is just here that the branch manager and his soundness of judgment, proved over the years and trusted by his head office, is of priceless value.

For customer and banker alike, however, better than any cure is prevention. The effects of serious and persistent over-trading can be so disastrous that it is better not to become involved at all.

Care should also be exercised in relation to borrowing schemes backed by Government or other agencies. The schemes that are continually being dreamt up are often hailed as new departures never thought of before but bankers with long memories will recall similar schemes being brought forward in the past. The fact that a guarantee may be forthcoming does not prevent overtrading. It often increases the risk. All such schemes should be examined against basic principles, although policy considerations may deem it wise to ignore some of the banking risks, on occasions.

CHAPTER 17

How much?

Balance sheet alone will not give the answer – Customer should state requirements – Why is advance necessary? – What for? – Nature of business – Effect on balance sheet – Is it enough? – Repayment – Relative size of banker's stake – What security – Character and capacity

Every reader who has followed the argument of this book so far will have realized that it is quite useless for a customer to hand his balance sheet to his banker and ask, 'How much can you lend against that?' The customer may have a trusting belief that a balance sheet is an 'open sesame' at once to the banker's heart and treasury. The banker himself should know better; he should not attempt an answer without much fuller information. There is no simple way of looking at a balance sheet and deciding on the amount which can be lent against it; there is no easy formula, and in any case a banker does not lend because a balance sheet is presented to him. He lends for a purpose; to finance a specific proposition. The proposition will have to be sound and worthy of support. Consideration of the strength of the balance sheet will then follow.

Fortunately the banker from whom an advance is sought is in a strong position to demand the fullest information and to require the production of balance sheets and full profit and loss accounts for a series of years, as well as detailed and up-to-date figures for current assets and liabilities. If full information is asked for at the outset *as a matter of course* it will be given with better grace than if it is asked for later with all the appearance of an afterthought. Where figures have to be examined in some detail it is advisable to defer full discussion until a second interview at which the presence of the customer's accountant will be invaluable. The contact thus made often enables the manager to clear up later queries direct with the accountant and with a minimum of trouble to the customer himself.

If the proposition is one the nature of which is outside the branch manager's own experience it cannot be too strongly urged that the advice of the head office advance specialist should be sought at the earliest possible moment and preferably before a second interview. Of necessity the latter's experience of all types of business will be wider than that of the branch manager, and he has at his disposal sources of information and assistance far more comprehensive. So often, where the manager is out of his depth and still tries to shape the proposal unaided, he will have to go back to his customer again and perhaps again for further information. This will at once irritate the customer and discredit the manager who should at all times be jealous of his position as the representative of the bank on the spot. He should endeavour to speak always with the voice of his bank; any reference at the interview to 'my head office' cannot fail to undermine his standing in the customer's eyes. The customer is quick to realize when the manager is a mere 'post office' between himself and the head office and is equally ready to be impressed when the manager handles the matter like a real banker.

The purpose of this chapter is to examine the extent and nature of that full information which a banker requires before he can give his decision. While it will confirm the impossibility of basing such a decision upon the accounts alone, it will show that nearly every further question is related to and often prompted by those accounts. Their place, their proper place, in bank lending will then be seen in clearer focus. The order in which the following points are set out has no significance: they may all be equally important in practice.

1. HOW MUCH?

Generally it is for the customer to indicate his requirements: not for the banker to say how far he is prepared to go. What the head office want, and are entitled to, is a proposition thoroughly hammered out in the manager's room after the manager has shaped it *as a banker*. But at whatever level the decision has to be given, whether at the branch or in the board room of the bank, the same rule applies: the customer should submit his complete proposal.

2. WHY DOES THE CUSTOMER REQUIRE BANK ASSISTANCE?

The last balance sheet may show a satisfactory liquid position: the banker will want to know what factors have brought about the need for further cash. Here up-to-date figures, preferably supplied by the accountant, may shed some light. Has working capital been depleted by the purchase of fixed assets, by dividends, by directors' fees, or by the repayment of fixed liabilities? Is the work in progress figure swollen: if so, why? Are there bottle-necks in production? Is the business over-stocked: if so, again, why? The causes may be over-trading, the development of consumer resistance or the emergence of competitive lines at more attractive prices. Have losses been made? Is current trading profitable?

3. WHAT WILL THE BANK'S MONEY BE USED FOR?

This question must be considered in the light of the following comments:

(a) will the money borrowed to pay tax and dividends deplete working capital unduly? If so, the self-liquidating character of a bank loan will be lost. Naturally, if profits are being made and sufficient are retained to restore the working capital to the right level for the business there should be no objection to providing bank funds for these payments, but if not the depletion of the working capital will cause strain;

(b) is money lent to pay creditors sound business? Money once obtained by a borrower is soon amalgamated into the overall business of circulating funds, or used for expenses, but if creditors have been pressing and bank funds are used to take off the pressure all that will have been achieved will be that the bank will have stepped into the shoes of the creditors and will likewise have to press for payment. If the money to pay creditors is required for normal business and perhaps to obtain discounts a valid reason for lending exists. The banker will then have to decide, as in (a), whether retained profits will repay the advance, or if it will be covered by the swing in the banking account;

(c) money required to finance stock or debtor tie-ups should not be lent without close enquiry into the liquid position. The banker will want to know why turnover and collections are slow. Where the money will be lent to subsidiaries special care is necessary. It is, however, often sound business to borrow from the bank in order to finance a special buying opportunity, promising a quick return;

(d) does increased turnover justify increased overdraft facilities? Not automatically. If a company's resources are relatively small a rapid increase in turnover could be a sign of over-trading. An increased overdraft may be justified to support increased turnover, but it may well be the case that more capital is required. What must be judged is the swing in the banking account in relation to increased turnover and whether any solid borrowing will be repaid over a short period by profits retained in the working capital of the business?

(e) advances granted to repay loans or capital are open to the criticism noted in (a) above. The result is often that the bank will merely stand in the shoes of the loan creditor and with just as little chance of reductions out of liquid resources as his predecessor had. Nevertheless there will be many occasions when such lending is quite satisfactory. It will depend on the profits being made and ploughed back to provide repayment;

(f) advances for the purchase of fixed assets may be quite sound business provided:

  (i) there are ample resources to finance any increased turnover which may result; and the transaction does not also involve an undue depletion of the working capital; as when the company is borrowing the loan value of the assets and finding the equity itself;

  (ii) reasonable reductions are in prospect out of profits after tax and the element of permanent lock-up is avoided.

There should be strong reasons for any departure from the sound rule that all fixed capital should be provided by the proprietors or long-term lenders, as well as at least a portion of the working capital. If this is not the case the company will have a negative amount of working capital.

It will be seen from the comments made that there is a common theme about lending to businesses. Overdraft lending is granted to deal with the uneven flow of receipts and outflow of payments, and is essentially related to working capital. It does not increase working capital as an overdraft is repayable on demand, and the amount of working capital remains the same. If the inflow and outflow cause a wide and frequent swing in the banking account to such an extent that the banking account at times reverts to credit the banker can feel quite happy about the overdraft facilities (security, if necessary, being satisfactory) and need not be concerned about reductions. If there is any hardcore borrowing or a loan account a reduction programme will be necessary. From what sources will reductions come? If fresh money is not to be injected then the business must make profits, part of which it must retain to provide the repayments, and the retained profits must, of course, be reflected in the working capital and not put into fixed assets. Similarly even if retained in the working capital the profits will not provide repayment if they are used to increase stock, or debtors, or to reduce creditors.

4. WHAT IS THE NATURE OF THE BUSINESS?

(a) any advance is to a business, not to a balance sheet. The banker will want to know whether the business is firmly established; with a good record; showing a satisfactory net return; and with a sound financial position. The trend of profits is significant. A balance sheet can have a great deal of strength and yet a change in management or conditions can reverse the profit experience and produce annual losses. Regardless of the strength of the balance sheet bank advances will not then work satisfactorily as, in the normal course, working capital will be depleted, and the banking account will show the strain and, if not controlled firmly, will reflect the losses with an increasing overdraft.

(b) how far does the success of the business depend on special contracts or concessions or a monopoly in a particular field? Contracts and concessions will terminate and a virtual monopoly may be undermined by new inventions and discoveries. In such cases it is important to delve thoroughly into the circumstances to establish that such advantages that are enjoyed are likely to continue;

(c) how far are the operations of the business confined to established lines? It may be attempting to exploit a new invention or to launch a new product. The risk of any such venture is normally not a banker's, but a proprietor's, risk. The invention or new product should first be *proved* at the expense of the company: then, and not until then, should the banker come in to finance further development. To use a simple illustration, it is for the customer to buy the vehicle and test it on the road: then the banker may be asked for some help to extend its range of operation. Inventors are notorious optimists. The banker must be on his guard against becoming involved with providing a banking advance which takes the risk which should properly be taken by the holders of the equity stake;

(d) what are the prospects for the applicant's *kind* of business? The banker's knowledge of affairs is usually wide enough to warn him when certain industries or commercial activities are running into difficulties. Sometimes it is farming which is in the doldrums; now the building industry; then motor servicing and garage business; later perhaps light engineering; or hotels. Budgetary and other government measures are potent influences today. A banker must continually keep up-to-date with the conditions surrounding the businesses to which he is lending and with economic conditions generally. This experience will then enable him to judge when the time has come to be wary.

(e) what are the prospects for that *particular* business? The factors to be considered are the quality of its management; the political and economic state of the normal market for its particular goods or services; and the suitability of its location in relation to supplies, transport, labour, and markets. Many a banker will know of retail businesses which have failed because of being opened on the wrong side of the street. That is why large retail chains now research thoroughly the sites of new premises before opening.

5. EFFECT ON THE BALANCE SHEET

How will the balance sheet look when the advance has been taken and used in the way proposed? This should always be considered with care. A balance sheet is a matter of nice equipoise. Will the balance of fixed and current assets be upset? Will the working capital be increased or decreased? The more far-reaching or complicated the proposal, the more important is this second look at the balance sheet.

6. WILL THE ADVANCE BE ENOUGH?

There is nothing a banker dislikes more than to put his hand to the plough and be unable to see it through to the end of the furrow. On occasions he has to say, 'You ask for £10,000. It is not enough. I will lend £20,000 or nothing. Let us see if £20,000 can be justified.' Obviously it is unwise to agree to the £10,000 only to find that in six months time the alternative is to break the business or put up more money. The long view will ensure that the banker does not become involved until the full extent of his possible commitment has been explored. It is here that the working capital ratio provides, if not an absolute criterion, at least the starting point for a carefully worked out budget for as long a period and in such form as the nature of the proposal requires. Ideally an estimated profit and loss account and a cash budget on a monthly basis should be provided as dealt with in Chapter 1, but so often these important financial planning documents are not available. A banker then has to make estimates which, of necessity, must be more cautious than would otherwise be the case.

7. THE SOURCE OF REPAYMENT

It must be stressed once more, in connection with the questions a banker should ask before making or enlarging an advance, that basically, bank lending should be temporary. It is not a bank's function to embark with its eyes open on lock-up lending. No banker should make a house-purchase advance to a widow of slender means if he knows (or should know after making suitable enquiries) that he can obtain repayment only by turning her into the street or waiting until she dies. The first will involve damage to his reputation; the second the surrender of essential banking liquidity. Exactly the same considerations apply to large-scale advances to companies. Before the advance is made is the time to remember that reduction or repayments can only come from:

(a) non-revenue cash receipts;

(b) conversion of circulating assets into cash.

Excepting to the extent that circulating assets are standing at, or will be built up to, an abnormal level; or are augmented by profits *after tax*; source (b) can produce reductions only by a running down of the scale of operations.

It is not the function of a bank to provide from its customers' funds the permanent capital of a business. The only time when this is justified is on a temporary basis pending the raising of more capital, or the injection of long-term funds.

8. RATE OF REPAYMENT

The examination of the rate or repayment involves two considerations:

(a) what period of profitable operation can be relied on in view of the nature of the business? This is of paramount importance where it depends on patents, concessions, rapidly wasting fixed assets, or generally on the temporary nature of the conditions essential to the earning of its profits. It is often possible to say that the advance is justified only if it can be repaid in, say, five years. That brings us to the second question;

(b) will the rate of reductions considered essential under (a) be within the capacity of the business? If not, clearly the banker will ask to be excused. In considering the many imponderables involved – the rate of profit, the risk of competition, the possibility of fiscal charges, the chances of heavier or lighter official controls – the banker may properly give some weight to:

(i) the scope for curtailing dividends or drawings if his requirements cannot otherwise be met. Where such drawings are already small the banker must normally rely on actual profits after tax to meet his requirements;
(ii) the cushion provided by the solid fixed assets.

9. THE PROPORTIONATE STAKE

At every stage in the granting or control of a bank advance, the banker must be on his guard against having too large an interest in the success of the business. No banker can reasonably be asked to play with the business community on the basis of 'Heads I win, tails you lose'. Bank finance is normally the cheapest finance, and while finer rates may be quoted for lending against first-class security even the banker's highest remuneration is not assessed on a risk-bearing basis. The proprietors' or shareholders' stake, as represented by the true net worth figure, must therefore always be large enough to cover the area of risk. If the business succeeds the proprietors reap the reward of their enterprise and efficiency; if it fails they should stand the loss. The banker asks no more than his interest and a reasonable remuneration for his services. He is certainly entitled to ensure that the commercial risk, which he is not paid to carry, is squarely borne on other shoulders. Kaleidoscopic changes, as swift as they are startling, sometimes catch him unawares: then losses are made. But the principle is sound: the proprietors' stake should cover all forseeable risks.

10. SECURITY

After the customer has formulated his requirements and presented his proposals the banker will have to judge whether he can support the request, and will also have to judge whether he needs security. If the security is strong the banker may be able to go further than he would otherwise be prepared to go, but he will not wish to be in a position of thinking that the most likely way of retrieving his advance will be to realize the security. It is the proposition which is important and the money generated from it should provide the repayment.

It will suffice here to mention that when third party security is lodged conferring a right of double proof the banker may be able to go a little further than if the same security were lodged by the actual borrower. Briefly this means that in the event of bankruptcy or liquidation the banker can prove for the full amount of the debt against the debtor's assets and still look to the full value of the third party security for any shortfall. The general consideration of various types of security is outside the scope of this book: but the margin required ought always to be sufficient to throw the burden of value fluctuation on the shoulders of the borrower.

11. CHARACTER

Bankers have traditionally looked at three aspects when considering advances. These are known as the three C's: capital, capability, and character. All are important. A man without capital is not afraid to lose someone else's money; he does not become the risk taker himself. Obviously capability is important or the funds lent may be written off as lost at the outset. Character is a very vital ingredient, especially in times of adversity. The personal evaluation by the lending banker is crucial.

(a) *Frankness* is vitally important. A banker likes to know that the customer has put all his cards on the table, face upwards;

(b) *Integrity* is the first consideration, and not mere fair-weather integrity. In any advance which is not fully secured on solid saleable assets, and particularly in an advance where substantial amounts are lent against current assets under a floating charge, the lender has to rely on periodical figures supplied by the directors (certainly as regards stocks and work in progress) and is very much in his customer's hands.

One case – fortunately not of a kind which occurs frequently – comes to mind where a receiver was appointed under a debenture. Before he could take over the stock which should have been ample to clear the bank debt it was spirited away and some of it was finally tracked down hidden in empty bricked-up shops all round the perimeter of London. Debtors had been collected with a similar disregard of normal business honesty: no doubt it was felt that the bank was fair game.

The accounts of a private company will sometimes show that the business has been milked by the directors, a potent cause of deficient working capital. Where this has been carried so far that the safety of the creditors is threatened it verges on dishonesty;

(c) *business capacity* is almost as important. The bad debt experience of the banks would be happy indeed if losses were made only when dealing with rogues. Serious and frequent losses arise also from incapacity which will now be considered under three sub-headings:

(i) *inexperience.* The past record of those responsible for a business which seeks financial assistance from a bank should always be closely examined. The rolling stone is a poor credit risk. Such weakness should be apparent to any alert banker. What is not so easy to detect is the risk of failure in a new enterprise of people who have been successful in their previous line of business. It requires nice judgment to decide whether a retired stockbroker will succeed as a farmer, or an ex-army officer as an hotel-keeper. No rules can be suggested; but the closest enquiry into the borrower's background is essential;

(ii) *financial acumen.* The lack of financial experience can wreck a sound business. Technical knowledge, drive and energy are not enough. The banker can often save himself and the customer worry and even loss by judicious advice; or by recommending a knowledgeable partner or introducing a sound accountant. Even then he has to assess the extent to which his customer can be relied on to accept and follow sound advice. This brings us to the third consideration;

(iii) *defects of temperament.* There are many characteristics which can make a borrower a poor credit risk. Pigheadedness will keep a man on his chosen course long after he should have recognized its unwisdom; over-trading is one such course. Greed, an anxiety to get-rich-quick and 'hang the risk', is nearly always dangerous. Allied to a gambler's temperament it may be fatal. Reluctance to cut a loss, often allied to a facile optimism, is a menace to customer and banker alike. To some, early success and achievement produces the over confidence which leads to disaster. The man who is reluctant to learn his business thoroughly and expects to start half way up the ladder may find it easier to borrow than to repay.

The moral of all this is, 'Know your man.'

CHAPTER 18

Practical Advance Control

Accounts record form – Its value in use – Adequacy of facilities – Importance of clear lending basis – Interim figures: their nature and use – The importance of wages – Loans by directors – Creditors' reaction to debentures

Advances in which the main consideration is the balance sheet position fall into two main classes. There are those where the position is so manifestly sound that the advance can be left to take care of itself. No security whatever is considered necessary and the annual balance sheets suffice. There are those where a debenture is taken and reliance is placed not only on a charge on the fixed assets but also on a floating charge over the current assets. Where the lending is against current assets to any substantial extent, quarterly or even monthly figures are desirable: the nearer to the risk-line, the closer the supervision necessary. Much of this chapter will be devoted to the figures which are necessary – throwing a progressively wider net as the need for watchfulness grows – and to the use which can be made of such figures.

Whether, and how frequently, confirmation of interim figures by the company's auditors is required, or by investigating accountants appointed independently by the bank, depends largely on the extent of the lending and the banker's estimate of the reliability of the management and the standing of the company's own auditors. It has already been pointed out that normally little direct protection is afforded by an auditor's certificate as far as the stock figures are concerned. There is no doubt, however, that in certain cases the fact that accountants (whether the company's or appointed by the bank) will supply certificates to the bank which will be placed alongside figures already provided by the directors, will often have a salutary psychological effect. An accountant's interim report is therefore a safeguard not to be discarded lightly.

Accounts record forms

The starting point of all balance sheet advances is a series of accounts, preferably for three or more years, which should be uniformly analysed and recorded in a way which will facilitate year by year comparisons and bring to the surface the salient points of both balance sheet and profit and loss accounts. The ideal form, as far as the balance sheet is concerned, would be that set out in Chapter 2, Example 12, but it would require a double column for each year, and some compactness and ease of comparison with the figures of previous years would be sacrificed. Example 42 shows a suitable compromise form, completed for 'Manufacturers Limited' for three years. The working capital figures for three years (Example 18) have already been given. The complete accounts for the three years will be found in Appendix 1.

EXAMPLE 42 Accounts record form

Customer: **'Manufacturers Limited'**

	A	B	C
	£	£	£
I CURRENT LIABILITIES			
Bank	—	—	5,000
Corporation tax	12,000	10,000	14,000
Creditors	5,000	17,000	43,000
Provisions	5,000	15,000	10,000
Bills payable	—	—	—
Loans	—	—	—
Total current liabilities	22,000	42,000	72,000
LONG-TERM LIABILITIES			
Mortgages	—	—	—
Debentures	70,000	70,000	70,000
Loans	—	—	—
CAPITAL AND RESERVES			
Capital	100,000	100,000	100,000
Reserves	30,000	30,000	30,000
Profit and loss account	10,000	14,300	13,600
	£232,000	£256,300	£285,600
II CURRENT ASSETS			
Cash	9,000	10,000	—
Marketable investments	3,500	—	—
Debtors	24,500	17,000	17,000
Bills receivable	7,500	5,000	—
Stock	25,000	50,000	60,000
Work in progress	7,500	15,000	50,000
Total current assets	77,000	97,000	127,000
FIXED ASSETS			
Freeholds	98,600	98,600	98,600
Leaseholds	—	—	—
Plant and machinery	50,000	55,000	55,000
Motor vehicles	—	—	—
Fixtures, fittings, tools and equipment	5,000	5,000	5,000
Investments (not marketable)	—	—	—
Loans	—	—	—
INTANGIBLE ASSETS			
Discount on debentures	1,400	700	—
Adverse profit and loss	—	—	—
	£232,000	£256,300	£285,600

	A	B	C
	£	£	£
III BALANCE SHEET NOTES			
[1]Net worth	138,600	143,600	143,600
Working capital	55,000	55,000	55,000
Current ratio	3.5	2.3	1.75
[1](after deducting intangible assets)			
REVENUE ACCOUNT NOTES			
Sales (or production)	212,000	390,000	354,000
Gross profit	97,000	87,250	49,000
Gross profit, per cent	45.8	22.4	13.9
Overheads	41,900	33,500	28,500
Net profit on ordinary activities before taxation	56,600	53,750	20,500
Taxation	35,000	23,750	10,500
Net profit on ordinary activities after taxation	21,600	30,000	10,000
Drawings or dividends	25,000	25,000	10,000

Without unduly enlarging the analysis it is not possible to record on the accounts record form all the matters of interest. Essentials only have been retained. The vital totals of current liabilities and current assets can be seen at a glance. The main classes of liabilities and assets are clearly segregated. The proprietors' claims items appear separately at the end of the first section; the intangible assets which should be deducted therefrom, to ascertain the true net worth, are last in the second.

The third section is invaluable. A word is, perhaps, desirable about the profit and loss account figures. The figure – sales (or production) – will indicate the magnitude of the total operations for the year, and can be usefully compared with the working capital position. An expansion in turnover without an expansion in resources can be embarrassing, and even dangerous. If there has been a material rise (or fall) in the amount of work in progress during the period the amount of such rise (or fall) must be added to (subtracted from) the sales figure to ascertain the true out-turn of the business.

The inclusion of the overheads (which is the total of the debits to the profit and loss account) focuses attention on the most important source of gross profit leakage. If net profit plus overheads exceed the gross profit shown, it indicates non-trading credits in the profit and loss account which should be referred to if the difference is of significant amount. No attempt has been made to devise headings for the appropriation account as the items may vary a great deal from year to year. Only the most significant figure, dividends, has been extracted. If the remaining amount of net profit (not shown) does not agree with the increase in the final profit and loss balance in section I, the appropriation account itself should be referred to for the explanation.

The following notes will demonstrate how this accounts record form can be read: the salient points are:

1. the progressive disappearance of cash and marketable investments: £12,500, then £10,000, then bank overdraft, £5,000;
2. the marked fall in the current ratio;
3. a very definite deterioration in the liquidity of the circulating assets. Expressed as percentages of the total current assets, the figures are:

	Year A	Year B	Year C
	%	%	%
Cash and marketable investments .	16	10	—
Debtors	32	17	13
Bills receivable	10	5	—
Stock	32	52	47
Work in progress	10	16	40
	100	100	100
Current liabilities	29%	43%	57%

4. the upward trend of stock and work in progress is out of step with the fall in debtors: they should all rise together if the business, i.e. both production and sales, is expanding normally;
5. the fall in debtors in year B is out of step with the increased sales and suggests a big falling off in sales in the last few months of the financial year, and possibly pressure to increase collections;
6. in step with increased stocks, creditors have increased faster than debtors; substantial over-buying is indicated;
7. bills receivable, which in year B fell with sales rising, disappeared in the following year. The suspicion that they may have been discounted is borne out by a footnote to the year C balance sheet.[1]
8. there does not appear to have been any provision for depreciation of plant and machinery and the other fixed assets in years B and C, in spite of the increased production and probable increase in actual wear and tear. This is confirmed by the accounts themselves;[1]
9. there was insufficient cash in hand to meet the final dividends in years B and C. In the latter year the proposed dividend could only be paid by substantially increasing the bank overdraft. In each year adequate profits had been made, but dividends exceeded the net profit after tax in year A; in year B the surplus of £5,000 ploughed back went into plant and machinery and in year C the current assets had become very illiquid;
10. in spite of the increased sales and (from the accounts[1]) production in years B and C, both working capital and net worth remained static. The resources of the business have not kept pace with its expansion;
11. the apparent fall in overheads is revealed by the accounts[1] to be due to the omission of depreciation provisions in years B and C; an explanation must be obtained;

[1] Appendix 1.

12. the fall in net profit is due to the fall in the gross profit: had adequate depreciation been charged, the fall in net profit would have been greater. In year C the net profit might well have disappeared altogether, and no dividend could properly have been declared;
13. looking to the accounts[1] for the explanation of the fall in gross profits, it will be seen that in year B the main fall was in the factory profit, while in year C both factory and merchanting showed reduced profits, the greater fall being in the latter;
14. a reasonable general inference from the figures is that:
    (a) the first year was normal, the second opened in boom conditions under which a large expansion was initiated;
    (b) towards the end of year B conditions deteriorated, production was affected, and sales began to fall away;
    (c) in year C a slump developed, and sales resistance caught the company in an over-stocked position;
    (d) the fall in the rate of trading profit is consistent with a break in selling prices, reducing both sales and end-year stock valuations.

Some uses of the record form

From an examination of the accounts record form alone it is therefore possible in practice to detect many material trends. It will nearly always repay close and thoughtful study. But, as the foregoing analysis will have made clear, its main value lies in directing the banker to the accounts themselves for further information.

In one instance it was noted that the stock figure in the accounts of a manufacturing company, which was earning good profits, was rising steadily year by year, without any corresponding increase in sales. Nor was there an excessive increase in creditors, or a loss of swing in the bank account, from which over-trading could have been inferred. Enquiry revealed that the stock growth was accounted for mainly by the accumulation of a by-product for which there was no outlet valued year by year on the basis established sometime before when there had been a ready market. The banker thus found that his lending value for the stock had to be drastically reduced. But he did more. He put his customers in touch with a live firm of chartered accountants who were able to persuade the Inland Revenue that for years past profits had been mistakenly overstated by reason of the progressive and erroneous over-valuation of stock and that a substantial refund of taxation was due to the company. Later he contacted some industrial friends who were able to use the by-product. The result was the receipt of much-needed cash capital and a permanent addition to the company's profit-earning capacity: and for the bank a satisfactory advance in place of one which had begun to give some cause for anxiety.

[1] Appendix 1.

EXAMPLE 43

Extract from accounts record form of 'XYZ Limited', Contractors

	Year A	B	C	D	E	F	G	H
	£	£	£	£	£	£	£	£
Bank overdraft	84,480	111,140	139,180	201,700	165,240	178,260	188,680	183,480
Creditors	39,200	48,200	43,700	50,200	53,800	70,850	23,000	36,200
Debtors	104,000	131,000	132,000	106,000	95,000	116,000	95,000	60,400
Work in progress	97,500	150,500	143,500	209,700	163,700	171,000	144,000	171,300
Adverse profit and loss	32,000	25,880	31,360	58,500	82,080	89,000	101,980	117,900
'Net worth'	126,700	132,820	127,340	100,200	76,620	79,700[1]	66,720	50,800
Sales	450,000	400,000	345,000	410,000	284,000	398,000	362,000	267,500
Gross profit	85,500	82,000	72,120	58,020	54,460	73,740	71,040	68,160
Per cent	19	20½	21	14½	19	18½	21	25
Overheads	99,300	75,880	77,600	85,160	78,040	80,660	84,020	84,080
Net loss	13,800	6,120 (profit)	5,480	27,140	23,580	6,920	12,980	15,920

[1] Share capital increased by £10,000

In a previous chapter some comments were made on over-trading following a succession of trading losses and consequent depletion of the company's working capital. The salient figures have been extracted from the accounts record form of such a company and are set out in Example 43.

The following points will be noted:

1. in only one of the eight years has a net profit been made;
2. the main cause is high and apparently irreducible overheads;
3. as a result of the accumulated losses the bank's stake increased in the period from 66% of the 'net worth' to 361%;
4. the bank overdraft had been held at £180/190,000 only by diminishing the scale of operations and with disastrous effects on production and on the burden of overheads per unit of production. The tie-up in debtors and work in progress at the end of year H represented no less than 78% of the total year's production (£294,800, made up of sales £267,500 plus increase in work in progress, £27,300);
5. the marked fall in creditors disproportionate to falling production suggested the curtailment of credit on a substantial scale.

At an interview the managing director stated that production could easily be expanded by 60% if the bank would grant additional facilities of, say, £50,000. Accepting the company's figures as a basis for investigation, the banker was able to present the following picture:

	£	£	
Turnover, year H		295,000	
60% increase		175,000	
Estimated turnover		£470,000	
Gross profit thereon @ 25%		117,500	
Less Overheads, year H	84,000		
Estimated increase (say 30%)	25,200		
Increased bank charges	5,000		
			114,200
Estimated net profit			£3,300

Even on this optimistic estimate, based on an expansion which would involve a great deal more work and worry for the management, there would only be a profit of £3,300 to provide a reward for the extra work and for reductions in the bank borrowing. But the scheme had to be rejected because:

1. the bank's stake in the business was already excessive;
2. the £50,000 asked for would not be nearly enough. On the year H figures an increase of £175,000 in production would require £115,000 more working capital, calculated as follows:

	£
60% increase in debtors and work in progress	136,500
Less Increased creditors, 60% of £36,200	21,700
Increased working capital required	£114,800

It was not possible for the proprietors to find the necessary new money, even if it could have been justified on business grounds. With the support of the company's accountant it was not difficult to convince the directors that they were 'flogging a dead horse' and the interview terminated with an agreed decision for the bank to put in a receiver and manager under its debenture, with the full co-operation of the company. The position had long since been reached when the only way in which the bank borrowing could be cleared was by the winding up of the business; it was only because the character of these old customers was first class that the decision taken had been deferred. A position of acute over-trading had been brought about by progressive shrinkage of working capital, the result of successive losses.

A strong argument available in this case was that the managing director was already working near breaking point for a mere pittance, which was all the business had been able to afford for years: and the suggested expansion would have produced a negligible reward for even greater efforts. It was agreed that only one criticism of the bank could possibly be made: that it had carried an obviously deteriorating position for far too long.

Adequacy of facilities

The need to test at the outset the adequacy of facilities sought for the purpose of financing an increased turnover has already been stressed. An actual case will illustrate the necessary calculations.

EXAMPLE 44

Manufacturing account. Year ended 30th June, year A

	£		£
Opening stock	120,000	Sales	1,480,000
Purchases	650,000	Increase in work in progress	50,000
	770,000	Total production	1,530,000
Less Closing stock	110,000		
Materials used	660,000		
Wages	410,000		
Other expenses	30,000		
Cost of production	1,100,000		
Manufacturing profit (28%)	430,000		
	£1,530,000		£1,530,000

Profit and loss account

	£		£
Directors' fees . . .	80,000	Manufacturing profit .	430,000
Rent	15,000	Sundry receipts . .	20,000
General overheads . .	200,000		
Net profit	155,000		
	£450,000		£450,000

Appropriation account

	£		£
Proposed dividend . .	40,000	Balance from last year .	65,000
Corporation tax . .	80,000	Net Profit . . .	155,000
Balance	100,000		
	£220,000		£220,000

In August year A 'Home Supplies P.L.C.' seek an overdraft of £200,000 to finance the purchase of a factory £250,000 and additional plant and machinery £100,000 and to finance an increase of £300,000 (say 20%) in turnover, guaranteed under firm long-term fixed price contracts; and produce the above revenue accounts and balance sheet. A regular supply of raw materials is assured. It will take three months to establish the increased production in the new factory.

To meet the £350,000 cost of the additional fixed assets, the customers propose to borrow £200,000 from the bank, utilizing £150,000 of their existing cash resources to cover the balance; and to reduce the overdraft by £50,000 in the first year out of anticipated profit, viz. 28% on £300,000=£84,000.

The working capital ratio,

$$\frac{220,000}{1,530,000} = 14.3\%$$

will provide a check on the adequacy of the amount sought.

	£	£
14.3% of increased turnover, £300,000 . .		42,900
Fixed assets to be bought	350,000	
Add Legal expenses (say)	10,000	
		360,000
Total additional capital required . . .		402,900
Less Cash available	200,000	
Less dividend	40,000	
		160,000
Overdraft necessary		£242,900

In these figures no allowance has been made for any margin for unforeseen events, and it would not have been unreasonable for the company to have added on a margin making their actual requirement, say, £270,000 and not £242,900. However, a margin must not be just a figure for which there is no basis, but should be carefully assessed.

BALANCE SHEET AS AT 30TH JUNE YEAR A

	£	£
FIXED ASSETS		
Intangible assets		
Goodwill		50,000
Tangible assets		
Plant and machinery at cost less depreciation		80,000
		130,000
CURRENT ASSETS		
Stock	110,000	
Work in progress	80,000	
Trade debtors	160,000	
Cash	200,000	
	550,000	
CREDITORS: AMOUNTS FALLING DUE WITHIN ONE YEAR		
Trade creditors	190,000	
Other creditors – taxation	80,000	
expenses	20,000	
Proposed dividend	40,000	
	330,000	
Net current assets		220,000
Total assets less current liabilities		£350,000
CAPTAL AND RESERVES		
Called up share capital		250,000
Profit and loss account		100,000
		£350,000

Working capital £220,000

Our figures which have brought into account certain items omitted by the company indicate that the £200,000 sought will not be enough and prompts a further analysis of the position as set out in Example 45.

EXAMPLE 45

Immediate cash requirements

	£		£
Present cash in hand	200,000	Purchase of factory	250,000
Overdraft required *now*, to balance	225,000	Legal costs	10,000
		Plant and machinery	100,000
		Installation costs	5,000
		Dividend	40,000
			405,000
		Minimum cash in hand *Note (iii)*	20,000
	£425,000	Required *now*	£425,000

Estimated position by end of year 30th June

	£	£		£
Estimated net profit as last year		155,000	Total brought down	225,000
Note (i) *Add* Gross @ 20% on £300,000 for nine months		45,000	Taxation	80,000
Saving in rent		15,000	Increase in normal overheads (estimated)	30,000
20% Increase in creditors:			Bank charges	20,000
Trade	38,000		Loss of profit due to transfer to new factory (estimated)	30,000
Expense	4,000	42,000		
		257,000		
Note (ii) Deduct 20% increase in circulating assets		70,000		
		187,000		
Note (iii) Closing bank overdraft (to balance)		198,000		
		£385,500		£385,000

Note (i). For the purpose of this calculation a conservative 20% gross profit has been assumed on the increased turnover for the nine months, instead of the 28% earned in the previous full year.
Note (ii). This is a *cash* analysis: consequently a deduction must be made for cash absorbed in increased non-liquid assets.
Note (iii). On the footing that £20,000 is kept available in case of need, but is not actually required at 30th June, the overdraft will be £20,000 less at £178,000 as shown in the balance sheet which follows.

These figures foreshadow the following balance sheet position in June year B (Example 46).

EXAMPLE 46

ESTIMATED BALANCE SHEET AT 30TH JUNE YEAR B

	£	£
FIXED ASSETS		
Intangible assets		
Goodwill		50,000
Tangible assets		
Freehold factory at cost		260,000
Plant and machinery at cost subject to depreciation		185,000
		495,000
CURRENT ASSETS	420,000	
CREDITORS: AMOUNTS FALLING DUE WITHIN ONE YEAR		
Trade creditors	252,000	
Bank overdraft	178,000	
	430,000	
Net current liabilities		(10,000)
Total assets less current liabilities		£485,000
CAPITAL AND RESERVES		
Called up share capital		250,000
Profit and loss account (subject to tax on £135,000)		235,000
		£485,000

Negative working capital £10,000 with taxation still to be assessed

	£		£
Profit calculated as follows		*Less* increase in overheads	30,000
Estimated net profit as last year	155,000	bank charges	20,000
Add profit on increased turnover	45,000	loss on transfer to new factory	30,000
Saving on rent	15,000		80,000
		Profit for year	£135,000
	£215,000		£215,000

This estimated balance sheet is subject to provision for taxation on the profits of the year, which will not however affect the cash position immediately. This analysis shows that the original estimate of £200,000 as the peak requirement is totally inadequate. Although the overdraft can be brought down to £178,000 (because of the profit earned) by 30th June year B, it will be seen that the promised reduction of £50,000 (from £200,000 down to £150,000) cannot be achieved. If debtors were pressed and creditors extended it might be possible, but there could be some harm to the company in adopting such measures. Also, of course, the dividend of £40,000 paid for year A could not be repeated for year B, and it must not be forgotten that tax has to be paid on the profit of £135,000. It will be seen that the request for a limit of £200,000 with reductions of £50,000 in the first year is totally unrealistic; there is no point in asking for inadequate facilities. For efficiency, the amount of bank facilities must be correct for the company or its business will suffer.

The request should really have been for £270,000 (dependent, of course, on the margin necessary over the figure of £242,900). As for the reduction programme this must be within the capabilities of the company. We see that profits of £135,000 (subject to a deduction for depreciation of plant and machinery) could be expected, but corporation tax must eventually be paid; meanwhile the company will have the use of the money. If, for this exercise, we assume that the corporation tax rate is 35% a substantial liability for tax could exist. However, the profit will have to be adjusted for tax according to the tax rules, and this cannot be estimated from the figures which have been presented. If a first year allowance of 100% is claimable on plant and machinery all the purchase price of £100,000 can be set against the profit figure, and little corporation tax will be payable. However tax rules change, and without detailed knowledge of a company's finances no reliable estimate of tax payable can be made. If, in this case, there were no allowances to be deducted from the profit figure the tax bill could be approximately £47,250 and the remaining £87,750 would be available to cover both reductions and dividends. Enquiry will be necessary to establish the true position.

The bank will be concerned with reduction of any solid element in the borrowing, and with a turnover of £1,800,000 per annum a reasonable swing should be seen in the banking account. Without examining past fluctuations we cannot tell how much the swing could be but, for the sake of this exercise, let us suppose that there is a swing of £100,000. If the bank is prepared to look to a five year term for repayment of the solid element of £170,000 annual reductions of around £35,000 will be required. We now have a revised situation. Banking facilities of £270,000 are necessary with reductions of £35,000 per annum to be met from profits of £135,000, subject to reduction for tax. It must also be kept in mind that the previous dividend level absorbed £40,000 of the profits after tax. It will be necessary for the directors to satisfy the bank that the after tax sum will be sufficient to cover the dividend, plus reductions. If there is a shortage the directors may, of course, decide to cut the dividend, or make other economies. Subject to satisfaction on this point a reasonable proposition could be presented. It will then be necessary to see if there is enough security to support lending of £270,000.

A factory is being bought for £250,000 and if this is a genuine price a lending of 50% should be safe. For the remaining £145,000 the bank could look to the net current assets which at 31st June year A were £220,000. Lending unsecured against this would be too thin, but a debenture would pick up current assets (ignoring cash) of £350,000 and this would be satisfactory for the remaining security. Monthly certificates of current assets and liabilities should be submitted and a reasonable arrangement would be that current assets should be at least twice the amount by which the bank debt exceeds £125,000. The assets and liabilities, and the bank debt, should be extracted from the company's books to give a correct comparison. It is quite wrong to take the bank debt from the bank's books and the other figures from the company's books; unbanked items and unpresented cheques might well make the bank debt in the bank's books greatly different from that shown in the company's books.

Finally we have to consider how the amount which the company wishes to borrow compares with the proprietors' stake. In June year A the proprietors had a capital and profit and loss balance of £350,000 but from this should be deducted the £50,000 item for goodwill giving the proprietors' stake of a net £300,000. It will be seen, therefore, that a bank facility of £270,000 almost matches the proprietors' stake. The proposition as revised, however, is satisfactory and the facilities could be agreed on the following basis:

1. limit of £270,000 subject to (2);
2. any excess over £125,000 to be covered by twice the amount of current assets;
3. certificates of current assets and liabilities to be submitted monthly;
4. reductions to be a minimum of £35,000 in the first year;
5. annual review of the facilities to be made;
6. a regular swing of around £100,000 will be expected;
7. a debenture to be given to the bank as security;
8. interest and commission rates to be specified.

Interim figures

1. CURRENT ASSETS ONLY

Even when the agreed lending basis does not involve any direct reliance on the current assets under a debenture, the regular supply of interim figures provides a useful and desirable barometer of current trading. The usual bank debenture contains what is known as a maintenance clause which incorporates an undertaking by the company to maintain the aggregate of its stock, good book debts and cash at a fixed figure or at a stated margin over the bank debt, and to supply a certificate of the amount at specified intervals. Its minimum requirement is therefore a periodical certificate 'In the terms of the clause . . . of the debenture dated . . . the aggregate of the company's stock, good book debts and cash on . . . amounted to (or was not less than) £*x* . . .' There may be accounts where this will suffice, but no watch on changes in the make-up of the current assets will then be possible. It is usual, therefore, to require at least separate totals for:

work in progress;
stock;
debtors;
cash;

in such detail as the nature of the business and the generosity of the bank lending require. A reminder may not be out of place here that the debtors' figure should be net (i.e. after deducting any set-off amounts included in the company's creditors): retentions should also be excluded. *Estimated* figures for stock or work in progress are common in interim figures and care is therefore necessary. They should be viewed with suspicion especially if the same figures appear unchanged month after month.

It must be borne in mind too that claims under a floating charge in a debenture are postponed to any creditors which, in winding up, would be preferential. This is one reason why at intervals full schedules of debtors and creditors are desirable. If only the current assets figures are supplied, the existence and effect on the position of preferential creditors will not be disclosed. Nevertheless the figures alone are not without value, as the following example (47) shows.

The lending basis was limit £22,500, £4,500 against a fully supported guarantee, the balance up to £18,000 not to exceed 50% of the current assets.

Throughout the six months' period the account was therefore within the lending basis, but the following points are noticeable:

EXAMPLE 47

Monthly figures

Work in progress	Stock	Debtors	Percentage of debtors to current assets	Total current assets	Bank debt	Debtors/ bank ratio
£	£	£	%	£	£	%
6,464	14,898	8,258	28	29,620	15,976	52
6,722	14,168	8,420	29	29,310	16,520	52
7,500	15,446	9,744	30	32,690	19,078	51
8,338	15,914	10,446	30	34,698	21,466	48
11,428	17,102	7,326	20	35,856	20,636	35
11,762	17,294	9,544	25	38,600	22,340	43
13,310	17,012	5,976	16	36,298	20,450	29

(a) the increasing use of the bank's facilities;
(b) a fall in debtors, suggesting a reduction in sales – debtors have fallen from highest figure of 30% to 16% of the total current assets;
(c) a parallel increase in work in progress and stock;
(d) at the beginning of the period the debtors provided 50% of the cover for the bank debt: at the end, under 30%.

The warning was clear. Further enquiry revealed that the company had devoted a substantial part of its productive capacity to developing a new and untried product and by the end of the period no less than £10,000 of the ostensible current assets consisted of completed or partly completed prototypes. This accounted for the fall in sales and the increase in stocks. As the £10,000 expenditure was clearly of a capital nature, the current assets available as cover for the bank should be reduced to £26,300; and debt exceeded the agreed lending basis by £2,800, thus:

	£	£
Bank debt		20,450
Guarantee	4,500	
50% of current assets (as amended) .	13,150	
		17,650
Excess		£2,800

The position was forthwith adjusted by taking additional supported guarantees as a temporary measure until the necessary capital was obtained.

2. CURRENT ASSETS AND LIABILITIES

The value of all the figures necessary to ascertain the changing amounts of working capital, and the use of this figure to estimate current profits has been dealt with in a previous chapter. The changing working capital figure is one of the most valuable tools in the control of balance sheet advances, and its use could be profitably extended. If the ways in which alone working capital can be changed are clearly understood, a close watch on its fluctuations may give an early warning of over-investment in fixed assets or excessive drawings, as well as of reduced trading profits. It should be added that the interim current liabilities figures should show preferential creditors separately.

3. CURRENT ASSETS AND LIABILITIES, PLUS WAGES, PURCHASES AND SALES

An even closer picture of current trading can be obtained if monthly purchases and sales figures are added to the items previously mentioned; the wages figure can usually be obtained from the bank account itself. Where the lending is 'near the bone', there need be no hesitation in calling for the additional information. Its preparation for the bank involves little extra work in the company's office, and the actual preparation of the figures will often be of great practical assistance to the directors themselvees in shaping production or business policy. Indeed, with the increased employment of budgetary control techniques it will often be found that all the figures required are already produced monthly for the Board. An extra copy for the bank will be readily forthcoming and, incidentally sheds useful light on the efficiency of the management.

EXAMPLE 48

Full monthly figures

QUARTER ENDED 30TH SEPTEMBER

	Purchases	Sales (for the month)	Creditors	Debtors	Stock	Work in progress	Bank debt
	£	£	£	£	£	£	£
30 June .	—	—	5,625	8,988	7,984	17,392	13,429
31 July .	3,299	5,744	5,660	9,363	9,015	16,421	14,016
31 Aug .	4,612	5,994	6,062	8,376	8,783	18,103	13,845
30 Sept .	4,244	6,217	7,014	9,309	9,716	18,457	14,802
	£12.155	£17,955					

	£
Wages (from bank account) . .	7,558
Estimated overheads (from previous year's account)	1,800

From these figures it is possible to construct:

(a) a trading and profit and loss account for the quarter;

(b) a cash reconciliation statement.

(a) Interim trading and profit and loss account for 3 months ended 30th September

	£		£	£
Opening stock	7,984	Sales . . .		17,955
Purchases	12,155	Work in progress		
		Opening . .	17,392	
	20,139	Closing . .	18,457	
Less Closing stock . .	9,716			
		Increase . . .		1,065
Materials consumed . .	10,423			
Wages	7,558	Total production .		19,020
		Net loss . . .		761
Prime cost of production .	17,981			
Overheads	1,800			
	£19,781			£19,781

(b) Cash reconciliation statement

RECEIPTS	£	£	PAYMENTS	£	£
Sales . . .	17,955		Opening bank overdraft . .		13,429
Less Increase in debtors . .	321		Purchases . .	12,155	
		17,634	Overheads . .	1,800	
Closing bank overdraft . .		14,802		13,955	
		32,436	*Less* Increase in creditors . .	1,389	
Unexplained balance		1,117			12,566
			Wages . . .		7,558
		£33,553			£33,553

In this particular account the figures quoted show an increase of working capital during the quarter of £356 which, in the absence of any information about non-revenue receipts would be *prima facie* evidence of profit earnings. The second computation enables the banker to infer a non-revenue receipt of £1,117 which, after deducting the loss of £761, exactly accounts for the increase in working capital.

Enquiry prompted by these fuller calculations elicited the information that vehicles which had appeared as a fixed asset in the balance sheet had been sold for £1,050. The slight discrepancy still unexplained could, of course, be due to the difference between the estimated overheads, £1,800, based on the figures from the previous accounts, and the actual overhead expenditure.

Where the cash reconciliation statement shows an unexpected balance of payments of any magnitude, the reason should be ascertained. There may have been unwise purchases of fixed assets, excessive drawings, or repayment of long-term loans; all of which will have reduced the liquid resources – one of the basic concomitants of over-trading. In this as in many other killing diseases the value of early diagnosis cannot be overstressed.

4. RECORDS

For interim figures to reveal their full story, they should be entered in columnar form on an interim figures record sheet to be kept in the front of the case file. Changes can then be readily detected and further enquiries made as necessary. A system of monthly or quarterly cards in conjunction with an efficient diary will help to ensure that all necessary figures are received promptly.

The record sheet will often be the most valuable document in the file. When the next audited balance sheet is received, the interim figures supplied previously for the balance sheet date should be checked against the balance sheet itself. Substantial differences should be explained by the company. The banker's estimate of the reliability of the interim figures may have to be revised as a result.

Wages

Reference has already been made to the added protection enjoyed by a banker who advances money to a company for the payment of wages.[1] It is advisable, although not absolutely necessary, to keep such advances on a separate wages account and to make such transfers from the general account from time to time as will ensure that only preferential advances (equivalent to not more than four months' wages and salaries) will be left on the wages account. This device has many times enabled a banker to see a *company* through its difficulties without undue risk. It should be noted that no preferential status is given under ordinary bankruptcy rules to wages advances made to individuals, partnerships or unincorporated bodies.

The usual automatic disclosure of the weekly wage total to the banker when the wages cheque is cashed, places a very valuable pulse under his fingers. The requirement that a company and a group (Companies Act 1985 section 235 (5) and (6) and Schedule 10) must disclose in the directors' report a statement of the average number of persons employed by the week (if numbering 250 or more) and their aggregate remuneration for the financial year, is of little help to the watching banker. The statutory information is too little and too late. Particularly in industry, the rise and fall of wages is a very fair index of changes in current production: certainly much more so than purchases or sales. In any case, where a tendency to over-trading is suspected, the banker who makes it his business to watch the wages should be well forewarned. One case comes to mind where the banker had expressly warned a company of the danger, and, had the precaution of watching the rising wages closely been taken, he could have acted promptly to save the customer, the bank and other creditors from heavy losses. Where the wages cheque also includes substantial and variable petty cash drawings, the weekly cheque figure may lose some of its value.

Loans by holding company or directors

There is a tendency, mainly in private companies, for the proprietors to provide the bulk of the cash capital, not by taking up shares (involving liability for capital duty) but on loan. From the company's point of view, this is sound enough. But for general creditors and lending bankers it raises several problems which want careful watching.

[1] Companies Act, 1985, Secs 475 (1) and (2), 614 (1) and Schedule 19.

1. Such loans can be repaid wholly or in part at any time, and without the banker's knowledge. Where a banker is lending substantially to provide working capital he usually relies on the profits earned by the working capital to service his advance. If the working capital is depleted to repay loans, the whole safety of the advance may be undermined, and the repayment programme defeated.

Although it is unusual the banker may take a charge from each lender over the company's promissory note, payable on demand, for the amount of the lender's loan, as security for the company's debt. The banker will then have a right of double proof in liquidation, first for the amount of his debt, and secondly for the amount of the note.

Alternatively, or in addition, a letter of postponement can be taken from the loan creditors, and acknowledged by the company, which provides:

(a) that the creditor will not receive nor the company make repayment of the loan in whole or in part (or sometimes so that the loan will not be reduced below £*x*——), during the currency of the bank advance;
(b) in event of liquidation (when the question of repayment will be taken out of the company's hands) any amounts received by the loan creditor on account of his loan will be held in trust for the bank, and as security for any part of the bank's advance not recovered by way of dividend or otherwise.

2. The broad effect of such a letter of postponement is to make the postponed loan quasi-capital, *as far as the position of the bank is concerned,* though the significance of the qualifying 'quasi' will appear later. Often in liquidation the position of the bank will be stronger with a letter of postponement, in the above form, than if the loan were capitalised, as the following example shows.

A financial house of the highest standing, satisfied that under good management a business which had fallen on evil days could be turned into a sound undertaking, bought the shares and provided loans to modernize the plant and machinery and to finance the inevitable losses during a period of complete reorganization. At the end of the new regime's first year the subsidiary's balance sheet showed the following position:

	£	£
FIXED ASSETS		225,000
CURRENT ASSETS		
Stock and work in progress	90,000	
Debtors	290,000	
	380,000	
CREDITORS: AMOUNTS FALLING DUE WITHIN ONE YEAR		
Trade creditors	160,000	
Bank overdraft (unsecured)	50,000	
Other creditors – preferential	40,000	
	250,000	
Net current assets		130,000
Total assets less current liabilities		355,000
CREDITORS: AMOUNTS FALLING DUE AFTER ONE YEAR		
Loan from parent company (postponed to bank loan)		350,000
		£5,000
CAPITAL AND RESERVES		
Called up share capital		200,000
Profit and loss account		
deficit balance forward	(80,000)	
loss for year	(115,000)	195,000
		£5,000

It will be noted that:

(a) owing to accumulated losses the company, on book figures, is barely solvent, the net worth being £5,000 only;

(b) the current position is strong and reasonably liquid;

(c) the bank has granted unsecured facilities of £50,000 because of the high standing of the parent, and the letter of postponement gives substantial cover: how substantial is worth investigating.

If the company had gone into liquidation on the balance sheet date, the bank's position would have worked out as shown in table I below.

Table I

Assets realize	Divdend in £ to non-preferential creditors	Received and held in trust for the bank by parent company	Dividend on bank advance	Total cover for bank	Bank's £50,000 covered
£		£	£	£	
400,000	64p	224,000	33,000	257,000	5.14 times
300,000	46p	161,000	23,000	184,000	3.68 ,,
200,000	28p	98,000	14,000	112,000	2.24 ,,
100,000	10p	35,000	5,000	40,000	0.80 ,, (loss £6,000)

Thus with a 50% realization of the book value of the assets – not unreasonable to expect with debtors alone representing nearly half the total assets – the bank debt is covered over three and a half times. This strong position arises, of course, from the fact that the postponed loan is seven times the bank overdraft, and the bank has the benefit, in effect, of proof for *eight times* its debt. Had the postponed loan been capitalized, however, the position would have been far otherwise (table II).

With a realization of the assets at £300,000 there is a margin of £134,000 over the bank debt in table I, but only £12,000 in table II with realization at £200,000, margin £62,000 and shortfall £12,000 respectively. The disparity between the two cases will be narrowed progressively as the excess of the postponed loan over the bank advance decreases.

Table II

Assets realize	Dividend in the £	Dividend on bank advance	Margin available	Bank's £50,000 covered
£	£	£	£	
400,000	1.71	50,000	35,500	1.71 times
300,000	1.24	50,000	12,000	1.24 ,,
200,000	76p	38,000	—	Loss £12,000
100,000	28p	14,000	—	Loss £36,000

The history of this particular case brought out an additional point of importance. A reduced operating loss of £75,000 was made in the second year. This would have produced a deficiency (negative net worth) of £70,000. For understandable prestige reasons such a deficiency was considered undesirable by the parent company which accordingly waived its loan and accrued interested on it to the extent of £75,000, the adverse profit and loss balance being reduced by that amount by a contra credit in the profit and loss account. The banker's natural enquiry whether such a waiver was permissable under the terms of the letter of postponement disclosed that it was: and if waiver of part, why not waiver of the whole debt? . . . which would result in the same reduction in cover for the bank as if the loan had been capitalized. Failure or refusal of the loan creditor to prove for the whole debt in liquidation – apparently also permissable – would have the same effect.

It would seem therefore as if, for the proper protection of the bank, the terms of the letter of postponement might well be extended to:

(a) preclude waiver of the loan in whole or in part;
(b) ensure that in liquidation the loan creditor must prove for the full amount of his loan.

Such a letter can increase the safety of unsecured lending in a large number of cases, though it cannot be overstressed that it falls far short of providing legal water-tight security: it is only a 'gentlemen's agreement'. If more is necessary a legal assignment of the debt should be taken by the bank.

3. Where a banker holds a floating charge he would naturally expect his debt to take priority over any director's loan. Without his knowledge, however, such director may have been advancing cash to pay wages, and such advances would be preferential and entitled to payment ahead of the bank, to the extent that the wages advanced would themselves have been preferential in liquidation.[1] Provided he appreciated the existence and significance of such a positon, an alert branch manager would at once take whatever action might be necessary.

Effect of debenture on creditors

Where a company is operating on the brink of 'going-concern' insolvency, the banker, when making his summing up of the position, will make some allowance for the possibility – experience suggests that it would be putting it too high to say 'probability' – that the registration of debenture (which will receive due publicity in the commercial gazettes and in the appropriate trade papers) may lead to some curtailment of his customer's credit. Should this occur to any significant extent, estimates of the cash required for future working and of the adequacy of the facilities sought, may have to be revised. The fear of repercussions following the inescapable publicity is usually, however, more real to the customer than to the bank. And in practice this fear is groundless in the majority of cases.

Misuse of facilities

In the previous chapter it was pointed out that the purpose for which an advance is sought is a crucial factor in deciding whether the advance is sound bank lending. It follows, therefore, that one of the most important aspects of control is to ensure that the facilities are used for the agreed purpose *and nothing else*. It is here that a watchful branch manager can so effectively protect the interests of his bank.

[1] Companies Act, 1985 Secs 475 (1) and (2), 614 (1) and Schedule 19.

For example, consider an advance which has been approved for normal trading to finance a seasonal peak or a special contract. If, in the event, it is used wholly or to a significant extent, to finance:

(a) the purchase of fixed assets;
(b) the payment of dividends or arrears of taxation;
(c) the making or repayment of directors' loans;
(d) in developing a new project;

the whole picture as envisaged by the banker when the facilities were agreed will be altered, and the expected self-liquidating character of the advance may be fundamentally changed.

The daily examination of the paid cheques will often give invaluable information. It is an indispensable precaution where the lending is marginal.

This chapter will have emphasized the fact that there are no easy formulae for the lending banker. The technique of practical advance control must emerge as a slow and natural growth from the application of established principles to individual cases. The banker's proper equipment is a sound understanding of accounts, a wide knowledge of men and affairs together with an alert, vigorous and flexible mind; and above all, plenty of common sense.

CHAPTER 19

Term Lending

Reasons for term loans – Roll over – Types of company – Monitoring of performance – Additional information necessary – Considering a proposition – Example of a term loan – Financial covenants

Although aspects of financial accounts have been examined in detail we have so far been considering these in relation to normal bank overdraft lending or for loans which are subject to annual reductions and are repaid over a relatively short period of time. We have also considered hard-core borrowing and its similarity to loan finance. Emphasis has been placed on the importance of the net current assets and the circulation of current assets and current liabilities.

However, of recent years, additional banking finance has been required by large company customers and this has brought about the development of term loans. With the economy of the country going through a difficult period and government pressure and directives on banks to reduce lending commitments from time to time, companies have not been able to plan ahead in the knowledge that the finance they require will be available at the right time. Some companies, therefore, have requested commitments from the banks for term loans which will not be repayable on demand, and the banks have found a way of providing such loans.

This chapter will not confine itself entirely to financial statements but will also consider some aspects of term loans as, without this knowledge, it will not be easy to follow why there are stipulations and ratios agreed between banker and customer when term loans are arranged.

With banks obtaining most of their funds from current and deposit accounts which are repayable on demand or short notice it has been necessary to match these liabilities with loans which are themselves as near liquid as possible. Overdraft lending is, therefore, the most appropriate form for this to take. Naturally, because of the large amount of deposits, banks are able to commit a limited proportion of them to lending which is not on overdraft. For the remainder of their term loans they have tended to look to the wholesale market. The wholesale market is provided with surplus funds by banks and other institutions, which are then lent on varying terms: overnight, a week, a month, three months, six months, etc., but substantial sums for a period of a year or more are at times very difficult to obtain.

The problem for the banks is, therefore, how to provide this short-term money to borrowers who require it for longer periods. The market in these funds is large and growing and the banks have therefore felt able to commit themselves to raising wholesale funds for a period, but putting the responsibility for changes in interest rates on to the companies who wish to borrow. For example, if a term loan for five years is required a bank could agree to this loan on the basis that it is rolled over every six months, and the customer is to be responsible for changes in the interest rates. The loan will then be available for the entire five year term, and the customer will be certain of his finance. The customer has, however, to realize that the interest rate on the loan will fluctuate according to market conditions. The bank and the customer are, therefore, locked in for the full term of the loan, but there can be variations on this straightforward method, and provisions can also be made for withdrawal from the loan under penalty.

When dealing with overdraft lending a company's liquid position has been looked at to see how it can cope with short-term borrowing, but the liquid position of a company will hardly be sufficient to estimate its ability to repay borrowing which may not be due for, say, five years. It is not easy to estimate what the liquid position will be in five years' time, and whether a company will be able to repay its borrowing then. It has been necessary, therefore, to develop a new technique when looking at financial statements to consider proposals for term loans. When long-term liabilities were discussed it was shown that in a properly proportioned balance sheet such liabilities were more than covered by the fixed assets. However, term loans are generally for a medium term of around five to seven years, and if cover by fixed assets was the only criterion there would be a problem of repayment at the end of the term. Other term liabilities such as debenture stocks are generally outstanding for a much longer period and repayment is not such an urgent problem at the outset when the borrowing is arranged. The question of providing for repayment of such long-term liabilities can often be left for many years before it is considered.

With a medium-term loan, however, the repayment must generally be considered at the outset. Except in the case of very strong companies term loans are normally secured, but it is hardly sufficient for a banker to rely on his security; this merely ensures his safety in an emergency, not that he will get repayment at the correct time. How then can this be achieved?

Types of company

Although many companies do not fall exactly within the four types suggested here, this division will be sufficient to indicate which companies are suitable as borrowers on a medium-term basis.

1. Companies with substantial assets and good profit records. For companies in this category there should be no great difficulty in arranging term

loans. The assets will provide backing for the borrowing, and the profit performance, if it continues at the same rate, should enable the loan repayment to be made at the correct time. Even so, profits can be distributed or used for buying fixed assets and, if so, the money for repayment of a term loan will not be available when required. There is, therefore, a certain amount of monitoring of performance to be carried out by the banker;

2. companies with substantial assets and poor profit records. These companies are not good candidates for term loans. Although the substantial assets can provide good cover for borrowing this will not ensure repayment. If the poor profit record continues there will be no money from profits for repayment, and it will also prove difficult for such a company to raise money elsewhere. The only way to achieve repayment would, therefore, appear to be sales of assets. In many cases companies such as these produce forecasts showing good profits to come, but without a record to prove ability a banker would be naïve to accept the forecast without any qualms;
3. companies without substantial assets but with good profit records. If the profits continue these companies should be able to service a term loan, but if their trading performance declines they may not then be able to repay from profits and their assets may not provide sufficient cover for the companies to borrow elsewhere. Sales of assets may mean their complete downfall. However, it is not beyond the bounds of possibility to arrange term loans for these companies, but very strict arrangements have to be made for monitoring the performance, and also to decide the time when action must be taken towards early repayment if the good profit record is not maintained;
4. companies without substantial assets and with poor profit records. These companies are difficult candidates for term loans and in most cases lending will not be advisable. The only way in which a banker can make such arrangements will be if the company has some easily saleable assets which are available as security.

Monitoring performance

In all cases where term loans are granted it is necessary to see that money for the repayment will be available at the appropriate time. A company should, therefore, be asked to provide a cash projection showing details of estimated balance sheet movements over the period of the loan. The banker, of course, will have to decide whether the proposition is a satisfactory one, and whether to rely on the ability of the customer to keep reasonably well to the estimates. Subsequently regular figures must be provided to compare with the original estimates, and to see whether the actual performance of the company is satisfactory. If the actual figures are worse than the estimate a banker will have to consider at what stage he will take action in order to extricate himself without loss.

It must be kept in mind that a term loan is arranged for a fixed period, even though there are roll over provisions and once a banker has lent money it is not easy to get out mid-term. In many facility letters there are provisions for quicker repayment on the happening of certain events, and it is these trigger clauses which give the banker scope to obtain early repayment.

Additional information

With all lending propositions a certain amount of basic information is necessary to assess whether to lend or not, but when dealing with term loans additional information has to be sought. There is obviously more risk, other things being equal, in lending for five years than there is in lending on overdraft. Some of the areas which should be examined are:

1. strength and weaknesses of management. Has it the strength to see the project through the entire term of the loan and is there sufficient depth of management?;
2. how long is the trading cycle for the particular industry? At what point in the cycle is the industry now, and what are the prospects of the industry in these times of rapid change?;
3. if the project involves high technology, or other difficult areas, should an independent feasibility assessment be obtained?;
4. what assumptions have been used in the projected results and how sensitive is the viability of the project through changes in the assumptions?;
5. have past cash projections and budgets worked out satisfactorily and, thereby, given confidence to the bank?;
6. the past performance of the company should be examined, covering both good and bad years, and it is advisable to look backwards for as long a period as the loan is required forwards;
7. the past statement of sources and applications of funds should be examined to see the uses to which the company has applied the funds made available to it;
8. although a correct balance between the various assets and liabilities in future balance sheets is important, a term loan must be examined in conjunction with the projections for future profit and loss accounts. It is from this source that repayment will be obtained. A term loan is unsuitable for the provision of funds for normal trading purposes.

A banker will also have to keep in mind the company's own assessment of the profitability of the project, and if a loan is required for a longer period than seven years (excluding the start up period) a banker must ask whether sufficient return is being generated on the project.

The remuneration from term loans lends itself to assessment by DCF methods. Considerable variations can be quoted for commission and commitment fees, and allied to these variations the worth of other accounts could also be incorporated into an evaluation exercise.

Considering the proposition

After obtaining the normal basic information and the additional information as set out above a banker will then be able to assess the request on the following lines:

1. he must consider the proposition and whether the retained profits will enable the company to repay at the stated time. Not only must the profits be retained in the company, but they will have to be retained in the liquid assets. It they are used for buying fixed assets then, of course, the funds will not be available for repayment of the term loan;
2. the cash projections and profit forecasts, together with the estimated future balance sheets, will have to be examined over the period of the loan. The banker will then be able to see whether the appropriate funds will be available at the right time. Also, by regular monitoring of the company's performance, he will be able to see whether it is measuring up to its forecasts;
3. the banker will have to consider at the outset how he will get his money back if the company's forecasts prove to be incorrect. Will there be assets to sell, or will the company be able to raise further funds, even if the profit performance is not good?;
4. the banker will have to consider the timing of any action if he sees that it will be necessary to obtain repayment before the term of the loan expires. He will have to look at the company's present balance sheet and estimate the worst position he is prepared to see in the deterioration of the balance sheet figures before taking action. When he has decided on this he can word his facility letter with the ratios that he wishes the company to keep and with the proviso that if these ratios are not kept action will be taken to recover the debt. It is no use waiting too long as a company with poor profits will find difficulty in raising alternative forms of finance and will also not achieve good prices if its assets are sold under pressure. It is better, therefore, to leave a margin in hand to enable a company after breaching its loan covenants to have time to raise funds or sell assets.

Example of a term loan proposition

Let us now consider a proposition for a term loan. In the example which follows not all the aspects mentioned above have been examined in detail as the object is not to assess fully a term lending proposition, but to examine financial statements to see how they help in the assessment and in the fixing of the financial covenants.

You have a good customer, Heavy Engineering Limited, which has banked with you for many years and which has an overdraft limit of £400,000 with an adequate swing. The customers have given you advance warning that they will be calling to discuss a proposition for borrowing for a period of five or six years. Before the customers arrive you have a look at their balance sheets and those for the last three years are set out as in Example 49 in a form which enables comparisons to be seen easily.

EXAMPLE 49

Term loan proposition

Heavy Engineering Limited

BALANCE SHEET FOR THREE YEARS AT END SEPTEMBER ('000s)

	Year A £	Year B £	Year C £
FIXED ASSETS			
Freeholds	1,100	1,100	1,100
Plant and machinery	700	500	500
	1,800	1,600	1,600
Add CURRENT ASSETS			
Stock	1,400	1,500	1,800
Debtors	820	890	900
	2,200	2,390	2,700
	4,020	3,990	4,300
Less TAX AND CURRENT LIABILITIES			
Corporation tax due in 3 months	100	160	150
Corporation tax due in 15 months	160	150	170
Creditors	350	400	500
Bank (secured by debenture on floating assets)	490	280	380
	1,100	990	1,200
	£2,920	£3,000	£3,100
Provided by:			
Long-term liability (secured by mortgage on freeholds)	1,800	1,800	1,800
Capital	1,000	1,000	1,000
Reserves	20	80	180
Profit and loss account	10	50	50
Deferred taxation	90	70	70
	£2,920	£3,000	£3,100

	Year A	Year B	Year C
	£	£	£
Turnover	4,700	5,000	5,300
Net profit on ordinary activities before tax .	360	380	400
Taxation	170	200	200
Net profit on ordinary activities after taxation .	190	180	200
Dividend	100	100	100

The balance sheets show that the current assets are well in excess of the current liabilities, although stock takes up rather a large proportion of the current assets. The bank overdraft limit of £400,000 is covered by a floating charge over the current assets which amount to £2.7 million. There is a long-term liability of £1.8 million secured by a mortgage on the freeholds, but the freeholds appear in the balance sheet as only £1.1 million. The plant and machinery reduced in year B but had been constant since, and this appears to be reflected in the deferred taxation account. Profits are made annually and there is some plough back after payment of the dividend.

Altogether the company seems to be progressing well. It has a good record of profits, but not very substantial assets in view of its turnover and borrowing. The next stage would be to prepare percentage balance sheets and ratios, and these are set out as in Example 50.

EXAMPLE 50

Term borrowing proposition

Heavy Engineering Limited

PERCENTAGE BALANCE SHEETS AND RATIOS

	Year A	Year B	Year C
Proprietor's funds . . .	27.8	30.1	30.2
Long-term liabilities . .	44.8	45.1	41.9
Tax and current liabilities .	27.4	24.8	27.9
	100%	100%	100%
Fixed assets	44.8	40.1	37.2
Current assets	55.2	59.9	62.8
	100%	100%	100%
Current ratio	2.0	2.4	2.3
Liquid ratio	0.75	0.90	0.75
Debtors/creditors . . .	2.3	2.2	1.8
Stock/sales.	108 days	110 days	124 days
Debtor/sales	64 days	65 days	62 days

This shows that proprietors' funds and long-term liabilities well cover the fixed assets. There is a good current ratio and the liquid ratio, although less than 1, is quite satisfactory in view of the large turnover. The ratio of debtors to creditors is good, but the amount of stock on hand in relation to sales seems to be somewhat heavy and has increased over the three years from 108 days to 124 days. The ratio of debtors to sales is reasonable at around 60 to 70 days. Other ratios could, of course, be calculated from the full profit and loss account, but the calculations made are sufficient for our purpose. There seems to be only one particular query as far as the balance sheet figures are concerned, and that is the question of the long-term liability of £1.8 million secured against freeholds of only £1.1 million, and this would be a matter for enquiry when discussing the term lending proposition with the customers, unless the circumstances were already known. When the directors call they tell you that although the freeholds are in the balance sheet at £1.1 million they are, in fact, worth £2.5 million. This, of course, puts up the proprietors' stake by £1.4 million to £2.7 million from £1.3 million. The long-term liability, however, at £1.8 million against freeholds of £2.5 million seems to be full borrowing. The customers agree that this is so and remind you that five years ago when the outside borrowers put up an additional £500,000 they asked for a charge over the floating assets to bolster their security. Neither the company nor the bank was happy about this as, although the bank would have had a prior floating charge, any subsequent charge would have been restrictive. It was eventually agreed that the outside borrowers would rely solely on the freeholds. The customers tell you that they now wish to modernize their plant and equipment as this will enable them to increase their turnover greatly. The additional capital expenditure will then be in the region of £2 million and most of it will be spent over a two year period. The increased turnover will enable much larger profits to be made, and with the contracts they already have in hand they can see a bright future ahead. With such a large capital expenditure it will take the company some years to generate funds for repayment and they have asked for term loan facilities of £600,000 to be repaid in six years' time. They have prepared extensive forecasts and leave a copy with you. An extract from the forecasts for six years is shown in Example 51.

EXAMPLE 51

Term lending proposition

Heavy Engineering Limited

EXTRACT FROM FORECASTS FOR SIX YEARS (£'000)

End of year	D	E	F	G	H	I
Net worth	1,500	1,800	2,100	2,600	3,100	3,600
Net current assets . .	1,400	1,300	1,600	2,100	2,600	3,000
Net profit on ordinary activities before tax . .	450	500	600	900	1,000	1,200
Capital expenditure . .	750	700	200	150	300	400
Turnover	5,700	6,000	9,000	10,000	10,000	10,000

The net worth and net current assets both increase over the period, but the increase is more rapid towards the end of the six years. Profits also have an upward movement towards the end of the period. Net profit on ordinary activities before tax is shown; there will be a writing down allowance of 25% (on the reducing balance method) on the capital expenditure and if we work on the basis of corporation tax being at 35% the customer should be able to provide the shortfall between the £600,000 provided by the bank and the cost of the capital equipment.

Dividends, of course, have to be met. It does appear, therefore, as if all of the funds are not required in year D, and probably £400,000 could be provided in year D, and £200,000 in year E. Repayment in year I looks feasible with the current assets increased to £3 million, but it will be necessary to examine this figure more closely to see that not too large a proportion consists of stock. It will be necessary to examine closely the assumptions on which the forecasts have been based. This will include the expected interest rates, the inflation rate, rate of exchange if foreign transactions are contemplated, and rates of taxation. The estimates will have to be examined to see if they have been prepared on a conservative basis because it is very difficult to look ahead as far as six years. A good margin must, therefore, be left in hand for contingencies. If, after a thorough examination of the forecast, it is considered that the proposition is a good one and could be supported by the bank the security aspect will have to be examined. With the bank being asked to put up a total of £1 million, and current assets at £2.7 million including a large proportion of stock, security, although adequate, does not leave much margin. The lending is, therefore, full enough, especially when £600,000 is on a term lending proposition. It is obvious, however, that it will not be possible to ask for a second mortgage over the freeholds as this will bring the outside lenders into the fray once again asking for a second charge over the floating assets.

It will be necessary now to decide on the state of affairs when action will be required by the bank to recover its lending. Firstly we must look at the current assets and decide to what extent we can allow them to deteriorate. Stock of course, is a problem being high in relation to debtors, and debtors are more important as far as the bank is concerned. If the current assets dropped from £2.7 million to £2 million there would be something radically wrong with the company's trading if the bank lending was still at £1 million. It would not be too early to take action if this happened as, although a serious situation would have developed, it would not be so critical that the bank could not salvage itself. This, therefore, should be one possible situation which should be noted.

Debtors are shown in year C as being at £900,000, and with total lending of £1 million there is some reliance on stock. This is satisfactory as it stands, but too great a reliance on stock would be wrong. If therefore, debtors dropped to £700,000 it would show that some radical change had taken place, and perhaps this, too, should be a situation which should be noted.

Therefore, as far as current assets are concerned, the bank would not wish the total to drop below twice the liability to the bank, and debtors not below 70% of the liability to the bank. This would still give the company adequate room for manoeuvre.

The bank need not get too worried if the current liabilities build up because it will have a floating charge over the current assets. Nevertheless, it will show that a dangerous situation is developing if the current asset ratio deteriorates rapidly. As it has built up in the three years from a ratio of 2 to 1 to 2.3 to 1 any deterioration in the current ratio below 1.5 to 1 would be serious, and would require action.

This, therefore, has dealt with the current assets and current liabilities, and we now have to look at the fixed assets and the long-term liabilities. We know that we cannot get more security and yet relying on current assets alone for a lending of £1 million in the particular circumstances does leave something to be desired because there is no fixed asset base to the bank's security. It is necessary, therefore, to see that no one else obtains the security on the margin of fixed assets above long-term liabilities and this can be done by requiring the company to agree that it will not give a further charge over its assets, or arrange any other substantial borrowing without permission of the bank. With these requirements we have a reasonable bank lending proposition, which is now as follows:

Overdraft	£400,000
Term lending	£600,000
with £400,000 to be drawn down in year D	
and £200,000 in year E	

The overdraft to be fully swinging and the term loan to be repaid in year I.

In the facility letter for the term borrowing the following covenants should be given by the customer:

1. current assets to be maintained at twice the level of the bank liability;
2. debtors to be maintained at at least 70% of the bank liability;
3. the current ratio to be in excess of 1.5 to 1;
4. a pledge to be given that no further security will be given, or substantial borrowing obtained (say in excess of £100,000), without the prior consent of the bank.

The clauses in a facility letter can have a great deal of variety and can cover the stages of drawing the money, repayment stages, roll over times, and it will also be necessary to define any terms used. Clauses can be inserted concerning the amount of the net worth of the company, or the debt equity ratio, or any other ratio, and it is usual to include in any negative pledge that the company should not give guarantees without the consent of the bank. Often there are limitations imposed on additional financing by leasing. Apart from the default clauses in failure to keep to stated proportions and amounts it is usual to provide for the debt to be called in if repayment is not made at the right time, if interest is not properly paid, and if a receiver is appointed. Specifically also interest rate, commission and commitment fees will be mentioned. These covenants and stipulations are beneficial to both parties. They provide warnings and with careful monitoring will enable appropriate action to be considered if the project is not turning out as envisaged.

There can be considerable variety in term loans, but the interpretation of the balance sheets and other financial statements follows a similar pattern:

1. interpretation of the balance sheets and profit and loss accounts for past years to establish the strengths and weaknesses of the company;
2. examination of future cash projections and estimates to see if repayment is possible and the whole project feasible;
3. estimating a deteriorating position to the point when it will be necessary for the bank to take action to safeguard its funds.

CHAPTER 20

Inflation Accounts

Current purchasing power – Current cost accounting – Cost of sales adjustment – Depreciation – Profit and loss account – Appropriation account – Balance sheet – Hyde guidelines – SSAP 16 – Abandonment of persuasion – The banker's view

In the previous chapters we have been dealing with accounts which have been drawn up on an historic cost basis. This is a perfectly suitable method of accountancy when prices are stable, but at times when there is rapid inflation the results produced by historic cost accounting fail to show the effects of inflation, and comparison of results year by year cannot be accurately undertaken without some adjustments.

The point is that when rapid inflation is taking place, the £ at the beginning of one year has more purchasing power than a £ at the end of the year and, therefore, the accounts year by year are measured in £ units which do not have the same value. This is similar to measuring distance with a chain twenty-two yards long, but changing the length of the chain year by year.

Numerous systems have been proposed for dealing with this problem stretching backwards over many years and the accounting profession, although tackling the conceptual aspects, has had difficulty in proposing a standard method which is generally acceptable. Historical accounts are therefore still used even though, in times of rapid inflation, they are bound to be inaccurate in many respects.

It is important for bankers to be able to understand the inaccuracies which can occur in order that they may make reasoned assessments of the worth of the accounts which they see. Also, of course, a knowledge of what has been proposed will enable them to follow the continuing twists in the debate concerning the most acceptable way of presenting inflation accounts.

Current purchasing power (CPP)

This method envisages that accounts should be adjusted at the end of each year according to variations in the retail price index. The result would be that instead of accounts being expressed in £s they would be expressed in units of purchasing power. In fact, the units of purchasing power proposed to be used are also designated as being in £s, and it can easily be seen that after a few years a very confusing situation would arise in that many people would not have been able to differentiate between a £ as a unit of account, and a £ as an amount of purchasing power. However, the system would be fairly easy to operate, and would enable comparisons to be made year by year. A disadvantage of using the retail price index is that although this index is perhaps suitable for comparisons of household purchases year by year, it is not suitable for comparing the costs of goods and services which are used by large companies.

Current cost accounting (CCA)

This system was first suggested by the Sandilands Committee when reporting on inflation accounting in September 1975. Subsequently the Morpeth Committee produced an exposure draft and guidance on how to put current cost accounting into practice. The system proposed that the £ monetary unit, although of variable value, should continue to be used as the unit of account, and that the values in the balance sheet and profit and loss account should be adjusted to reflect the changes caused by inflation. This means that with the measuring unit, the £, being a fluctuating measure many problems would remain. It was suggested that this method of accountancy should be introduced for United Kingdom companies starting on 1st January 1979, but the wide-ranging proposals received a severe jolt when it was found in July 1977 that general acceptance by practising accountants was not possible. There were five major constituents of the proposals which were as follows:

1. THE BALANCE SHEET

This, it was proposed, should show current values for the assets and not their historical cost. The theory is that all assets and liabilities would be shown at their current value to the business, but it was conceded that there were great difficulties in applying these valuations throughout all the assets and liabilities, and, initially, it was proposed that alterations in valuations would only apply to tangible assets. This means that fixed assets and stock were to be revalued, but debtors, monetary assets, goodwill, and liabilities would not be revalued. Any differences in the revaluation of assets would be taken to revaluation reserves.

2. DEPRECIATION

Depreciation which is worked on an historic cost basis does not retain sufficient funds in a business to provide for the eventual replacement of assets during a period of inflation, and on the CCA method depreciation would be calculated on the current value to the business of the assets concerned instead of on the historic cost of the assets, and this would thus give a more realistic charge in the profit and loss account of the cost of the resources used in each accounting period. However, the depreciation provided would not, even then, go far enough, because during each accounting period the calculation of the amount of depreciation required would be on the value of the asset during that accounting period. It would still not provide sufficient retention of profits to enable the asset to be replaced at the end of its useful life. This is because depreciation, although it would have been calculated on the increasing value year by year during the useful life of the asset, would not have been calculated on the final replacement cost. Some backlog depreciation would also have to be provided and it was proposed that an amount to cover this purpose would be made by a book entry and deducted from revaluation surpluses. Bankers would have had to keep in mind that this would be a book entry only as far as backlog depreciation was concerned, and that it would not conserve resources in the business, out of profits, to provide for the replacement of the asset.

3. COST OF SALES ADJUSTMENT

In a period of inflation stock which is purchased at the beginning of an accounting period is worth more at the end of the accounting period, but such a profit is not due to the operations of trading, but due to holding the stock. Current cost accounting proposed that an attempt would be made to differentiate between the two types of gain, and that instead of the profit being a composite figure the profit shown in the profit and loss account would be for the operating profit only. The remaining gain on the holding of stock would be transferred to an appropriation account.

4. APPROPRIATION ACCOUNT

This was a new statement which was to appear in the annual accounts, and its intention was to bring together the current cost profit from the profit and loss account, together with holding gains and surpluses, or deficits, arising from the revaluation of assets. Also included was to be the amount appropriated by the directors to or from revaluation reserves, and the amount of the dividend. This appropriation account would have required much study by bankers because a great amount of subjectivity was to be introduced. Directors would have had to consider how much should be retained within the business, having regard to their assessment of its needs, and the amount could be large or small dependent upon the whim of directors. The directors would have had to make subjective judgments on whether the company needed to finance a higher level of trade debtors, and if money should be retained for this purpose. Other aspects to be considered would be whether the company needed to finance a higher level of net monetary assets, or if it would be necessary to provide for backlog depreciation. Then, again, if the company wished to maintain the purchasing power of the shareholders' equity an adjustment would also have to be made in the appropriation account. Conversely a decrease in the amount appropriated to reserves would also have to be considered by the directors in making their adjustments in the appropriation account. If they thought that the company had increased its stock by relying on increases of trade creditors an adjustment (which would in effect offset some of the appropriation to reserves) would be made. Similarly, if the company financed itself by increasing its borrowing a decrease in its appropriations would be made.

5. STATEMENT OF CHANGE IN THE SHAREHOLDERS' EQUITY INTEREST

It was proposed that the retail price index should be used to show the change in the amount of the shareholders' equity interest. It would, therefore, be possible to examine accounts and see if sufficient profit and appropriations had been made in order to maintain the value of the shareholders' equity interest.

The idea of introducing CCA was not just to make adjustments to profit and loss accounts and balance sheets, but it was envisaged that management accounts would also be adjusted on CCA principles. This, of course, is important, as otherwise a company could not adopt a proper pricing policy for its goods and services, and if it ignored dealing with management accounts on the CCA basis it would have been in a situation whereby its annual accounts would have shown that it had not coped with its inflationary problems, and yet during the accounting period it would have been unaware that it had not been making the correct assumptions as far as pricing and costs were concerned.

Monetary items

During the time the Sandilands and Morpeth committees were deliberating over the methods to be used for inflation accounting considerable controversy occurred over how to adjust for inflation when a company had large monetary assets or liabilities. Money depreciates during times of inflation and it seems natural therefore to consider that a company which holds large monetary assets is losing value, and vice versa. The difficulty occurs, however, in using the monetary unit of measurement (£) for measuring its own loss of value. It is easy to account for the inflationary change in the value of, say, stock in units of £s but not so easy to account for changes in money in the same units.

Both the Sandilands and Morpeth committees were inclined to ignore adjusting monetary items for inflation but the banks put forward strong opposition to this view. As the largest holders of net monetary assets they would have suffered greatly in comparison with other companies if no adjustment in the profit and loss account could be made in a similar way to the cost of sales adjustment. The banks' profits would have been shown at higher figures than would otherwise have been the case. It was argued that monetary items were the stock in trade of banks and it is very necessary in times of inflation to increase reserves to support what appears to be increased liabilities which need not necessarily be so after taking into account the fall in the value of money.

The Hyde Guidelines

After the rejection in July 1977 of the Morpeth Committee's proposals for a wide ranging system of current cost accounting it was decided that a simpler method should be introduced quickly. A sub-committee was formed under the chairmanship of Mr. William Hyde and it put forward recommendations to the Accounting Standards Committee. These recommendations were issued as interim guidelines in November 1977.

These guidelines (popularly known as the 'Hyde Guidelines') were intended to be used by all companies listed on the Stock Exchange for their accountancy periods ending on or after 31st December 1977. It was hoped that out of the practical application a suitable method of dealing with inflation accounts would evolve which would be acceptable to a large body of people. A separate statement was proposed to accompany published accounts setting out the adjusted figures.

The recommendations were kept to a simple form and dealt only with the profit and loss account. Three adjustments were proposed:

1. *Depreciation*

An adjustment was proposed for the difference between the depreciation calculated on the historical cost basis and that based on the current cost of fixed assets. If a business had already devised an appropriate method of dealing with this aspect, it was proposed that it continued with its method. If a method had not already been devised, it was recommended that the calculations could be based on indices of appropriate prices. Such indices could be selected from specific industry indices or from the Central Statistical Office booklet 'Price Index Numbers for Current Cost Accounting'. For assets in a country outside the United Kingdom, where no such indices are available, the general price index for the particular country could be used instead.

2. *Cost of Sales*

The adjustment proposed was for the difference between the current cost of stock at the date of sale and the amount charged in computing the historical cost result. If a business had already devised a system, it was recommended to continue with its method, otherwise the calculations were to be based on an averaging method using index numbers.

3. *Gearing*

The result of both the depreciation and the cost of sales adjustments in inflationary periods is to reduce the profit. It was, however, recognized that if a business was relying on borrowed money a further adjustment should also be made. However, no consensus on the correct method was available and it was decided to experiment. The recommendation was that if total liabilities (including preference share capital) exceeded total monetary assets, the adjustments for depreciation and cost of sales need not be provided in full when computing the profit. The adjustment should take into account that the operating capability of the business was partly financed by net monetary liabilities. Alternatively, if there were net monetary assets, the adjustment for depreciation and cost of sales would have to be increased.

Here again, companies were not discouraged from following their own methods of adjustment, but for all three adjustments the methods used were to be disclosed in a short note to the separate statement.

Hyde Guidelines in Practice

As the guidelines were rushed into being after the failure of the Morpeth Committee's recommendations in July 1977, they did not deal comprehensively with all aspects of inflation accounts. They dealt only with profit and loss accounts and left individual companies to decide whether to use the methods suggested, whether to use alternative methods or not to use any adjustment at all. One cannot help thinking that the Accounting Standards Committee brought in these guidelines in order to save face and have something to show for the large amount of time and effort devoted to studying inflation accounting.

In the event, the Hyde Guidelines were not successful and were ignored by the majority of companies reporting after 31st December 1977.

Statement of Standard Accounting Practice No. 16 (SSAP 16)

In April 1979 another attempt was made by the Accounting Standards Committee to bring in a form of current cost accounting by the issue of a further exposure draft. This one proposed that it should become effective from 1st January 1980, and that it should be used in annual financial statements by all listed companies on the Stock Exchange and other entities with a turnover of £5 million or more. Certain companies were exempted. These were: insurance, property investment and dealing companies, and investment and unit trusts where the methods proposed did not appear to be appropriate.

The Accounting Standards Committee in this Exposure Draft abandoned its previous ideas of trying to introduce a comprehensive system for current cost accounting and instead decided to use the ideas of the 'Hyde Guidelines' as a practical solution and merely expand them.

Where the 'Hyde Guidelines' proposed three adjustments to the profit and loss account, Exposure Draft No. 24 proposed four, and, additionally, proposed that a current cost balance sheet should be provided. Historical cost accounts were still to be prepared and the current cost profit and loss account and current cost balance sheet were to be provided as additional statements with explanatory notes. Listed companies were to state the amount of current cost earnings per share. Where group accounts were concerned, it was only necessary to produce the additional statements for the consolidated accounts. The Exposure Draft was quickly followed in March 1980 by SSAP 16 with little practical alteration.

PROFIT AND LOSS ACCOUNT UNDER SSAP 16

In the profit and loss account Hyde had proposed adjustments for cost of sales and depreciation with the resultant combined figure being further adjusted for gearing. SSAP 16 continued with both the cost of sales and depreciation adjustments and with no alteration in the methods of calculation as proposed by Hyde. However, a further adjustment was required for monetary working capital. Then all three adjustments were combined and further adjusted for the gearing aspect.

CURRENT COST BALANCE SHEET UNDER SSAP 16

This was to be in summarized form and accompany annual financial statements in the same way as the current cost profit and loss account. Where appropriate, assets were to be included at their value to the business (normally net current replacement cost). A reserve known as Capital Maintenance Reserve was to be created to reflect the revaluation surpluses and deficits in the assets to the extent that they were not already included in the historical cost accounts.

Abandonment of persuasion

Towards the end of 1985 the proportion of Stock Exchange listed companies complying with SSAP 16 had fallen to only 15% and the Accounting Standards Committee announced that it had exhausted its powers of persuasion to get companies to make adjustments for inflation and said that it considered that legislation would be necessary to compel companies to give the requisite information. It accordingly withdrew SSAP 16.

What did it all mean?

The original proposals of the accountancy bodies to establish an all-embracing form of current cost accounting failed to get acceptance. They were undoubtedly too complicated for general use and an exact system cannot be devised when using a value of account (£) which is constantly moving.

The 'Hyde Guidelines' were simple to allow for development, but they had been ignored by the majority of companies and accountants. SSAP 16 brought in an adjustment for monetary working capital which was an improvement on Hyde as also was the provision of a current cost balance sheet. However, the use of so many different index numbers for relatively simple calculations seemed to be returning to the complications of the earlier proposals for current cost accounting. Aiming to be precise with certain isolated figures is pointless when so many other requirements for an accurate system have been ignored. For example, the monetary working capital was generally to be related to debtors and creditors only. The index numbers relating to stock were to be related only to approximate periods. The average of index numbers is a simple average and may not be in accordance with the facts, and averaging numbers solely between those applying at the beginning and the end of a financial period cannot be a true representation of the facts.

Where group accounts are prepared, the current cost figures were to be prepared for the consolidated accounts only and this is little help to a banker unless he is lending with the benefit of cross guarantees from all companies in the group.

Nevertheless, there were some advantages, but these apply regardless of the particular system of inflation accounting which is used. An indication is given that in times of inflation the whole of the historical profit cannot be distributed without, in effect, distributing part of the capital of the business. Some of the historical profit must be kept to maintain the operating capability of the business. Also, fixed assets would be valued at their current worth to the business instead of at out-of-date values. This has the effect of increasing the shareholders' funds through increases in reserves and this can be salutory when considering whether a proper return is being obtained on shareholders' funds.

In all, inflation adjusted accounts, although not perfect, can provide additional information which is useful to bankers in helping them to understand more thoroughly the business with which they are dealing. Such accounts help in showing whether companies are efficient on trading performance alone, bring out more forcibly the gearing aspects of borrowing, and produce more accurate figures for asset values.

The banker's view

A banker must view balance sheets and profit and loss accounts not just as numbers to be accepted but must look at them as being the result of a trading period in the environment in which the companies are operating. Booms and slumps in the particular industry concerned must be taken into account as well as individual aspects appertaining to the company being considered. Obviously, therefore, inflation must also be considered by a banker.

As far as turnover is concerned a certain increase in the sales receipts is necessary in an inflationary period merely to stand still. As for balance sheet figures, inflation affects the various items in different ways. For example, the increased values of properties have far exceeded the inflation rate in many years. Stock in a balance sheet, being valued at the lower of cost or market price may be of much greater value at the balance sheet date.

Long term borrowing is of advantage to businesses if they are eventually able to repay in depreciated money.

A banker must look at all aspects when considering a borrowing proposition and inflation is one which, in the absence of agreed procedures, must require experience and common sense to be applied to the figures submitted.

CHAPTER 21

Requirements for Company Accounts

Company accounts have to be produced in accordance with legal requirements but additionally they have to comply with the requirements of the Accountancy profession and, if they are listed companies or have quotations on the Unlisted Securities Market, with the rules of the Stock Exchange.

The legal requirements are set out in Schedule 4 of the Companies Act 1985 (except for banking, insurance and shipping companies which have to comply with sections 258 to 262 of Schedule 9). The Act is a consolidating act of the Companies Acts 1948 to 1983 and, as such, incorporates the proposals in the EEC Fourth Directive designed to harmonize accounting practices in the member states of the Common Market.

The Accountancy profession's regulations are contained in Statements of Standard Accounting Practice (SSAPs) and are designed to make more uniform the ways in which assets and liabilities are valued in balance sheets and income and expenditure are treated in profit and loss accounts. Should the requirements of the Act not be followed or any SSAP not be observed the auditors, who have to be qualified accountants, must qualify the accounts in their report.

The Stock Exchange regulations are contained in their publications 'Admission of Securities to Listing' (Yellow Book) which apply to listed companies, and 'General Undertaking' (Green Book) for companies dealt in on the Unlisted Securities Market. These rules are partly designed to see that individuals do not get an unfair advantage in share dealings through inside knowledge and, therefore, the rules govern such matters and the ways in which announcements of results, both interim and final, are made. Additionally, when such announcements are made it must be stated if any SSAP has not been followed and the reason why it has not been followed.

Statutory requirements

The Companies Act 1985 lays down the format in which accounts must be presented. There are two formats for the balance sheets, a vertical one and a double-sided balance sheet. For profit and loss accounts there are four formats, two vertical and two double sided as the profit and loss accounts can be shown with the items on an expense basis (i.e. suitable for companies which do not have their own manufacturing capability) or on a function basis (where manufacturing forms part of the activity).

The Companies Act is strict on the use of the formats and lays down that the items listed in the formats must be shown in the order given and under the headings and sub headings set out. Greater detail is permitted to be given but if there is any combining of items details of each item must be given in notes to the accounts. Once a choice of format has been made the same format is to be used every year. However, it is possible to change to an alternate format as specified in the Act but the change must be brought to attention through a note to the accounts and the reasons for the change must be given.

If, by following the requirements of the Act a true and fair view is not portrayed further information must be given to enable a true and fair view to be portrayed to readers of the accounts.

Companies are also required to observe the following:

1. They must be a going concern because their accounts will be prepared on this assumption. If there is any doubt the auditors must qualify their report. Quite often, whether a company is a going concern or not depends upon whether bank overdraft and loan facilities are available for a certain period ahead. If not, the auditors will state this as the reason for a qualification.
2. The accounting policies must be consistently applied year by year. If not, a note to the accounts must state the reason for any change.
3. All values shown in the balance sheets must be on a prudent basis. Only profits which are realized at the date of the balance sheets are to be included. In contrast to this, all liabilities made at the balance sheet dates have to be included together with any liabilities for losses likely to be made including any which may become apparent between the date of the balance sheet and the date of its signing by the directors. If this was not the case a large loss could unexpectedly occur after a company's financial year end and yet financial statements would be sent to shareholders giving a totally false impression. This requirement is also a help to bankers.
4. All income and charges relating to the financial year must be taken into account regardless of the date of receipt or payment.
5. Values of each individual item of assets or liabilities must be separately determined.

It is also laid down in the Act that the accounting policies used must be stated and, in particular, the depreciation policies used for writing down or reduction in value of fixed assets and the policy used for dealing with foreign currency sums. It is also not permitted for assets to be set off against liabilities or for income to be set off against expenditure. Corresponding figures for the previous financial year have to be given both in the balance sheet and the profit and loss account and in the notes to the accounts where figures are quoted.

The Act specifically states that the following items cannot be treated as assets:

1. Preliminary expenses
2. Expenses and commission on the issue of shares or debentures
3. Costs of research

Numerous matters have to be disclosed when accounts are sent to members (i.e. shareholders). Many of these do not affect the financial requirements of the company but a number of them are important and give valuable information to a lending banker.

For example, the total of the directors' remuneration has to be quoted and the chairman's remuneration and the remuneration of the highest paid director. Details of any loans to directors must be shown and these are only permitted by companies where the lending of money is part of its ordinary business. As for employees, the number receiving remuneration above certain levels must be quoted together with the aggregate amount of loans to officials. This is all useful information to bankers particularly as regards the smaller companies, as they will be able to relate the amounts shown to the success or otherwise of the company and decide whether or not those in charge are 'milking' the company unnecessarily.

The average number of employees and their total cost must be shown but these figures have to be treated with care. Averages can be misleading and as part-time employees are included an incorrect impression can be gained. This is particularly so when group accounts are being read.

The auditors' remuneration has to be quoted and this may give some idea as to the difficulty of the audit if a comparison is made year by year.

Of particular interest to lending bankers will be the transfers to and from reserves which have to be specified, and the contingent liabilities such as guarantees or securities given to third parties for the liabilities of others, or provisions for legal damages. This last item is generally resisted by directors as it might give comfort to the other side in the legal action. Where security has been given for liabilities this must be stated.

The Act lays down that proper books of account should be kept and a balance sheet, profit and loss account, directors' report and auditor's report should be presented to members and that subsequently a General Meeting should be held at least once a year. These documents also have to be filed with the Registrar of Companies within specified time limits from the end of the company's financial year – seven months for a public company and ten months for a private company. Unfortunately many sets of accounts are not, at the moment, registered within the time limits.

Small and medium-sized companies can file modified accounts in which the main exceptions are that they may omit turnover, profit and loss accounts and directors' reports and submit abbreviated balance sheets. These companies do, however, have to submit full accounts to their members. Small companies are those which can satisfy two of the following points. Turnover must be less than £1.4m per annum, total assets less than £0.7m and the employees must be less than 50. To qualify for the medium-sized category the figures are; turnover £5.75m, total assets £2.8m and employees 250.

As far as lending bankers are concerned modified accounts are of little use and full accounts should be requested.

The Directors' Report

The Directors' Report should not be confused with the Chairman's Statement. The Directors' Report is required under the Companies Act 1985 and must cover certain specified points. The details therein are subject to audit. This is not the case with the Chairman's Statement. There is no statutory requirement for such a Statement and in many private companies no Statement appears. Most public companies produce a Chairman's Statement and, although auditors like to see it and, if necessary make comments about any inaccuracies, before it is published, the auditors can only influence the Statement; they have no statutory power concerning it. In consequence, some chairmen are over-enthusiastic about future trading prospects and, although much valuable information may be gleaned from the remarks of a chairman, a lending banker should beware of giving too much emphasis to stated prospects of expected good times ahead.

The points which have to be covered in the Director's Report or, in the case of listed companies anywhere in the annual report are:

1. The recommended dividend and transfers to reserves.
2. The principal activities of the company together with any significant changes in the activities during the year reported upon.
3. A fair review of the business activities during the year.
4. Any post balance sheet events of importance.
5. Comments on future developments in the business.
6. Comments (if any) on research and development.
7. The names of all persons who, at any time during the year, have been directors together with details of their and their spouses' and infant children's interests in the company.
8. Details of any purchases of its own shares.
9. Any significant changes in the fixed assets.
10. Any substantial difference in the value of the freeholds and leaseholds between book value and market value.
11. Political or charitable donations if in excess of £200.
12. Details of any contracts between directors and the company, apart from service contracts.

There are also some non-financial points to be covered concerning employees and consultation with them over matters which affect their interests and in keeping them informed about the company's performance. The company's policy on employing disabled persons must also be stated if it employs 250 or more people.

Apart from these statutory requirements the Stock Exchange also requires from both listed companies and those dealt in on the Unlisted Securities Market the following to be covered:

1. Geographical details of turnover and contribution to results of activities outside the United Kingdom and the Republic of Ireland.
2. Details of any material difference between trading results and any published forecast.
3. Details of any director's interest in shares or options in the company.
4. Names of shareholders who hold 5% or more of shares in the company which have voting rights.
5. Any non-observance of any SSAP.

Are there standard accounts?

Although it could be thought that with such regulations, most company accounts would follow a standard pattern this is far from the case. There is a great deal of variety between what is shown in the balance sheets and profit and loss accounts as opposed to the notes accompanying financial statements. There are also, unfortunately, ways of expression when explanatory notes are prepared which, to other than the initiated, give a bland form of words which cloud the real facts.

There is only one way for the student to get an overall view and that is by studying the published accounts of limited companies, both public and private. For lending bankers detailed enquiries are often necessary concerning individual items in the accounts and the notes.

Balance Sheet Format 1.

The format as specified in the Companies Act 1985 is as follows:

FORMAT 1

A Called up share capital not paid

B Fixed assets

I Intangible assets
1 Development costs
2 Concessions, patents, licences, trade marks and similar rights and assets
3 Goodwill
4 Payments on account

II Tangible assets
1 Land and buildings
2 Plant and machinery
3 Fixtures, fittings, tools and equipment
4 Payments on account and assets in course of construction

III Investments
1 Shares in group companies
2 Loans to group companies
3 Shares in related companies
4 Loans to related companies
5 Other investments other than loans
6 Other loans
7 Own shares

C Current assets

I Stocks
1 Raw materials and consumables
2 Work in progress
3 Finished goods and goods for resale
4 Payments on account

II Debtors
1 Trade debtors
2 Amounts owed by group companies
3 Amounts owed by related companies
4 Other debtors
5 Called up share capital not paid
6 Prepayments and accrued income

III Investments
1 Shares in group companies
2 Own shares
3 Other investments

IV Cash at bank and in hand

D Prepayments and accrued income

E Creditors: Amounts falling due within one year

1 Debenture loans
2 Bank loans and overdrafts
3 Payments received on account
4 Trade creditors
5 Bills of exchange payable
6 Amounts owed to group companies
7 Amounts owed to related companies
8 Other creditors including taxation and social security
9 Accruals and deferred income

F Net current assets (liabilities)

G Total assets less current liabilities

H Creditors: amounts falling due after more than one year

1 Debenture loans
2 Bank loans and overdrafts
3 Payments received on account

4 Trade creditors
5 Bills of exchange payable
6 Amounts owed to group companies
7 Amounts owed to related companies
8 Other creditors including taxation and social security
9 Accruals and deferred income

I Provisions for liabilities and charges

1 Pensions and similar obligations
2 Taxation, including deferred taxation
3 Other provisions

J Accruals and deferred income

K Capital and reserves

I Called up share capital

II Share premium account

III Revaluation reserve

IV Other reserves
1 Capital redemption reserve
2 Reserve for own shares
3 Reserves provided for by the articles of association
4 Other reserves

V Profit and loss account

Fixed assets

It will be seen that these are divided into three sections

1. Intangible
2. Tangible
3. Investments

The statutory requirements are that valuations in accounts must normally be at cost or market price, whichever is the lower, and that depreciation must be provided if any fixed assets have a limited useful life. If any other method of valuation is used it must be stated. SSAP 12 also deals with depreciation and requires that the depreciation methods used are disclosed and if there is a change in method used it should be explained.

It has already been mentioned that preliminary expenses, costs of research and commission on the issue of shares or debentures cannot be treated as assets. However, it is possible to carry some development costs forward in special circumstances. This can only be if the development is virtually certain to bring benefit to the company and the costs must be written off over the expected time of economic advantage to the company. The reasons for capitalization and the write-off period must be disclosed.

Goodwill can only be carried in accounts if it has been purchased and it must be written off over its useful economic life. Details must be disclosed.

As intangible assets generally prove to be worthless when a company gets into trouble bankers will ignore the value of intangible assets when assessing balance sheets.

Among the tangible assets the land and buildings must be sub-divided between freeholds and leaseholds with short leases of 50 years or less unexpired being shown separately.

A banker will, of course, not be relying on balance sheet values to support any advance but may require specific valuations.

The investments in this part of the balance sheet are fixed assets which means that they are held for the long term. As such, there is no necessity to apply a market value in the accounts. The directors may carry the investments at a value which, to them, seems appropriate. If listed investments are held the market value should be shown if this is less than the balance sheet value. Details have to be given of any holdings where the nominal value exceeds 10% of the issued share capital.

If a banker takes investments from a company as security he should note whether they are held as fixed or current assets. If they are fixed assets they are held for the long term and they may not easily be sold without some damage to the owner. This is not the case with investments held as current assets.

The Stock Exchange regulations require details to be given of interests in equity capital of 20% or more and SSAP 1 details how associated companies investments should be treated in accounts (see Chapter 12).

Current assets

The general rule is that current assets are valued at cost or market value whichever is the lower but stocks can be carried at current cost if desired. If so, this fact must be stated. Stocks can also be valued using F.I.F.O., L.I.F.O., weighted average or similar methods (see Chapter 4).

Debtors must be divided between the various groups and amounts falling due after more than one year have to be stated separately. Even though they are stated separately they are still included in the current assets. A banker should use a prudent approach when considering such items and would do well to exclude them from current assets in his own analysis form.

Separate details must be given for amounts due from subsidiaries and other group companies. This is useful to bankers when lending to one or some of a group of companies as it enables them to see the picture more clearly.

Investments in current assets can be shown at current cost.

Current liabilities

Apart from the separate items shown it should be noted that the liabilities are those shown falling due within one year. If security has been given for any sum due it should be noted on the front of the balance sheet or in the notes.

Creditors: amounts falling due after more than one year

If security has been given it must be stated. Figures also must be given for those amounts falling due after five years. There is a Stock Exchange requirement that for bank loans and overdrafts, both in this section and under current liabilities, separate figures are to be given for those loans repayable in one year or less, between one year and two years, between two years and five years, and in five years or more. This requirement also applies to loans other than bank loans.

In a similar way to the treatment of sums due from subsidiaries and other group companies in the current assets, separate figures must be given for amounts due to subsidiaries and other group companies.

Provisions for liabilities and charges

Transfers to provisions must be disclosed and also transfers from provisions if the purpose was not that for which the provision was established. SSAP 15 deals in detail with taxation matters and this is important to bankers as amounts can be large and if they are not paid when due a company can be placed in a serious position. A company can then put pressure on its bank to provide the funds to pay the tax and a banker who wishes to avoid stepping into the shoes of the tax creditor should see that he is aware of the liabilities and when they are due. Bankers must be conscious, however, that the amounts shown for both current and deferred taxation are estimated amounts. The actual amounts are agreed with the tax inspectors well after the preparation of accounts. If the taxation liabilities cause some unease a banker should ask for a full explanation of the position. As for deferred taxation SSAP 15 requires that it should be shown separately and that the full amount of deferred taxation not provided for in the accounts should be shown in the notes.

Capital and reserves

Both the authorized and paid up capital should be shown together with details of share options and convertible securities. Any movement on reserves must be shown.

Balance Sheet Format 2

This format is as follows:

FORMAT 2

ASSETS

A Called up share capital not paid

B Fixed assets

I Intangible assets
 1 Development costs
 2 Concessions, patents, licences, trade marks and similar rights and assets
 3 Goodwill
 4 Payments on account

II Tangible assets
 1 Land and buildings
 2 Plant and machinery
 3 Fixtures, fittings, tools and equipment
 4 Payments on account and assets in course of construction

III Investments
 1 Shares in group companies
 2 Loans to group companies
 3 Shares in related companies
 4 Loans to related companies
 5 Other investments other than loans
 6 Other loans
 7 Own shares

C Current assets

I Stocks
 1 Raw materials and consumables
 2 Work in progress
 3 Finished goods and goods for resale
 4 Payments on account

II Debtors
 1 Trade debtors
 2 Amounts owed by group companies
 3 Amounts owed by related companies
 4 Other debtors
 5 Called up share capital not paid
 6 Prepayments and accrued income

III Investments
 1 Shares in group companies
 2 Own shares
 3 Other investments

IV Cash at bank and in hand

D Prepayments and accrued income

LIABILITIES

A Capital and reserves

I Called up share capital

II Share premium account

III Revaluation reserve

IV Other reserves
 1 Capital redemption reserve
 2 Reserve for own shares

3 Reserves provided for by the articles of association
4 Other reserves

V Profit and loss account

B Provisions for liabilities and charges

1 Pensions and similar obligations
2 Taxation including deferred taxation
3 Other provisions

C Creditors

1 Debenture loans
2 Bank loans and overdrafts
3 Payments received on account
4 Trade creditors
5 Bills of exchange payable
6 Amounts owed to group companies
7 Amounts owed to related companies
8 Other creditors including taxation and social security
9 Accruals and deferred income

D Accruals and deferred income

It will be seen that, contrary to tradition, the assets appear first i.e. on the left side if a double-sided balance sheet is prepared, while the capital and liabilities appear afterwards and would be on the right side on such a presentation. There is also a difference from Format 1 in that the creditors do not have to be divided between those falling due within one year and those falling due after one year.

Most companies are following Format 1 as it is generally considered that this is more comprehensible to the general body of the public.

Profit and loss formats

There are four Formats. 1 and 2 are vertical forms and 3 and 4 are double-sided ones. 2 and 4 are suitable for companies which manufacture whereas 1 and 3 are suitable where manufacturing does not form part of a company's activities.

The Formats are as follows:

FORMAT 1

1 Turnover
2 Cost of sales
3 Gross profit or loss
4 Distribution costs
5 Administrative expenses
6 Other operating income
7 Income from shares in group companies
8 Income from shares in related companies
9 Income from other fixed asset investments
10 Other interest receivable and similar income
11 Amounts written off investments

12 Interest payable and similar charges
13 Tax on profit or loss on ordinary activities
14 Profit or loss on ordinary activities after taxation
15 Extraordinary income
16 Extraordinary charges
17 Extraordinary profit or loss
18 Tax on extraordinary profit or loss
19 Other taxes not shown under the above items
20 Profit or loss for the financial year

FORMAT 2

1 Turnover
2 Change in stocks of finished goods and in work in progress
3 Own work capitalised
4 Other operating income
5 (*a*) Raw materials and consumables
(*b*) Other external charges
6 Staff costs:
(*a*) wages and salaries
(*b*) social security costs
(*c*) other pension costs
7 (*a*) Depreciation and other amounts written off tangible and intangible fixed assets
(*b*) Exceptional amounts written off current assets
8 Other operating charges
9 Income from shares in group companies
10 Income from shares in related companies
11 Income from other fixed asset investments
12 Other interest receivable and similar income
13 Amounts written off investments
14 Interest payable and similar charges
15 Tax on profit or loss on ordinary activities
16 Profit or loss on ordinary activities after taxation
17 Extraordinary income
18 Extraordinary charges
19 Extraordinary profit or loss
20 Tax on extraordinary profit or loss
21 Other taxes not shown under the above items
22 Profit or loss for the financial year

FORMAT 3

A Charges

1 Cost of sales
2 Distribution costs
3 Administrative expenses
4 Amounts written off investments
5 Interest payable and similar charges
6 Tax on profit or loss on ordinary activities
7 Profit or loss on ordinary activities after taxation
8 Extraordinary charges
9 Tax on extraordinary profit or loss

10 Other taxes not shown under the above items
11 Profit or loss for the financial year

B Income

1 Turnover
2 Other operating income
3 Income from shares in group companies
4 Income from shares in related companies
5 Income from other fixed asset investments
6 Other interest receivable and similar income
7 Profit or loss on ordinary activities after taxation
8 Extraordinary income
9 Profit or loss for the financial year

FORMAT 4

A Charges

1 Reduction in stocks of finished goods and in work in progress
2 (*a*) Raw materials and consumables
(*b*) Other external charges
3 Staff costs:
(*a*) wages and salaries
(*b*) social security costs
(*c*) other pension costs
4 (*a*) Depreciation and other amounts written off tangible and intangible fixed assets
(*b*) Exceptional amounts written off current assets
5 Other operating charges
6 Amounts written off investments
7 Interest payable and similar charges
8 Tax on profit or loss on ordinary activities
9 Profit or loss on ordinary activities after taxation
10 Extraordinary charges
11 Tax on extraordinary profit or loss
12 Other taxes not shown under the above items
13 Profit or loss for the financial year

B Income

1 Turnover
2 Increase in stocks of finished goods and in work in progress
3 Own work capitalised
4 Other operating income
5 Income from shares in group companies
6 Income from shares in related companies
7 Income from other fixed asset investments
8 Other interest receivable and similar income
9 Profit or loss on ordinary activities after taxation
10 Extraordinary income
11 Profit or loss for the financial year

Turnover has to be shown and if the turnover comprises two or more types of business which are substantially different from each other separate details must be given together with the profit or loss before tax derived from each type. Also, if the geographical areas in which sales are made are substantially different from each other the turnovers in each area must be stated. However, it is easy to see that the disclosure of this information could be of use to a competitor and if the directors consider that giving the information would be seriously prejudicial to the company's interests it need not be given. In such circumstances the reason for non-disclosure must be given.

If the amount paid to and from group companies include interest elements the amount of interest must be shown separately as also must the interest paid to banks and on other loans.

The main disclosures are self evident from the items shown in the Formats and it will be seen that extraordinary items have to be shown separately and not netted. The Act requires that the basis on which tax is computed must be given together with the rate of corporation tax used. Separate figures have to be given for U.K. corporation tax, double taxation relief, U.K. income tax and foreign tax.

If any director has waived emoluments this must be disclosed. The Stock Exchange regulations for listed companies go even further. They require disclosure of any dividends waived by shareholders.

Group Accounts

These have to be produced for the ultimate parent company of a group and, generally, must be consolidated accounts and subject to similar requirements as laid down in the Act for company accounts. If a consolidated profit and loss account is prepared, a holding company need not prepare its own separate profit and loss account. The same rules apply that sufficient information should be given for a true and fair view to be portrayed.

There are occasions when directors feel that instead of consolidated accounts some other form of group accounts is preferable. If so, they must give their reasons for not producing consolidated accounts. The Stock Exchange regulations, however, require consolidated accounts for listed groups.

Statements of Source and Application of Funds

These statements form part of sets of accounts but they are not called for under the Act. They are a requirement of SSAP 10.

CHAPTER 22

Statements of Standard Accounting Practice

In order to appreciate thoroughly the requirements of these standards it is necessary to study the full texts. These can be obtained from the Institute of Chartered Accountants of England and Wales and purchased singly. Alternatively the full texts of all current standards 'Accounting Standards' can be obtained from the same source. This latter comprehensive publication is brought up to date annually.

Comment on the individual standards and how they affect the lending banker follow, but it is emphasized that more benefit will be obtained from reading and understanding the actual text of each standard.

SSAP 1. Accounting for Associated Companies

In the circumstances of a simple investment a company would bring into its profit and loss account the dividends received. However, where a company carries on a significant part of its business through an associated company a false impression would be given if, in the consolidated accounts, only the dividend income from the associated company was included. It could well be policy to restrict the dividends in the associated company in order to build up the capital base and this would be hidden from shareholders.

This standard of accounting practice was brought in to deal with this problem and the general principle is that the investing company should bring into its profit and loss account the dividends received (and thereby show its correct position as a legal entity) while in the consolidated accounts the investing company's share of the associated company's profits or losses will be brought into the consolidated profit and loss account and its share of the associated company's post-acquisition retained profits or accumulated deficit would be reflected in the consolidated balance sheet. This method is known as the equity method of accounting.

All that is now necessary is to know what is an associated company. First of all we should remember that a subsidiary company is one where a holding company either holds more than 50% in nominal value of its equity share capital or controls the composition of its board of directors. A company would not be classed as an associate if such conditions existed. There is a clear division between subsidiary companies and associated companies.

A temporary investment cannot make one company an associate of another. The investment must be for the long term and substantial in relation to other shareholdings and the investing company or group must be in a position to exercise a significant influence over the company in which the investment is made.

The standard says that significant influence over a company involves participation in the financial and operating policy decisions of that company (including dividend policy) but not necessarily control over those policies. Representation on the board indicates such participation but is not conclusive evidence and neither is it the only way in which participation in policy decisions can be obtained.

It will be seen, therefore, that whether or not a company is an associated one will depend on the facts in any particular instance. However, the standard says that if a company owns 20% or more of the equity voting rights it should be presumed that the investing company can exercise significant influence.

In summary, therefore, a holding company or a group will class another company as an associate if it;

1. is holding its investment for the long term, and
2. can exercise a significant influence over the affairs of the company in which it holds the investment, and
3. it is presumed to exercise such influence if it holds 20% or more (not of course exceeding 50% when it will be a subsidiary) of the equity voting rights.

For further details of the accounting treatment and the bankers' view see Chapter 12.

SSAP 2. Disclosure of Accounting Policies

The directors of companies have commercial judgements to make while the accountants have to decide how to reflect the results in accounts. There obviously can be several ways in which to reflect the results depending upon whether an optimistic or pessimistic view is taken. It can be seen that if one view is taken one year and a different one the following year that no real comparison year by year can be obtained. It is necessary, therefore, that there should be consistency in the policies adopted by each company.

There are four fundamental accounting concepts which, in particular, are mentioned in this standard.

1. Going concern. That is that there is no intention to liquidate or curtail significantly the scale of operation.
2. Accruals. Revenue and costs are accounted for as they are incurred not when money is received or paid.
3. Consistency. As explained above.
4. Prudence. Profits are not anticipated and provision is made for all known liabilities.

Within these concepts it is possible to have considerable variations in, for example, depreciation of assets, valuation of stocks and raw materials, leasing transactions, conversion of foreign currencies and dealing with long term contracts.

Many other items can be dealt with in a variety of ways and the standard lays down that specific accounting bases should be selected and followed consistently.

These policies have to be shown in the notes to the accounts and a banker should read and understand them in order to interpret thoroughly the figures shown in each set of accounts.

SSAP 3. Earnings per share

This standard applies to listed companies and stipulates that the earnings per share on a net basis should be shown on the face of the profit and loss account together with the figure for the corresponding previous financial period.

The method of calculation is laid down in order to make comparisons between companies on a like basis. Earnings per share are calculated on the profit in the consolidated balance sheet after deducting minority interests and preference dividends but before taking into account extraordinary items.

The net basis is that referred to after taking into account taxation including any irrecoverable advance corporation tax and any unrelieved overseas tax on dividend payments.

From a banker's point of view it is important to keep in mind that the earnings per share are based on the consolidated figures and that this includes the share of profits (not the dividends received) of associated companies.

SSAP 4. The Accounting Treatment of Government Grants

There are numerous types of grants. Those that are made with reference to revenue expenditure cause no problems as the grants should be credited direct to the profit and loss account to offset such expenditure. Those related to capital expenditure should not, however, be treated in the same way as this would boost profits in the year in which the grant was obtained whereas the economic advantage of the fixed asset would be spread over a period. This standard specifies that the grant should also be spread over the expected useful life of the asset.

Balance sheets will show, in such circumstances a deferred credit, a portion of which will be transferred to revenue annually. A banker should keep in mind that in many instances capital grants are only made because no such investment would be made on purely commercial grounds. The deferred credit should, therefore, be looked upon with caution.

SSAP 5. Accounting for Value Added Tax

This standard is not of great importance to a lending banker but he should note that the turnover shown in profit and loss accounts excludes V.A.T. (see p. 174).

SSAP 6. Extraordinary Items and Prior Year Adjustments

In order to avoid distortion in the profit and loss accounts many accountants used to favour putting extraordinary items and prior year adjustments direct to reserves. However, this standard considers that this does not give as correct a view of the progress of the business as is possible. The standard states that such items should generally be credited or debited to the profit and loss accounts in the years in which they occur but should be disclosed as separate items after the ordinary results have been obtained. This is the same treatment as indicated by the profit and loss formats in the Companies Act 1985.

There is an exception, however, for some prior year adjustments. If there are material adjustments arising from changes in accounting policies and from the correction of fundamental errors the adjustments should be made to the prior years with the result that the opening balance of the retained profit will be adjusted. Disclosure by a note to the accounts should be made. Normal recurring corrections, however, should go to the profit and loss account in the same way as extraordinary items and, if material, should be disclosed.

SSAP 8. The Treatment of Taxation under the Imputation System in the Accounts of Companies

The following points should be understood;

1. Advance Corporation Tax (A.C.T.). When a company makes a distribution to shareholders it is required to make an advance payment of Corporation Tax. This is not a deduction from the gross dividend with the shareholder receiving the net amount but a figure on top of the distribution to the shareholder. The shareholder receives a tax credit as he is chargeable to tax on the total of the dividend plus the tax credit.
2. Corporation Tax. This is the tax liability on a company's income and, when paying it, the A.C.T. already paid in the year is normally deducted.
3. Mainstream Corporation Tax. This is the net sum payable. Therefore, Corporation Tax is a combination of Mainstream Corporation Tax and A.C.T.
4. Franked Investment Income. This is the income received from another U.K. resident company with the addition of the related tax credit. The

net amount can be redistributed to shareholders of the recipient company without further payment of A.C.T. and the shareholder is entitled to a tax credit on the distribution.

5. Unrelieved Overseas Tax. If the rate of overseas tax exceeds the rate of Mainstream Corporation Tax part of the overseas tax will be unrelieved. In these circumstances it may not be available for calculating overseas tax credit and, if this is the case, it should be debited to the profit and loss account and separately disclosed.

There are some variations in the recoverability of A.C.T. although it is principally recovered by being set off against Corporation Tax in the year in which the related distribution is made to shareholders. The two previous years are also available to absorb the relief. A.C.T. can be carried forward indefinitely but if the A.C.T. is large and the foreseeable future profits are expected to be relatively small the prudent course would be to write off some or all of the A.C.T.

The accounting problem is whether to treat A.C.T. as part of the cost of the dividend or whether it should be treated as part of the tax on the company's profit. This standard says that dividends should be shown in the profit and loss account and that the charge for taxation shown in the accounts is to be the full Corporation Tax i.e. the A.C.T. plus Mainstream Corporation Tax.

Separate disclosure is necessary for the charge for Corporation Tax (and any transfers to and from deferred taxation account), tax on franked investment income, irrecoverable A.C.T., the relief for overseas taxation and the total of overseas taxation.

The balance sheet will treat the A.C.T. on proposed dividends as a current tax liability.

SSAP 9. Stocks and Work in Progress

As it is possible to value these items in so many different ways this standard is an important one. The normal method of valuation laid down is that of cost or, if lower, at net realizable value. Each item of stock should be valued separately or, if this is impracticable, groups or categories can be valued together. Costs can include related production overheads.

It is not permissible to use an estimated replacement cost if the effect is to take into account a loss which is greater than that expected to be incurred. On long-term contract work, if the outcome can be assessed with reasonable certainty, an attributable profit can be added to cost but this must be assessed with prudence.

There are many methods of costing and the standard states that the accounting policies followed in arriving at the amounts for stocks and work in progress must be disclosed in a note to the accounts.

SSAP 10. Statements of Source and Application of Funds

This accounting standard applies to all enterprises with a turnover or gross income of £25,000 per annum or more and it states that this funds statement should form part of the audited accounts of a company.

For details of how this statement is produced see Chapter 1.

SSAP 12. Accounting for Depreciation

The standard states that the allocation of depreciation to accounting periods involves managerial judgement and, as such, requires annual review in the light of possible changed circumstances.

In order to allocate depreciation to appropriate accounting periods managements must take into account the cost of assets, their useful life and the anticipated residual value. Where the residual value is expected to be small it should be regarded as nil with the depreciation calculated accordingly.

Financial statements should state for each major class of depreciable asset;

1. the depreciation methods used
2. the useful lives or the depreciation rates used
3. total depreciation allocated for the period
4. the gross amount of depreciable assets and the related accumulated depreciation.

If there is a change in the depreciation method used it should be brought to the attention of readers through a note to the accounts and it is not permitted to omit charging depreciation on a fixed asset on the basis that its market value has increased. If the new market value is to be used and the asset written up in the books, depreciation must be charged by taking the new value into account.

A banker will be able to see whether the depreciation rates used are prudent by comparing them with the rates used by other companies in similar businesses.

SSAP 13. Accounting for Research and Development

Research and development generally falls into three categories – pure research, applied research and development expenditure. It is difficult to lay down dividing lines between these three categories but the standard emphasizes that prudence in treatment is to be observed. The first two categories are considered to be normal continuing expenditure and should be written off in the periods in which they are incurred. The Companies Act 1985 also does not permit research expenditure to be treated as an asset.

Development work on new or improved products is quite different and it can be asserted that if such development work is expected to bring future commercial benefits, the expenditure should be matched against future revenue.

This is accepted by this standard which gives guidelines for assessing the uncertainties involved. Prudence is stressed, and if the available evidence gives justification, it is permitted to bring forward a balance on development expenditure to be written off over the period expected to benefit.

Detailed disclosure could raise considerable problems of definition and, therefore, disclosure is limited to the movements of unamortized development expenditure during the year. The accounting policy followed must, however, be clearly explained.

SSAP 14. Group Accounts

The normal accounts required by this standard are consolidated accounts and only exceptionally are alternative forms of group accounts permitted.

An overriding aspect is that the group accounts should present a true and fair view and that uniform group accounting policies shall be followed. If differing accounting policies are used this must be disclosed and the reasons given.

Whenever practical the financial statements of subsidiaries shall be prepared to the same accounting date as the holding company and associated companies shall be incorporated by the equity method of accounting (see SSAP 1 and Chapter 12).

SSAP 15. Accounting for Deferred Tax

Deferred tax is related to timing differences between profits and losses as computed for tax purposes. Timing differences are those which originate in one financial period and are capable of reversing in subsequent periods.

The deferred tax payable is computed according to the liability method which is calculated at the rate of tax which is expected to apply when the tax is payable.

Whether there will be a liability or not must be based on reasonable assumptions and a prudent view must be taken.

The amount of deferred tax relating to ordinary activities should be shown in the profit and loss account or in a note, as must deferred tax on extraordinary items. The full amount of any unprovided deferred tax must be shown in a note and analysed into its major components.

The balance on the deferred tax account must also be shown and transfers to and from deferred tax must be disclosed in a note.

For further information on deferred tax see Chapter 14.

SSAP 17. Accounting for Post Balance Sheet Events

Events occurring after the end of a financial period can be:

1. Adjusting events. Those which provide additional evidence relating to conditions existing at the balance sheet date.

2. Non-adjusting events. Events which concern conditions which did not exist at the balance sheet date.

This standard states that if material adjusting events occur after the end of a financial period and up to the time that the balance sheet is signed, changes in the financial statement should be made. In order to assess 'materiality' it is necessary to take into account all matters which will enable users of financial statements to assess the financial position.

If the non-adjusting events are material reference should be made to them in a note.

SSAP 18. Accounting for Contingencies

For the purpose of this standard a contingency is a condition which exists at the balance sheet date where the outcome will be confirmed only on the occurrence or non-occurrence of one or more uncertain future events.

Where it is probable that there will be a material contingent loss this should be accrued in financial statements. A contingent financial gain should, however, not be anticipated but if it is probable that the gain will be realized a note should appear with the financial statement.

Obviously, careful judgement is necessary by the directors to decide on whether to account for contingencies.

SSAP 19. Accounting for Investment Properties

A company can hold investment properties whether or not its main business is that of an investment holding company. It all depends on the facts.

The point is that such investments are not held for consumption in the business enterprise and the disposal would not materially affect the trading activities of the company.

For many investments the depreciation on the lines of SSAP 12 is inappropriate (although leases, especially short ones, provide an exception) and it is more important to know the current value of such investments in order to gain a proper appreciation of the financial position.

The standard requires investment properties to be included in the balance sheet at open market value although it is not necessary to employ an external valuer. If the company is a listed one an external review should be carried out, at least, every five years. The adjusting entries are made through an investment revaluation reserve account which is non-distributable. The balance of such an account is required to be shown in the balance sheet formats specified in the Companies Act 1985.

SSAP 20. Foreign Currency Translation

A company may carry out operations in a foreign currency either on its own behalf or through a foreign enterprise which keeps its own accounting records.

This standard deals with the treatment of both operations.

(a) If a company carries out operations on its own behalf it must translate each transaction at the exchange rate ruling at the time of the transaction. If there is little fluctuation in the rate during the period an average rate can be used.

At the balance sheet date the company may be holding non-monetary assets (generally fixed assets) and net monetary assets (generally net current assets) abroad. The non-monetary assets when first translated should be kept at that translation figure without subsequent movement because of exchange rate fluctuations. For monetary assets the closing rate at the balance sheet date should be used unless there are attributable forward or other contracts establishing a different rate. Any long-term contracts are generally dealt with at the closing rate.

It will be seen that there can be gains and losses on exchange differences on revenue and on net current assets and these are considered to be on ordinary activities and appear in the profit and loss account. If there should be gains or losses on extraordinary items they would be treated as extraordinary items in the same way as for non-currency items (see SSAP 16).

(b) If a company has a foreign enterprise carrying on its own activities the investment in the foreign enterprise is really in the net assets and not in the individual items.

The standard says that in these circumstances the closing rate at the balance sheet date is the appropriate rate to use, but it does allow, in certain circumstances, for an average rate to be used. Consistency year by year must apply.

Following the theme that the investment is in the net assets any exchange differences would not be akin to trading activities and gains and losses have therefore to be put through a reserves account.

There can be a combination of these two methods of conducting foreign trade. The situation can be as in (b) above but although there are separate entities they are so closely linked that the results of the overseas entity are more dependent upon the economic environment of the investing company. This would be similar to a head office and a branch. In these circumstances the 'temporal' method of translating is used. This is similar to that used in (a) above.

The standard also deals with borrowing by an investing company in a foreign currency to finance the foreign equity investment. In these circumstances, there is, at least, a partial hedge against exchange movements as foreign currency borrowings can be offset against foreign currency investments. Any translation differences should be dealt with through reserves.

For the banker, therefore, he should look to see which translations have taken place through the profit and loss account and which through reserves. He will then be able to judge the position accordingly.

SSAP 21. Accounting for Leases and Hire Purchase Contracts

Leases and hire purchase contracts have a great deal of similarity although legally they are quite different.

The ownership of a leased asset rests with a lessor who leases it to a lessee for an agreed regular payment. With the law as it stands at present, ownership cannot pass to the lessee at the end of the lease term. In a hire purchase contract the hirer is able to purchase the asset at the end of the hire period and this is usually for a nominal sum.

Leases are of two types, financial leases and operating leases. The operating lease is one where the lessee pays a rental for use of the asset for a period which is substantially less than the economic life of the asset. A finance lease is one whereby the lessee pays the lessor the full cost of the asset plus an interest amount. The contract provides that substantially all the risks and rewards are accepted by the lessee.

In both lease and hire purchase transactions during the term of the contracts the ownership of the asset rests with the lessor or the hire purchase company, and if legal ownership was the criterion for reflection of the asset in accounts the value of the asset would appear in lessor's or hire purchase company's books with only the lease or hire payments appearing in the accounts of the enterprise actually using the asset.

It will be seen that unless full disclosure takes place a lessee or hirer could produce accounts which would give no indication of the liabilities incurred.

This standard, therefore, provides for disclosure by setting out the method of accounting for these transactions.

Lessees of financial leases and hirers must enter the value of the assets in their balance sheets as if they owned them with a contra entry for the payments due. The methods for calculating these amounts are stated in the standard. A finance lease is, therefore, capitalized by a lessee by which he accounts for the right to use and enjoy the asset with simultaneous recognition of the obligations to make future payments. A hire purchase transaction is accounted for in a similar way but with an operating lease only the rental payments are taken into account by the lessee.

As far as lessors are concerned, the amounts due from a lessee should be recorded in the balance sheet under debtors while the earnings should be allocated to accounting periods to give a constant return on the lessors' net cash investment.

Disclosure in financial statements of both lessee and lessor have to be made in sufficient detail, as set out in the standard, to make the position plain.

SSAP 22. Accounting for Goodwill

The value of a business as a whole can differ from the value of its net assets. This can be either a positive or negative figure and is known as goodwill.

Goodwill can obviously apply to an existing business but it is not the practice to recognize a balance sheet value for goodwill in such circumstances. Where, however, a business has been purchased at a price above that of the net assets, a figure for purchased goodwill will have been paid.

This standard prefers that purchased goodwill should normally be eliminated by immediate write off. This would be consistent with the treatment for non-purchased goodwill. The write off should be against reserves and not as a charge in the profit and loss account.

Conversely, a business may have been purchased for less that its net assets, in which case, a negative amount for goodwill will appear. This should be eliminated by crediting it to reserves.

The standard, however, also allows a company to carry purchased goodwill as an asset subject to writing it off through the profit and loss account over its useful economic life.

The judgement to be made by directors is whether to eliminate goodwill immediately through the reserves account or whether to eliminate it through a reduction in future annual profits through the profit and loss account.

SSAP 23. Accounting for Acquisitions and Mergers

There have been many mergers and take-over bids in recent years and two different methods of accounting have developed.

1. Merger accounting. The financial statements of both enterprises are aggregated and presented as if the combining companies had always been together.
2. Acquisition accounting. The results of the acquired company are brought into consolidation only from the date of acquisition.

In both cases the accounts of the individual companies will be unaffected by the accounting treatment of the group. The legal entities are not disturbed, and it is only the consolidated figures which are affected.

The standard recognizes that there is merit in both methods and it considers that the most appropriate method to be used will depend upon the circumstances in each case.

Merger accounting is considered to be appropriate when two groups of shareholders combine and continue both businesses as before. Acquisition accounting is appropriate when full merger does not take place and substantial resources leave the group. Substantial resources are considered to be 10% or more.

Disclosure of the accounting treatment and any significant accounting adjustments must be made.

CHAPTER 23

Conclusion

Object – Deficiencies in balance sheets and management accounts – Important items not shown in balance sheets – Know your man

The object of this book has been to show how a careful study of balance sheets and other financial statements can help a banker to obtain a good knowledge of the financial aspects of businesses.

It has been shown that there are ways to control and plan efficiently all the individual items comprising assets and liabilities. It must be emphasized again, however, that there are deficiencies in published accounts which show the position on one particular day in each year, and which can, in fact, be very misleading. A more detailed knowledge is obviously obtained by looking also at a company's internal management figures and by intelligent enquiry.

However, regardless of the deficiencies in balance sheets and profit and loss accounts, and providing these drawbacks are understood, these accounts can reveal a vast amount of information, and this is particularly the case if trends from year to year are carefully watched. Even if the figures produced in published and internal accounts are given in full detail a banker will still not know sufficient about a company to satisfy him on all aspects of lending criteria because so much about a company is not revealed by the figures. The figures show only the facets of the business for which book-keeping entries have been passed. It records such matters as purchases, production, sales and administration expenses, but it does not record, for example, good or bad industrial relations, and this can affect a company far more than good or bad control of debtors, stock or creditors.

Labour relations do not only affect personalities within a company, but also working capital, profits, ability to raise further funds, and so on. There are, of course, many aspects of a like nature which affect a company. As an indication the following are important matters which are not revealed by accounts:

1. ability of management. This, of course, is vital and affects all aspects of a business;
2. knowledge of the management. So often managers can be knowledgeable but fail to keep up to date in their study of developments. With the rapid change we now see in all aspects of life it is not sufficient to finish

one's training at an early age. Retraining must continue throughout the active working life of managers;

3. resourcefulness. This is an attribute which is so important during difficult periods and alert management can make a considerable difference to the efficiency of a company;
4. inventiveness. In companies which deal in high technology the people employed in the research department play a very important role when it comes to future activities of a business. Past ability in this direction may well be shown by good profit figures, but future ability cannot, of course, be assessed;
5. picking the right people. This cannot be done in a haphazard way, but a great deal of care must be exercised, particularly for the people in a company who will have a large amount of authority;
6. incentives for the workforce. If a dull routine job is involved it is unlikely the workforce will make great efforts unless there is some incentive to encourage them;
7. care for people. It is no use treating the workforce as just a number of people. They are all individuals and proper systems should be instituted to see that their welfare is properly catered for at least during working hours. Adequate care and attention in this way will also help production as individuals who are well treated tend to give of their best;
8. drive for production. Although the care of people is important the object of a company is the production of its goods or services and this must have priority. It is no use having a very friendly atmosphere in a business if this affects the drive for production;
9. administrative procedures. If these are not good there will be waste of time and money and this will affect the profit and loss account;
10. ability in buying. The money saved by good buying is vitally important to a business as it can help the business in reducing its price on sales and making itself more competitive;
11. modern methods of production. A business which employs old machinery will have a great deal of expense on maintenance and will not be able to produce so quickly, efficiently and cheaply as other businesses with modern machinery;
12. efficient layout of all sections and departments. This naturally saves time and expense;
13. effective sales force. Naturally if the product is not good the sales force will not be able to sell it, but if there is a good product it is poor business to try and sell it with an inefficient sales force. This will tell immediately on the profit and loss account and balance sheet.

All these items, and many more, can affect a company's business, and no amount of examining profit and loss accounts and balance sheets will bring these items to light. The only way for a banker to assess these items in relation to a company is to visit it and by observation, questioning, and knowledge of the management, he should be able to get a good idea of whether all aspects of the business receive proper attention. Local knowledge will, of course, also help.

In fact, we come once again to the three 'C's, which are so important in banking. Capital, Character and Capability. The capital can be seen by examining accounts, but the character and the capability must be judged on wider observation. A banker must, therefore, know his man.

Appendix 1

Accounts of Manufacturers Limited

for the three years ended 31st March

FACTORY ACCOUNT YEAR A

		£		£
Stock at beginning of year		2,000	Transfer to trading account	99,000
Purchases		10,000		
		12,000		
Less stock at end of year		(5,000)		
		7,000		
Work in progress at beginning of year	£3,500			
at end of year	£7,500	(4,000)		
Materials consumed in goods transferred		3,000		
Wages, power and expenses		50,000		
Cost of production		53,000		
Factory profit		46,000 (46.5% on transfer £99,000)		
		£99,000		£99,000

TRADING ACCOUNT

Stock at beginning of year	7,000	Sales	212,000
Own manufacture	99,000		
Purchases	43,000		
	149,000		
Less stock at end of year	(20,000)		
Cost of materials	129,000		
Wages and warehouse expenses	32,000		
	161,000		
Gross profit	51,000 (24% on sales)		
	£212,000		£212,000

PROFIT AND LOSS ACCOUNT

Debenture interest (gross)	3,500	Factory profit	46,000
Directors' fees	5,000	Trading profit	51,000
Overheads	10,000	Sundry receipts	1,500
Provision for depreciation	23,400		
Net profit	56,600 (26.7% on sales)		
	£98,500		£98,500

PROFIT AND LOSS APPROPRIATION ACCOUNT

	£		£
Corporation tax . .	35,000	Balance from last year .	14,100
Written off discount on debentures . . .	700	Profit for year . .	56,600
Interim dividend paid .	20,000		
Provision for final dividend	5,000		
Balance	10,000		
	£70,700		£70,700

PROFIT AND LOSS ACCOUNT
(in a format in accordance with the Companies Act 1985)

	£
Turnover	212,000
(1) *Cost of sales	83,000
Gross profit	129,000
(2) *Distribution costs and administration expenses	70,400
Operating profit	58,600
Amount written off discount on debentures	700
	57,900
Interest payable on debentures	3,500
Profit on ordinary activities before taxation	54,400
Tax on profit on ordinary activities	35,000
Profit on ordinary activities after taxation	19,400
Extraordinary items less taxation	1,500
Profit attributable to members of the company	20,900
Dividends	25,000
Reduction in profit and loss account balance after dividends .	£4,100

* Note: the calculations are as follows:

1. Cost of materials £129,000 from trading account less £46,000 factory profit.
2. Wages and warehouse

expenses	£32,000
Directors' fees . . .	£5,000
Overheads	£10,000
Depreciation . . .	£23,400
	£70,400

BALANCE SHEET YEAR A

	£	£
FIXED ASSETS		
Intangible assets		
Discount on debentures	2,100	
less amount written off	700	1,400
Tangible assets		
Freehold factory at cost	100,000	
less depreciation	1,400	98,600
Plant and machinery	70,000	
less depreciation	20,000	50,000
Fixtures, fittings, tools and equipment	7,000	
less depreciation	2,000	5,000
CURRENT ASSETS		
Stocks		
Raw materials and consumables	5,000	
Work in progress	7,500	
Finished goods and goods for resale	20,000	
Debtors		
Trade debtors	24,500	
Bills receivable	7,500	
Investments		
Listed investments at cost (market value £3,841)	3,500	
Cash at bank and in hand	9,000	
	77,000	
CREDITORS: AMOUNTS FALLING DUE WITHIN ONE YEAR		
Trade creditors	5,000	
Other creditors – taxation	12,000	
Provision for dividend	5,000	
	22,000	
Net current assets		55,000
Total assets *less* current liabilities		210,000
CREDITORS: AMOUNTS FALLING DUE AFTER MORE THAN ONE YEAR		
5% debentures, secured		70,000
		£140,000
CAPITAL AND RESERVES		
Called up share capital		100,000
Reserves		30,000
Profit and loss account		10,000
		£140,000

YEAR B

FACTORY ACCOUNT

		£		£
Stock at beginning of year		5,000	Transfer to Trading account	274,750
Purchases		100,000		
		105,000		
Less stock at end of year		(10,000)		
		95,000		
Work in progress at beginning of year	£7,500			
at end of year	£15,000	(7,500)		
Materials consumed in goods transferred		87,500		
Wages, power and expenses		148,000		
Cost of production		235,500		
Factory profit		39,250 (14.3% on transfer £274,750)		
		£274,750		£274,750

TRADING ACCOUNT

Stock at beginning of year	20,000	Sales	390,000
Own manufacture	274,750		
Purchases	75,250		
	370,000		
Less stock at end of year	(40,000)		
Cost of materials	330,000		
Expenses	12,000		
	342,000		
Gross profit	48,000 (12.3% on sales)		
	£390,000		£390,000

PROFIT AND LOSS ACCOUNT

Debenture interest (gross)	3,500	Factory profit	39,250
Directors' fees	15,000	Trading profit	48,000
Overheads	15,000		
Net profit	53,750 (22.4% on sales)		
	£87,250		£87,250

PROFIT AND LOSS APPROPRIATION ACCOUNT

	£		£
Corporation tax . .	23,750	Balance from last year .	10,000
Written off discount on debentures . . .	700	Profit for year . .	53,750
Interim dividend paid .	10,000		
Provision for final dividend	15,000		
Balance	14,300		
	£63,750		£63,750

PROFIT AND LOSS ACCOUNT
(in a format in accordance with the Companies Act 1985)

	£
Turnover	390,000
(1) *Cost of sales	290,750
Gross profit	99,250
(2) *Distribution costs and administration expenses	42,000
Operating profit	57,250
Amount written off discount on debentures	700
	56,550
Interest payable on debentures	3,500
Profit on ordinary activities before taxation	53,050
Tax on profit on ordinary activities	23,750
Profit on ordinary activities after taxation	29,300
Dividends	25,000
Retained profit for year	£4,300

* Note: the calculations are as follows:

1. Cost of materials £330,000 from trading account less £39,250 factory profit.
2. Expenses £12,000
   Directors' fees . . . £15,000
   Overheads £15,000
   £42,000

BALANCE SHEET YEAR B

	£	£
FIXED ASSETS		
Intangible assets		
Discount on debentures	2,100	
less amount written off	1,400	700
Tangible assets		
Freehold factory at cost	100,000	
less depreciation	1,400	98,600
Plant and machinery	75,000	
less depreciation	20,000	55,000
Fixtures, fittings, tools and equipment	7,000	
less depreciation	2,000	5,000
CURRENT ASSETS		
Stocks		
Raw materials and consumables	10,000	
Work in progress	15,000	
Finished goods and goods for resale	40,000	
Debtors		
Trade debtors	17,000	
Bills receivable	5,000	
Cash at bank and in hand	10,000	
	97,000	
CREDITORS: AMOUNTS FALLING DUE WITHIN ONE YEAR		
Trade creditors	17,000	
Other creditors – taxation	10,000	
Provision for dividend	15,000	
	42,000	
Net current assets		55,000
Total assets *less* current liabilities		214,300
CREDITORS: AMOUNTS FALLING DUE AFTER MORE THAN ONE YEAR		
5% debentures, secured		70,000
		£144,300
CAPITAL AND RESERVES		
Called up share capital		100,000
Reserves		30,000
Profit and loss account		14,300
		£144,300

YEAR C

FACTORY ACCOUNT

		£		£
Stock at beginning of year		10,000	Transfer to trading account	232,000
Purchases		90,000		
		100,000		
Less stock at end of year		(10,000)		
		90,000		
Work in progress at beginning of year	£15,000			
at end of year	£50,000	(35,000)		
Materials consumed in goods transferred		55,000		
Wages, power and expenses		148,000		
Cost of production		203,000		
Factory profit		29,000	(12.5% on transfer £232,000)	
		£232,000		£232,000

TRADING ACCOUNT

Stock at beginning of year	40,000	Sales	354,000
Own manufacture	232,000		
Purchases	100,000		
	372,000		
Less stock at end of year	(50,000)		
Cost of materials	322,000		
Expenses	12,000		
	334,000		
Gross profit	20,000	(5.65% on sales)	
	£354,000		£354,000

PROFIT AND LOSS ACCOUNT

Debenture interest (gross)	3,500	Factory profit	29,000
Directors' fees	10,000	Trading profit	20,000
Overheads	15,000		
Net profit	20,500	(13.9% on sales)	
	£49,000		£49,000

PROFIT AND LOSS APPROPRIATION ACCOUNT

	£		£
Corporation tax . .	10,500	Balance from last year .	14,300
Written off discount on debentures . . .	700	Profit for year . .	20,500
Proposed dividend . .	10,000		
Balance	13,600		
	£34,800		£34,800

PROFIT AND LOSS ACCOUNT
(in a format in accordance with the Companies Act 1985)

	£
Turnover	354,000
(1) *Cost of sales	293,000
Gross profit	61,000
(2) *Distribution costs and administration expenses	37,000
Operating profit	24,000
Amount written off discount on debentures	700
	23,300
Interest payable on debentures	3,500
Profit on ordinary activities before taxation	19,800
Tax on profit on ordinary activities	10,500
Profit on ordinary activities after taxation	9,300
Dividends	10,000
Reduction in profit and loss balance after dividends . . .	£700

* Note: the calculations are as follows:

1. Cost of materials £322,000 from trading account less £29,000 factory profit.
2. Expenses £12,000
   Directors' fees £10,000
   Overheads £15,000
   £37,000

BALANCE SHEET YEAR C

	£	£
FIXED ASSETS		
Tangible assets		
Freehold factory at cost	100,000	
less depreciation	1,400	98,600
Plant and machinery	75,000	
less depreciation	20,000	55,000
Fixtures, fittings, tools and equipment	7,000	
less depreciation	2,000	5,000
CURRENT ASSETS		
Stocks		
Raw materials and consumables	10,000	
Work in progress	50,000	
Finished goods and goods for resale	50,000	
Debtors		
Trade debtors	17,000	
	127,000	
CREDITORS: AMOUNTS FALLING DUE WITHIN ONE YEAR		
Bank overdraft	5,000	
Trade creditors	43,000	
Other creditors – taxation	14,000	
Provision for dividend	10,000	
	72,000	
Net current assets		55,000
Total assets *less* current liabilities		213,600
CREDITORS: AMOUNTS FALLING DUE AFTER MORE THAN ONE YEAR		
5% debentures, secured		70,000
		£143,600
CAPITAL AND RESERVES		
Called up share capital		100,000
Reserves		30,000
Profit and loss account		13,600
		£143,600

Note: There is a contingent liability in respect of bills discounted.

Appendix 2

EXAMPLES OF BALANCE SHEETS

BALANCE SHEET A — SOLE TRADER: TENANT FARMER

Mr. J. B. Farmer

BALANCE SHEET AS AT 25TH MARCH 19—

	£		£	£
CAPITAL ACCOUNT		FIXED ASSETS		
Balance at start of year	38,046	Freehold house at cost		9,000
Add profit	26,505	Freehold cottages at cost		13,725
	64,551	PLANT AND MACHINERY		
Less drawings	1,494	Balance at start of year	38,883	
Balance at end of year	63,057	*Plus* additions, *less* sales	30,438	
Bank overdraft	72,864		69,321	
Sundry creditors	86,748	*Less* depreciation 10%	6,933	62,388
		MOTOR TRACTORS		
		At start of year	19,692	
		Plus additions, *less* sales	9,468	
			29,160	
		Less depreciation 22½%	6,561	22,599
		MOTOR LORRIES		
		At start of year	10,386	
		Plus additions, *less* sales	9,054	
			19,440	
		Less depreciation 20%	3,888	15,552
		Total fixed assets		123,264
		CURRENT ASSETS		
		Sundry debtors and prepayments	12,816	
		Valuation*	83,727	
		Implements and utensils	2,862	99,405
	£222,669			£222,669

*Valuation by A. P. Praiser F.V.I.

	£
Cattle and Sheep	10,629
Horses	675
Poultry	117
Crops, cultivations, manures and sundries	72,306
	£83,727

BALANCE SHEET B — FARMING COMPANY

Farm Produce Limited

BALANCE SHEET AS AT 31ST MARCH 19—

	£	£	£
FIXED ASSETS			
Tangible assets			
Buildings at cost		213	
Additions during year		327	540
Farm implements at cost		5,526	
Additions during year		129	
		5,655	
Less sales	663		
depreciation	693	1,356	4,299
Tractors at cost		1,116	
Less depreciation		528	588
Investments			
Farmers Trading Society Limited			30
			5,457
CURRENT ASSETS			
Valuation*		18,258	
Sundry debtors and prepayments		2,415	
		20,673	
CREDITORS: AMOUNTS FALLING DUE WITHIN ONE YEAR			
Sundry creditors		2,852	
Bank overdraft, secured by debenture		8,322	
Accrued charges		1,341	
Loan	10,536		
Addition during year	1,500		
	12,036		
Less repayment	126	11,910	
		24,425	
Net current liabilities			(3,752)
Total assets less liabilities			£1,705
CAPITAL AND RESERVES			
£1 Ordinary shares (Authorised £3,000)			2
£1 6% Preference shares (Authorised £15,000)			—
PROFIT AND LOSS ACCOUNT			
Profit for year		3,220	
Less balance brought forward		(1,517)	1,703
			£1,705

* Valuation by Mr.... F.V.I.

	£
Livestock	13,163
Stores	61
Provender	1,278
Produce	481
Manures and sundries	1,073
Tenant right	2,202
	£18,258

PROFIT AND LOSS ACCOUNT

	£
Sales	28,581
Subsidies	870
	£29,451
Net profit	£3,220

BALANCE SHEET C

G. Smith and Partners

Previous year £		£	£	£
	SUNDRY CREDITORS AND PROVISIONS			
12 } *6,893* }	Sundry creditors		12,566	
9,188	Provision for income tax		16,816	
12,114	Amounts payable under staff bonus scheme		11,226	
				40,608
—	Estate of G. H. Parker, dec.			26,573
978	Estate of C. C. Faull, dec.			—
29,185	Total current liabilities			67,181
	CAPITAL ACCOUNTS			
9,600	G. Smith		—	
4,800	F. Jones		10,800	
4,800	C. Brown		10,800	
4,800	H. Green		10,800	
				32,400
	DRAWINGS ACCOUNTS			
21,814	G. Smith			—
	F. Jones			
14,340	Balance at start of year		20,298	
958	*Add* Interest on capital and drawings accounts		1,255	
12,035	Share of profit		17,299	
27,333			38,852	
7,035 {	*Deduct* Drawings	5,542		
	Income tax	7,927		
			13,469	
20,298				25,383
	C. Brown			
13,976	Balance at start of year		20,041	
938	*Add* Interest on capital and drawings accounts		1,242	
12,035	Share of profit		17,299	
26,949			38,582	
6,908 {	*Deduct* Drawings	3,674		
	Income tax	7,891		
			11,565	
20,041				27,017
	H. Green			
7,610	Balance at start of year		13,352	
620	*Add* Interest on capital and drawings accounts		908	
11,554	Share of profit		17,299	
19,784			31,559	
6,432 {	*Deduct* Drawings	3,410		
	Income tax	7,575		
			10,985	
13,352				20,574
£128,690				£172,555

PROFESSIONAL PARTNERSHIP: CONSULTING CIVIL ENGINEER

BALANCE SHEET AS AT 31ST MARCH 19—

Previous year £		£	£
	CASH AT BANK		
25,627	Current account	32,817	
6,110	Deposit account	14,687	
			47,504
24	Cash in hand		76
12,000	Investments		12,000
43,761	Liquid assets		59,580
	DEBTORS		
30,912	For fees charged	16,880	
38,980	Estimated accrued fees	49,144	
7,640	Expenses not yet charged to clients	16,719	
712	Sundries	1,301	
			84,044
122,005	Total current assets		143,624
—	Freehold property at cost		22,700
	Motor vehicle	866	
758	*Less* Depreciation to date	325	
			541
	FURNITURE AND FITTINGS		
	Balance at start of year	1,247	
	Additions to date, *less* Sales	2,959	
		4,206	
	Less Depreciation to date	971	
3,367			3,235
	Drawing office and survey equipment at cost, *less* depreciation	760	
	Less Depreciation for year	225	
760			535
	PAYMENTS TO S. R. THOMAS		
1,800	On account of purchase of practice, *less* amounts charged to partners		1,920
£128,690			£172,555

PROFIT AND LOSS ACCOUNT

Previous year £		£
28,918	Salaries	35,770
12,114	Staff Bonus scheme	10,252
1,228	Consultant's fees	3,540
1,013	Travelling expenses	1,825
787	Drawing office expenses	1,811
131	Motor expenses not charged to clients (including depreciation)	136
4,117	Rent and rates	5,588
6,084	General office expenses	5,750
281	Accountancy and audit fees	345
—	Subscriptions and donations	395
443	Depreciation	428
98	Interest on deceased Partner's share	1,366
3,544	Interest on capital and drawings accounts	3,405
52,703	Divisible profit	51,897
£111,461		£122,508

YEAR ENDED 31ST MARCH 19—

Previous year £			£	£
99,996		Fees charged		111,143
38,980		Accrued fees at end of year	49,144	
27,787		*Less* ditto at start of year	38,024	
11,193		Increase in accrued fees		11,120
111,189		Total earnings		122,263
272		Bank deposit interest		216
—		Bad debt reserve – no longer required		29
£	£	*Interest on capital*	£	£
	480	G. Smith	—	
	240	F. Jones	240	
	240	C. Brown	240	
	240	H. Green	240	
1,200				720
		Interest on drawings account		
	548	G. Smith	—	
	716	F. Jones	1,015	
	698	C. Brown	1,002	
	382	H. Green	668	
2,344				2,685
£3,544				£3,405
£111,461				£122,508

BALANCE SHEET D — ASSOCIATION

Institute of . . .

BALANCE SHEET AS AT 31ST OCTOBER 19—

	£	£
ACCUMULATED FUND		
As at 31st October, start of year	45,631	
Deduct		
Deficit per income and expenditure account for the current year	2,270	
		43,361
PREMISES RESERVE		
As at 31st October, start of year	7,569	
Add Amount transferred from income and expenditure account	1,834	
		9,403
Staff contingency reserve		6,000
		58,764
Debentures		10,000
INCOME RECEIVED IN ADVANCE		
Balance of compounded subscriptions	16,118	
Fees and subscriptions	755	
		16,873
Creditors		2,970
		£88,607

	£	£
FIXED ASSETS		
Freehold premises and offices, at cost		19,234
Furniture and office equipment, at cost	3,187	
Less Provision for depreciation	1,808	
		1,379
Library books at cost *less* depreciation		228
		20,841
INVESTMENTS		
at cost		51,601
(Market value, £49,766)		
CURRENT ASSETS		
Debtors	4,104	
Stock at valuation	5,387	
Cash with bankers and on hand	6,674	
		16,165
		£88,607

BALANCE SHEET E — HOTEL COMPANY

Group Hotels P.L.C.

BALANCE SHEET AS AT 30TH SEPTEMBER 19—

Last year £		This year £	This year £
	FIXED ASSETS		
	Intangible assets		
480,000	Goodwill		430,000
	Tangible assets		
1,450,000	Sundry fixed assets		1,400,000
	Investments		
20,000	Associated companies		20,000
50,000	Trade loans		50,000
10,000	Listed investments (market value £10,000)		10,000
2,010,000			1,910,000
	CURRENT ASSETS		
250,000	Stock	350,000	
250,000	Debtors	250,000	
20,000	Cash at bank and in hand	20,000	
520,000		620,000	
	CREDITORS: AMOUNTS FALLING DUE WITHIN ONE YEAR		
450,000	Trade creditors	400,000	
185,000	Bank overdraft (secured)	200,000	
30,000	Taxation and social security	20,000	
10,000	Proposed final dividend	10,000	
675,000		630,000	
155,000	Net current liabilities		10,000
1,855,000	Total assets *less* current liabilities		1,900,000
	CREDITORS: AMOUNTS FALLING DUE AFTER MORE THAN ONE YEAR		
250,000	Loan stock 1995 (secured)	250,000	
	Other loans		
250,000	maturing within five years	250,000	
350,000	maturing after five years	350,000	
	Taxation	15,000	865,000
£1,005,000			£1,035,000
	CAPITAL AND RESERVES		
	Called up share capital		
300,000	Ordinary shares		300,000
50,000	Preference shares		50,000
600,000	Reserves		600,000
55,000	Profit and loss account		85,000
£1,005,000			£1,035,000

PROFIT AND LOSS ACCOUNT

Last year		This year £	This year
£3,200,000	Trading turnover		£3,600,000
£			£
130,000	Trading profit		150,000
95,000	*Less* interest on loans		95,000
35,000	Profit on ordinary activities before tax		55,000
4,000	Income from investments		5,000
39,000	Profit for the financial year after tax	£	60,000
20,000	Taxation – current	15,000	
	deferred	15,000	30,000
£19,000			£30,000

BALANCE SHEET F EXTRACTIVE INDUSTRY QUARRYING

BALANCE SHEET AS AT 31ST DECEMBER 19—

	£	£
FIXED ASSETS		
Intangible assets		
Goodwill at cost	8,573	
Less written off	8,573	—
Tangible assets		
Freehold and leaseholds at cost	122,374	
Less depreciation	42,652	79,722
Plant and machinery at cost	192,448	
Less depreciation	115,272	77,176
Motor vehicles at cost	34,224	
Less depreciation	19,888	14,336
Fixtures, fittings, tools and equipment at cost	1,007	
Less depreciation	625	382
Investments		
Trade		5,202
Total fixed assets		176,818
CURRENT ASSETS		
Stock, loose plant, stores etc. as valued by managing director	51,637	
Road developments	1,376	
Ridding values	32,206	
Work in progress *less* advances received	89,908	
Trade debtors	126,223	
Cash at bank and in hand	2,624	
	303,974	
CREDITORS: AMOUNTS FALLING DUE WITHIN ONE YEAR		
Bank loan (secured on certain of the companies properties)	51,938	
Trade creditors	121,422	
Corporation tax	30,954	
Proposed dividend	2,572	
	206,886	
Net current assets		97,088
Total assets *less* liabilities		£273,906
CAPITAL AND RESERVES		
Called up share capital		
£1 Ordinary shares		23,332
£1 6% Preference shares		12,334
Share premium account		3,966
Revaluation reserve		13,328
Other reserves – general		100,000
Profit and loss account		120,946
		£273,906

FROM PROFIT AND LOSS ACCOUNT

Gross profit	£127,000
Net Profit	£ 31,500

BALANCE SHEET G PROPERTY INVESTMENT COMPANY

Property Investment Company Limited

BALANCE SHEET AS AT 31ST MARCH 19—

Previous year £		£	£
	FIXED ASSETS		
	Tangible assets		
50,000	Freehold property at cost		50,000
	Investments		
2,000	Long term loan		2,000
	CURRENT ASSETS		
3,000	Trade debtors	2,700	
	Prepayments	900	
4,300	Cash at bank and in hand . . .	5,500	
7,300		9,100	
	CREDITORS: AMOUNTS FALLING DUE WITHIN ONE YEAR		
700	Trade creditors	900	
2,900	Taxation	3,800	
2,500	Final dividend proposed	2,500	
6,100		7,200	
1,200	Net current assets		1,900
£53,200	Total assets *less* liabilities		£53,900
	CAPITAL AND RESERVES		
40,000	Called up share capital		40,000
	Other reserves		
8,000	General		8,000
3,000	Repairs		3,000
2,200	Profit and loss account . . .		2,900
£53,200			£53,900

PROFIT AND LOSS ACCOUNT (SUMMARY)

Previous year £		£	£
8,000	Rent receivable	9,500	
500	Interest	500	10,000
2,500	*Less* expenses		3,000
6,000	Net income before taxation		7,000
2,900	Corporation tax		3,800
3,100	Net income after taxation		3,200
2,500	Dividend proposed		2,500
£600	Retained income		£700

BALANCE SHEET H — DRAPERY RETAILERS

Drapery Shops Limited

BALANCE SHEET AS AT 28TH FEBRUARY 19—

Previous year £		£	£
	FIXED ASSETS		
	Tangible assets		
1,000,000	Sundry fixed assets (note 1)		1,100,000
	Investments		
35,000	Endowment policy for redemption of mortgage (note 3)		40,000
1,000	Trade loan		1,000
1,036,000			1,141,000
	CURRENT ASSETS		
	Stocks		
300,000	Raw materials and consumables (note 2)	350,000	
45,000	Trade debtors	70,000	
2,000	Cash at bank and in hand	2,000	
347,000		422,000	
	CREDITORS: AMOUNTS FALLING DUE WITHIN ONE YEAR		
70,000	Bank loan (note 4)	160,000	
100,000	Trade creditors	130,000	
270,000	Associated companies	320,000	
12,000	Hire purchase creditors	30,000	
25,000	Taxation	22,000	
110,000	Proposed Dividends	11,000	
587,000		673,000	
(240,000)	Net current liabilities		(251,000)
796,000	Total assets *less* current liabilities		890,000
	CREDITORS: AMOUNTS FALLING DUE AFTER ONE YEAR		
200,000	Mortgage loan (note 7)	240,000	
100,000	Directors' loans (note 8)	80,000	
36,000	Other loans (note 9)	30,000	350,000
£460,000			£540,000
	CAPITAL AND RESERVES		
140,000	Called up share capital (note 5)		140,000
320,000	Reserves (note 6)		400,000
£460,000			£540,000

BALANCE SHEET H (continued)

Drapery Shops Limited

PROFIT AND LOSS APPROPRIATION ACCOUNT (SUMMARY)

Previous year £		£	This year £
£2,200,000	Turnover for the year		£2,500,000
93,000	Operating profit for the year *after charging*		113,000
32,000	Directors' remuneration	32,000	
2,000	Auditors' remuneration	2,000	
27,000	Depreciation	35,000	
16,000	Interest charges	19,000	
25,000	*Deduct* Taxation		22,000
68,000	Profit for year on ordinary activities after taxation		91,000
11,000	*Less* Proposed dividends	11,000	
12,000	Deferred taxation account (Note 11)	18,000	
5,000	Sinking fund for mortgage redemption	5,000	
28,000			34,000
40,000	Unappropriated profit for year		57,000
170,000	*Add* Balance brought forward		210,000
£210,000	Balance carried forward		£267,000

NOTES TO THE ACCOUNT AS AT 28TH FEBRUARY 19—

1. Fixed assets:

	Cost start of year £	Additions £	Cost, end of year £	Accumulated depreciation £	Written down value, end of year £
Freeholds	800,000	100,000	900,000	—	900,000
Fixtures, fittings, plant and machinery	215,000	15,000	230,000	75,000	155,000
Motor vehicles	50,000	20,000	70,000	25,000	45,000
	£1,065,000	£135,000	£1,200,000	£100,000	£1,100,000
(Previous year			*£1,065,000*	*£65,000*	*£1,000,000*)

2. Stock in trade has been valued at the lower of cost or net realizable value.
3. Endowment policy for redemption of mortgages.
   The surrender value of the policy at end of year was £43,000 (previous year *£37,000*).
4. Bank overdraft. This is secured by a mortgage over 25 South Street, Northtown.
5. Share capital.

	Authorized	Issued and fully paid
Ordinary shares of £1 each	140,000	140,000

BALANCE SHEET H (continued)

Drapery Shops Limited

6. Reserves:

	At start of year £	Additions £	At end of year £
Mortgage redemption reserve	35,000	5,000	40,000
General reserve	63,000	—	63,000
Revenue reserve	210,000	57,000	267,000
Deferred taxation account	12,000	18,000	30,000
	£320,000	£80,000	£400,000

7. Mortgage loans:

	Previous year £	This year £	Security
8% loan repayable 1990	*200,000*	200,000	21 South Street
12% loan repayable in two years' time		40,000	23 South Street
	£200,000	£240,000	

8. Directors' loans. Secured by a second charge over 21 and 23 South Street.
9. Other loans. This is provided by a wife of a director and is secured by a third charge over 21 and 23 South Street.
10. Capital commitments. At the end of the year these amounted to £57,000. (Previous year *£5,000*).
11. Deferred taxation account. This represents the reserve for tax deferred by excess tax allowances on fixed assets over the depreciation shown in the accounts.
12. Directors' remuneration:

		Previous year
Chairman	£18,000	*£18,000*
Other directors, £5,001 to £7,500	2	2

BALANCE SHEET I INSTALMENT CREDIT COMPANY

Hire Purchase Finance P.L.C.

BALANCE SHEET AS AT 30TH APRIL

	£	£	Previous year £
FIXED ASSETS			
Intangible assets			
Goodwill		200	*200*
Tangible assets			
Properties		200	*200*
Plant and equipment on lease		1,500	*1,200*
Rental equipment		2,800	*2,700*
		4,700	*4,300*
CURRENT ASSETS			
Stocks	200		*180*
Trade debtors	260		*250*
Cash at bank and in hand	10		*10*
	470		*440*
CREDITORS: AMOUNTS FALLING DUE WITHIN ONE YEAR			
Loans	220		*220*
Bank loans	100		*80*
Trade creditors	300		*290*
Bills of Exchange payable	800		*750*
Other creditors			
Deposits	200		*180*
Taxation and social security	40		*40*
Acceptance credits	100		*120*
Dividend	1		*1*
	1,761		*1,681*
Net current liabilities		(1,291)	*(1,241)*
Total assets *less* current liabilities		3,409	*3,059*
CREDITORS: AMOUNTS FALLING DUE AFTER ONE YEAR			
Loans	1,000		*1,000*
Bills of Exchange payable	300		*200*
Deferred taxation	400	1,700	*400*
		£1,709	*£1,459*
CAPITAL AND RESERVES			
Called up share capital		1,000	*1,000*
Reserves – general		400	*200*
Profit and loss account		309	*259*
		£1,709	*£1,459*

PROFIT AND LOSS ACCOUNT (summary)

	£'000	*£'000*
Turnover	£2,000	*£1,800*
Profit after tax	£ 250	*£ 230*

BALANCE SHEET J — CHAIN STORE COMPANY

Branch Stores P.L.C.

BALANCE SHEET AS AT 30TH JUNE 19—

	Current year £'000	Current year £'000	Previous year £'000
FIXED ASSETS			
Tangible assets			
Freeholds		1,500	*1,310*
Leaseholds		400	*500*
Short leases		100	*80*
Fixtures, fittings, tools and equipment		100	*60*
Investments			
Subsidiary		30	*30*
		2,130	*1,980*
CURRENT ASSETS			
Stock	200		*170*
Trade debtors	55		*50*
Cash at bank and in hand	100		*90*
	355		*310*
CREDITORS: AMOUNTS FALLING DUE WITHIN ONE YEAR			
Trade creditors	150		*140*
Taxation and social security	150		*140*
Proposed final dividend	65		*60*
	365		*340*
Net current liabilities		(10)	*(30)*
Total assets less current liabilities		2,120	*1,950*
CREDITORS: AMOUNTS FALLING DUE AFTER ONE YEAR			
7% debenture stock	200		*200*
Deferred taxation	100	300	*80*
		£1,820	*£1,670*
CAPITAL AND RESERVES			
Called up share capital		1,000	*1,000*
Reserves		700	*500*
Profit and loss account		120	*170*
		£1,820	*£1,670*

PROFIT AND LOSS ACCOUNT (summary)

	£'000	£'000
Turnover	£3,500	*£2,500*
Operating profit	410	*320*
Taxation	195	*140*
Profit after taxation	215	*180*
Dividends	65	*60*
Profit retained	£150	*£120*

Index